Eclectica Publishing Intl LLC Titles

2004   *Best Fiction Volume One (7th Anniversary)*

2015   *Tales of Choroni*

2016   *Best Poetry Volume One (20th Anniversary)*

2016   *Best Nonfiction Volume One (20th Anniversary)*

2016   *Best Fiction Volume Two (20th Anniversary)*

2016   *Speculative Edition Volume One (20th Anniversary)*

Eclectica Magazine Best Nonfiction

Celebrating 20 Years Online

Eclectica Magazine
Best Nonfiction

Celebrating 20 Years Online

Selected from *www.eclectica.org*
October 1996 through February 2016
by David Ewald

*With an Introduction by David Ewald
and a Foreword by Donna Talarico*

ECLECTICA PUBLISHING INTL LLC
ALBUQUERQUE, NEW MEXICO

In memory of Julia Braun Kessler, whose numerous contributions bolstered the nonfiction section, and Barbara Lefcowitz, who passed just as creating this anthology was getting underway.

Acknowledgments

Thanks to...

Emily, Elliott and Gregory, for allowing the time needed to make this book happen.

Tom Dooley and Chris Lott, without whom there would be no *Eclectica*.

Donna Talarico for her foreword as well as her support of nonfiction writing through the online journal she founded, *Hippocampus Magazine*.

Clinton Daniel McKay for his unique cover art.

The 113 contributors to our Kickstarter campaign who footed the bill for this and three other volumes.

Caroline Allen, John Wilson and Robyn Bell, faculty in the College of Creative Studies at the University of California Santa Barbara, who helped develop my interest in reading and writing nonfiction, and to Leonard Tourney, whose courses in professional editing gave me a foundation for the work that was to come.

Erin Elizabeth Smith, Melvin Sterne, and Charles Yu for some good blurbing.

Paul Sampson and William Reese Hamilton, who as nonfiction editors helped select many of these pieces.

The multitude of editors, authors, and supporters not already mentioned above who have helped keep the boat afloat for two decades.

Visit our website at www.eclectica.org.

ISBN 978-0-9968830-2-3

Printed in the United States of America

All works originally published in *Eclectica Magazine*
(www.eclectica.org) and reprinted by permission of the authors.

Contents

Foreword

IN 1996, a friend and I were featured in *The Pocono Record* newspaper as being "teenagers of the future." The Internet was still relatively new, at least from an at-home consumer point of view. But Jennifer and I were active on forums and we had personal websites, thanks to Geocities and HTML tutorials. We also had a column in our weekly school newspaper, *The Cardinal Quill*, called "Nothing but Net," where we reviewed websites for our classmates. You could say we were early adopters, and she and I would grow up to enjoy careers involving technology—but we had a lot to learn first.

While I was still making discoveries of what the World Wide Web could do for mankind (and experimenting with animated gifs), the founders of *Eclectica Magazine* had already realized literature had a place online. In 1996. When dialing up was still the only way to enter the newly paved information super highway.

Since then, *Eclectica* has consistently published quality writing in many genres, its content reaching far and wide. And now, we the readers are able to physically touch some of the best nonfiction from that output, which heretofore has only lived online. I'm delighted to have had the chance to read this collection while it was still in production, and I'll take a moment to share what you can expect inside.

The essays in this celebratory anthology flow into one another. The editor carefully arranged them as if they weren't plucked from dozens of different issues over the course of two decades. You'll trek to exotic locales, visit different eras, become immersed in new cultures, and explore deep philosophies. The essays in this collection highlight issues we as a society are still grappling with: the economy, the vulnerability of children, and identity—to name a few. This collection shows how timely *and* timeless creative nonfiction can be.

There's breadth and depth in this collection, from Stanley Jenkins' haunting and fittingly named essay "Twenty Years," where a pastor reflects on some of the many souls he has touched and been touched by during his tenure, to Monika Lange's "The World and I," where a Polish immigrant whose first husband was an Iranian is able to reflect—on the Saturday after the 9/11 attacks—that "The world and I have come a full circle, and we still have hope." Between those two remarkable pieces: Ana Doina's colorful and chaotic "Earthquake"; Ikhide Ikeola's humorous take on returning home to Nigeria after a decade in America; John Palcewski's page-turning essay about big city dreams, new love, and trust; Thomas Larson's relevant as ever "A Few Photographs of Molested Children"; Lyn Fuchs's macabre, graphic-in-a-good-way "Dying with Dignity, Mexican Style"; "You Can't Have Him," written by Anthony Brown while he was incarcerated, serving a life sentence for murder; Alan Kaufman's tale of recovery and friendship, "Things Carl Little Crow and I Did Together to Stay Sober in San Francisco."

With these and 22 other pieces, this collection has something for everyone—topics that, at first, might seem foreign (literally and figuratively), but after reading, we're better for having read them. It's telling when, days after flipping the last page, I am still thinking of characters, of places. This book reminds us that the world is bigger than we think, the people more diverse than we know—and it makes us want to dig deeper and travel farther. (If you're like me, you might take a pause between essays to search flights to an exotic land or scroll through photos of ancient ruins.) This is what good nonfiction does.

Eclectica encourages us by example to take risks, to try something new—not just in terms of the content they've presented to the world over the years, but in embracing a new medium. Twenty years on, the Web is still evolving, and it's still a novel territory for many people and organizations. Some print publications are just getting their webbed feet wet, and online-only magazines are still being launched. We can thank *Eclectica* for blazing the digital trail.

Donna Talarico is the founder and publisher of *Hippocampus Magazine.*

Introduction

WHERE WAS I in 1996? Certainly not on the Internet. That year my family situated our single desktop computer in a corner of the dining room, close to where we ate. It was an accessory then, something on which my sister and I completed homework assignments and our parents composed letters and work-related documents. I had no idea how pervasive the screen would become even two years later when, unable to get through to my family on their land line—my sister was on her umpteenth hour of dial-up connection—I was forced to walk the mile and a half in wicked summer heat from my job, arriving home sweaty and miffed.

Something else I had no idea about in 1996: the existence of *Eclectica Magazine*. Founded by Tom Dooley and Chris Lott, the e-zine launched in October of that year. It would be another ten years before I discovered it and submitted something for consideration. That piece was accepted, and my connection to this dynamic journal began.

I took on the role of nonfiction editor in June of 2012, after *Eclectica* published two of my essays. I thought, *What the heck, Tom is asking for help, I'd probably be good at this, why not go for it?* In my four years of editorship, I have not regretted my decision. Rather, I have been buoyed by the vast amount of quality writing I've gotten to read and the talented writers with whom I've gotten to work. I have discovered such greats as Stuart Gelzer, Bobbi Lurie, and Melissa Wiley, all three of whom point very much in the direction of where I'd like to see the nonfiction and travel sections go.

The aforementioned writers are in the pages of the volume you are now reading, but there are many others—28 other voices, to be exact. I confess I was unfamiliar with the majority of these writers and their work before selecting them for this anthology. I read every candidate carefully and chose based on the sole criteria of quality. Combing—or, rather, clicking—through the archives took considerable time. I had to go back, way back, and it was not without a smile that I looked upon those very first pages published in 1996, a reminder of just what the Internet was like then. Of every piece I asked myself, *Does this piece belong in an anthology celebrating a literary magazine's 20-year history?* Even though I knew each piece would be prefaced by the month or months and year in which it was published, I wanted to know if there was something of a *timeless* quality to the work. Again and again, *Will this work hold up 20 years from now? What does each piece have to offer? What does each author?*

In addition to serving as *Eclectica's* nonfiction editor, I am also the de facto travel and miscellany editor—hence several of the pieces in this anthology are set abroad. Having traveled widely and written about it myself, I can say I am proud to have included so much travel writing in these pages, for some of the very best nonfiction I have read would technically be labeled as such.

Another sub-category of nonfiction to be found in these pages is that of "creative nonfiction" or "autobiographical fiction." One piece I'd attribute to this category comes immediately to mind: "You Can't Have Him," Anthony Brown's intense yet controlled account of a prisoner murdering another prisoner at a federal correctional facility in California. "The killing was real," Brown wrote by way of introducing his piece when it was published online in 1997. "So are the nightmares." Despite the anguish and terror that gave birth to "You Can't Have Him," the piece remarkably presents itself as near-strict reportage, with the author taking an objective (albeit omniscient) stance. Brown did admit, though, in that 1997 introduction that "license [had] been taken with specific details in order to protect all involved," and, indeed, like Jon Krakauer with the ill-fated Christopher McCandless, he does get into the heads of his very real "characters." What then are we to make of this? Just how creative is it? Just how nonfictional is it? Perhaps it's best to set these questions aside and instead *feel* for those involved.

Going beyond creative nonfiction and into the realm, possibly, of autobiographical fiction is Alan Kaufman's "Things Carl Little Crow and I Did Together to Stay Sober in San Francisco," an amazing performance of language and humanity. How "true" is it? I suspect very much of it is. I suspect very little of it is. I suspect, ultimately, that the question of this piece's veracity is *Does it matter?* If it's true, as the line in Todd Solondz's *Storytelling* goes, "Once you start writing, it all becomes fiction," then it may be equally true, from this editor's perspective anyway, that once you start writing, it all becomes *nonfiction*.

The bottom line is it either works or it doesn't. If it works, it works—and these 31 pieces by 31 diverse and distinct voices without question *work*. They are the best of the best that *Eclectica* has published in the categories of nonfiction, miscellany, and travel in the past 20 years.

My colleague Donna Talarico, founder of *Hippocampus Magazine*, who was kind enough to provide the introduction to this volume, is correct when she writes that each piece flows into the next. This is how the arrangement came to me: from one voice connecting to the next, connecting to the next, each in its own, ever-so-slight or ever-so-pronounced way. The first piece of this anthology, "Twenty Years" by Stanley Jenkins, connects to *Eclectica's* celebration itself, and the final piece, Monika Lange's "The World and I," brings it all together with its final line. I'd like to think *Eclectica* still exemplifies the spirit she invokes. I know I strive to do so.

David Ewald is *Eclectica's* nonfiction, miscellany and travel editor.

STANLEY JENKINS

Twenty Years

1.

NEXT WEEK WE will celebrate the 20th anniversary of my
Ordination at my church. We will have a special celebration at coffee
hour. (I donated a cake.)

I have invited a number of ghosts.

The lady in Waterloo, New York, who gave me her dead husband's
fishing rod and then clung to my hand while her heart seized up and
the doctors pushed air into her lungs and she needed me to look her in
the eye when she might die and I was her Pastor and 25 years old—
which I did—look her in the eye—as she chose to either live or die—
and she chose to live—and I was holding her hand when I was twenty-
five.

Ghosts.

And the lady, who I hope is still living, who called me in the middle
of the night to tell me she had swallowed a bottle of sleeping pills and
was going to die and would I take care of her children?—and who I

knew didn't have the money to pay the ambulance, so I, in perfect panic, walked her up and down the apartment and then finally into my car so I could take her to the emergency room and left her there after having to call her husband who wasn't home yet when the deal went down and tell him—he of sad eyes—where his wife was this time. Again.

I have invited the ghosts.

The man who had the eyes of a pole-axed drunk, married to a mail-order Indonesian bride, who could not hold a job, keep himself from slapping his wife, or even keep himself from pulling the trigger. He's invited, too. I called the cops to pick him up because he was obviously suicidal. It's the law. My duty. They committed him involuntarily for a few days. On my say so—or at least instigation (there was a psych evaluation, but still...). His wife took him back—but left the church. She was too ashamed.

And Valerie. Elderly Jewish woman who lived in Forest Hills. In a once luxury apartment. Wore hats. Marlo Thomas "That Girl" outfits. She came to me when it was too late. In her 60s. Already in the process of eviction. I don't even know why she came to the church. She was Jewish. Throwing herself at the feet of mercy of the minister of Jesus.

I was annoyed, it's true. I thought to myself that surely there was a Rabbi out there with responsibility. I was peevish and selfish. But she came to us. And I knew it was going to be bad. I followed her into the shelter system. She descended and descended. I stood by her every step of the way. I watched as she descended. As if chosen to watch her.

There wasn't a damn thing I could do about it. The last time I saw her, she clung to my hand and implored me to save her. To make it all better. I looked at her and knew what I knew from the first time she came to me. She didn't want to be saved. She wanted to drown and make someone responsible. Make someone pay.

There had been a husband who had deserted her. There had been a brother who had died and not provided for her. Every contact I set up for her—she rejected. Every city program I came up with—she had a problem with. Every hope she vetoed. I exhausted every avenue I knew. She didn't want to be saved. She wanted to drown and make someone responsible.

Jesus! Ghosts.

All the ghosts are invited. I seem to be just about ready to accept that you can't do this without being touched—without losing something with every touch, something that matters. Jesus plays for keeps. Just about ready to accept what I have always known, always preached and am always learning anew: love heals. We are loved. Love sustains.

There's just a price you pay for knowing that.

It's worth it, though. The price you pay. I think I can say that after 20 years, at least for myself. Even all the fear and self-doubt—and even occasional self-loathing. Hellhound on my trail! It's worth it. All these ghosts. I—a man with a deep coldness at heart—have been allowed to be kind.

2.

And the surprising number of incest cases that came up when I was in Upstate New York. The first was the most startling. She came to me for a school project. She said she wanted to be a Minister. She was supposed to tag along with me on a typical day as a Minister—for her school project. Within 20 minutes she had let me know she could give me a blow job.

It was her grandfather. He was molesting her. Had been sleeping with her for a couple of years. Raping her.

She never testified. He never went to jail. The grandfather. I moved on, and I have no idea what became of her life. She was exceptionally bright. Her mother never seemed to fully grasp it—she spent most of her time trying to encourage her daughter to get me to marry her. As if I could erase it. As if my office could erase it. As if becoming a minister's wife could atone for what had happened to her.

That girl—she really wasn't much younger than me at the time—I'm telling you, she was bright and beautiful and doomed. Her family would not accept the horror. She descended into promiscuity and self-immolation. I don't think she graduated from high school.

She's invited too. That ghost.

3.

I don't even know what I am anymore. I have always experienced my faith as a volcanic eruption—I mean the actual event of cataclysmic eruption—contained and arrested in a stylish, fine leather, handtooled, convenient carrying case—a brief case, if you will—designed for the modern man on the go. If you act now, shipping and handling are free. Credit terms available.

That's not true.

Sometimes I have experienced my faith as the return of a longed for gaze—a meeting of eyes—when I have had reason to avert my eyes—avert my eyes in shame—a becoming visible after having erased myself.

Other times I have experienced it as if in a dream, walking on water that should not hold my weight. Standing in the pulpit delivering the Pastoral Prayer, gripping the pulpit like one of those fantastical sculptures that used to jut out the bow of sailing ships, opening my wooden mouth and letting loose, like steam screeching a valve, like water trickling a creek, and feeling the contented sigh of a nestling, the settling in of a congregation—while I am erased and really very ugly and bitter about it, like a thirsty pipe, with what is needed always passing through but never slaking.

Other times I have experienced it as a kind of frozen explosion. And me walking around the shards, filing away at the sharp edges, alone and frigid, as if the ghosts of windgusts chilled the room. I am amazed at the space between the broken pieces in which I walk. I shouldn't be able to be here in that space.

Other times I have experienced it as a kind of seduction: a slow dance of power, hints of dominance, the aggression of submission, San Juan de la Cruz's suspension on the breast of the Beloved, the ecstasy of Santa Teresa, the animal rutting of the soul behind the gates of Eden.

Other times I have experienced it as a deep calm and a foundation beneath which I trust I cannot fall.

As I get older I suspect the future of my faith lies less with cataclysms and more with putting my dishes in the dishwasher. I am grateful for the drama though. I have seen farther on stage.

I have seen the parade of days. I have been loved.

BARBARA LEFCOWITZ

Fiber, Hands, and Fig Trees

From March/April 1999

1.

ON THE ISLAND of Barbados, I once watched an old woman weaving a basket from the roots of a wamba tree; when she finished her elaborate braiding of the long, tapered roots, interspersing them every few inches with coils of dark green fiber, the basket was so tautly woven, it could hold water. Always I have admired such work, as well the deft finger movements of those who create it: how their fingers dance the same steps over and over without missing a beat.

I talk with my hands. No matter how hard I might try to control their movements, my hands rise, fall, arc, slice and mince the air, sometimes making zig-zags worthy of a stepped pyramid, sometimes waving as if I secretly wished my hands were wings, sometimes performing the dance of a maundering drunk, whirling dervish, or the Hindu god Shiva as he circles in ecstatic trance.

The concentric upward curves of a fig tree's branches resemble the arrangement of Shiva's multiple arms as he dances the Nadanta or cosmic dance. Particularly striking are the bronze statuettes of Shiva cast in the South of India around the 11th century AD. The best of these figures suggests a cadenced movement, its turning effect accomplished through the positioning of the arms one behind the other. A similar architecture of branches distinguishes the related sycamore tree (Gr. sukomoros: sukon, fruit of the fig + moron, black mulberry).

2.

Given my tendency to dance with my hands, it's lucky I'm not a Hindu god or goddess—though I've always found their multiplicity of hands a most curious sort of icon. Surely the depiction of numerous hands and arms is related to each god's diversity of roles, some even contradictory. Shiva, at times the lord of destruction, at other times the ecstatic dancer, sometimes a young ascetic, and at still other times a most benevolent protector god, has as many as 18 hands.

In a well known statue, his upper right arm holds a drum balanced by a flame in the upper left; the lower left hand is curved in a gesture promising relief from pain, the lower right raised in a benedictory position.

Though usually possessing only four hands, several of the savior god Vishnu's incarnations hold in each an object pertinent to Vishnu's powers: the wheel or chakra, the conch shell, the club, and that ubiquitous fertility symbol, the lotus.

But the mystery remains: how come other polytheistic religions, whose gods also play multiple roles—the Greeks, the Egyptians, the Mayans, among others—do not grant their gods the gift of multiple hands? Do not, as it were, provide any iconic means for a division of labor?

All fibers have spiraling, threadlike characteristics, whether we speak of bast fibers from the phloem or nutritive tissues of trees and plants like jute, ramie, flax (from Gothic flahta, plaiting), or silk removed from the boiled cocoons of the silk moth and spun many times around a spindle, or any of the long filaments that wind through muscles and nerves. Of course the worms that produce silk cocoons are quintessentially spiral, weaving their way through vast quantities of mulberry leaves, which they consume almost continuously until ready to spin and be spun.

Fig trees, identified often with the sacred Tree of Knowledge, combine both the masculine and feminine—the leaf associated with the phallus, or at least its shield, and the fruit with the vulva. In Buddhist terms, the leaf is the linga and the fruit is the yoni. But what about the flower?

3.

Rainer Maria Rilke's sixth Duino Elegy begins by invoking the fig tree's mysterious omission of the flowering stage: "Fig-tree, for such a long time I have found meaning / in the way you almost completely omit your blossoms/and urge your pure mystery, unproclaimed, / into the early ripening fruit" (tr. Stephen Mitchell). After associating the fig tree with the fusion of god and swan, he makes an invidious contrast between the tree and our own tendency to "linger" because of pride in the showy blossom, so by the time we come to fruition we are "betrayed." The flowerless fig tree, though still mysterious, thus becomes an ideal for the high romantic hero.

Some fibers weave themselves together naturally, strong enough to use prior to human intervention. I have often admired the rough brown cloth unfurling from the bark of palm trees: a natural source of raffia for making baskets and a raw version of burlap. Some varieties of seaweed intermesh their fibers into patches suitable for a sea-quilt, and the largest of the green algae, Ulva or sea lettuce, can create ribbons and sheets several feet long. In desperation, one could even shape a shawl from the gulfweed commonly found floating in patches on the Sargasso Sea. And who, if lucky enough to find some, could resist twisting a rope from already intertwined, stray hemp fibers?

Palm reading originated in India, back around 1500 BC. From there the practice and theory traveled east to China and west to Egypt, Greece, and eventually to the dowdy shacks one sometimes sees on the back roads of America, a large sign in front proclaiming EXPERT PALM READING, FORTUNE TELLING, TAROT READINGS, courtesy of Madame Evangelina Sorbet de Savon Yablonka. A clue to the mystery of those multiple hands in Hindu iconography? But then there are the *mudras* (the Sanskrit word for signs), that vast array of hand gestures in both Hindu and Buddhist art, each *mudra* expressive of a particular state of being—e.g., the Dharmachakra *mudra*, hands juxtaposed one slightly below the other against the chest, index finger and thumb forming a circle, a gesture that sets the wheel of *dharma* (law, doctrine) in motion. Or the simple inversion of the right hand reaching towards the ground, palm inward—a gesture calling upon the earth to witness Buddha's enlightenment.

But every culture has its vocabulary of hand gestures, some markedly obscene, to the potential embarrassment of the ignorant tourist. I've even seen supposedly reserved Scotsmen making gestures with hands and fingers. So I'd be hard pressed to say an extraordinary interest in hands is particularly germane to the climate, geography, or natural life of India. And if, say, an American sculptor created a statue with three hands, he would likely be accused of an obsession with the grotesque. So the mystery of the multiple hands persists.

4.

First the rippling, then the retting, the breaking, and the scutching: even the words suggest a process far more harsh, indeed near-violent, than the image of smoothly woven, cream-color linen napkins, each folded under elegantly aligned and gleaming silverware at a formal dinner party. Yet the transformation of flax fiber into linen begins with pressing the stalks through a coarse metal comb whose long, sharp teeth remove seeds and leaves. Then the rippled stalks are ready to be decomposed or retted—either by immersion into a tank of hot water that is allowed to stagnate, encouraging bacteria to consume some of the stalk's chemicals and thus break the inner fibrous core from the outer layers, or by dispersion of the stalks on the ground for six weeks so the combination of dew and bacteria will accomplish the same end.

Voila! Time to dry the flax and pass it through long, fluted rollers so any hard, scabby excrescences will be crushed away. All the better to enter the surviving fibers into a scutching machine. ("Scutch" derives via French from the Latin word *escutere*, to shatter.) Purpose? To beat the hell out of them so the long bundles will emerge thoroughly purified and ready to be spun, cut, stitched, dyed, pressed, and perhaps folded carefully onto a formally set dinner table so someone might have the liberty of staining them red with spilled wine or making them sticky with buttery fingerprints.

The rustling music of a silk kimono or gown may suggest a Zen-like calm, but the transformation from silkworm to silk thread is anything but. First comes the picking and plucking of the firmest young yellow worms. After they form cocoons comes the boiling, and then women traditionally retrieve the hot threads with their fingers, twisting and joining them to be spun on spindles or reels. At this point the women, at least in modern Indochina, eat what's left of the cooked worms.

After the spinning comes the drying of spun threads in the hot sun. In the words of Katharine Wardle, the threads at this point resemble "coarse blond hair," eventually to undergo a metamorphosis into raw silk, subsequently knitted or woven into textures with names like chiffon, charmeuse, matelasse, shantung, and *peau de soie*... and draped around the expensively perfumed bodies of expensive women, their silk gowns making a gently rustling music.

And let's not forget the Silk Wars—the 30 centuries of fanatic secrecy on the part of the early Chinese discoverers of silk—or the incursions of the Indians and Japanese, or Emperor Justinian's invasions of China to steal mulberry seeds and silkworm eggs, or the 17th century silk rivalry between Italy and France.

In Bursa, Turkey, Ibrahim Sansar calls the silk caterpillars "voracious as locusts." His wife keeps the larvae behind a dark curtain to protect them from the evil eye.

I am not aware of any superstitions about hands intertwining fibers, but I know a few linked with the intertwining of a hand's fingers themselves. Nearly universal is the notion that crossing one's fingers can bring about good luck, while clasping the fingers of one hand with those of the other may ward off punishment. Remember when you had to sit at your school desk with tightly clasped hands lest you do something naughty and invite the wrath of the teacher? I believe the practice is now much less common, but people of a certain age might identify with my memory of clasping my hands so firmly, they seemed to have converged into one and I feared I would never be able to pry the interlocked fingers apart.

A hand with an eye embedded in the middle helps ward off the evil eye, particularly in Islamic cultures. Sometimes called the talismanic hand, it also signifies clairvoyance.

Fig trees fare poorly in the Gospels. In the Parable of the Barren Fig Tree (Luke 13:6-9), the tree represents the Hebrew rejection of Jesus. After pleading with the owner of the vineyard to leave the barren tree alone for a year to give the Hebrews time to repent, Jesus eventually condemns the tree and orders it cut down. In Mark 11:12-14, Jesus curses a similarly fruitless tree:

And on the morrow, when they were come from Bethany, he was hungry. And seeing a fig tree afar off having leaves, he came, if haply he might find any thing thereon: and when he came to it, he found nothing but leaves; for the time of figs was not yet. And

Jesus answered and said unto it, No Man eat fruit of thee hereafter for ever...

Shortly thereafter, the fig tree dries up completely, roots to branches. Once again, the lack of fruit is interpreted as lack of faith in the teachings of Jesus.

5.

Figs and fig trees play an essential role in several mysterious transformations. While sitting under a fig or pipal tree, the Buddha attained enlightenment. Mohammed swore by a fig, thus transforming it to a sacred fruit to which he attributed an intelligence nearly on the level of an animal's. In both Italy and parts of Africa, women are anointed with the milky sap of the fig (and sometimes tied to a fig tree) in order to encourage fertility. The milk of the wild fig in particular has been widely savored for its curative properties. Folktales tell of magical figs bringing on sleep or causing horns to grow on the heads of people—is the latter a veiled reference to cuckoldry, the adulterous escapades of the errant mate having taken place while the husband or wife was deep in an enchanted fig-sleep? And let's not forget the particular association of a basket of figs with woman as earth goddess or mother.

Baskets themselves have a long history related to the use of fibers, especially reeds, roots, grasses, and raffia. Celebrations of the Dionysian Mysteries involved baskets covered with ivy, containing both fruit and a concealed phallus. Ceres often carried a basket. No one knows who made the basket used to rescue the infant Moses, but he was not the only person to be so rescued. Thinking back to when I watched the woman of Barbados weaving wamba roots and reeds into a basket, I wonder if it was ultimately used to hold an infant, a supply of wheat or barley flour, stray threads and buttons, mangoes or starfruit—or perhaps she used it as a receptacle for various fibers gathered until she had enough to transform them into yet another basket?

In ancient Hinduism, nine basic types of handicrafts were not only deemed honorable by the divine artisan Visvakarman but considered part of any worldly man's education. To manipulate a particular material or substance in its raw state and transform it into a thing of beauty, utility, or both, was thought both morally and intellectually worthy. Many treatises laid out the rules for the various crafts. Among the nine basic crafts is the hand weaving of not only cotton, silk, and wool, but coconut fiber into textiles and rugs. "Stem-working," or the twisting of fresh stems into garlands and joining of reeds to create rush mats and baskets, was considered important enough to warrant a separate category.

Perhaps the next time I catch myself talking with my hands, I will make sure to have some string or threads nearby. Maybe even reeds, wamba roots, coconut fibers, fig roots. Then I can transform my words into something beautiful, useful, or even both.

ROLF POTTS

Greenland is Not Bigger Than South America: A Memoir of the 1994 Northridge Earthquake

From August/September 1998

(Joshua Tree National Monument, California, January 25)

I AM SITTING exactly 5,461 feet above sea-level, atop Ryan Mountain in the midst of Joshua Tree National Monument, looking skyward. Above me, manic clouds are hovering and morphing against the blue sky, but they can hardly compete with the static, brown magnificence of this Mojave landscape.

Below me to the east, the lack of vegetation makes the desert basin look particularly barren and moonlike, as if it is impassable without space suits and a lunar rover. Below us to the west, out of sight and 140 miles away, Los Angeles sits in a disarray of broken sewer mains, collapsed freeway overpasses, and condemned houses: the result of a 6.6 magnitude earthquake that shook the city eight days ago. On that morning, I was jolted awake before sunrise, convinced in a moment of groggy confusion the world was coming to an end. From what I can tell, it didn't—except for the 55 individuals who died in the process. Apocalypse is subjective, I guess.

I arrived at Joshua Tree last night under a full moon, which lit everything in a colorless glow and made me feel like I was in a giant indoor arena illuminated by dying fluorescent lights. I hiked a bit in the dim light, navigating a route over the sandy soil between the scrub brush and cacti, through the arroyos. I stopped at a cluster of aplite granite boulders to watch the clouds form. To the west, the sky was clear and starry, but directly above wisps of clouds magically appeared and sped with time-lapse quickness to a growing mass over Ryan Mountain. The clouds occasionally blocked out the neon glow of the moon, and every time the illumination returned, I expected to grow suddenly warmer, as if the moon brokered the sun's heat. I felt charmed as I watched the clouds form, like I'd caught America in her dressing room: unassuming, beautiful, and half-clothed.

I have not seen any other people all day, and I am enjoying the deluded euphoric feeling that I am the first person ever to reach this stark mountaintop. A bright red canister here at the summit cairn speaks otherwise. Inside the canister, a roll of paper bears the comments of people who have made the ascent in recent weeks:

"Nuthin' like this in Michigan."

"New Year's Day. My name is Joe, I am too drunk to know where I am or how I got here."

"Sitting and reading in the old birthday suit. Took a picture of my clothes. This is great."

"Unemployed and having fun."

"There will be no gloom and doom. I can do it."

"Sufi sez, "It's the sides of the mountain that support life, not the summit."

"Unplug your TV and give it away. Read a book. Talk less. Look more."

Supposedly, prophets operate in the desert to avoid temptations, but I get the feeling the emptiness of the desert itself is what makes a prophet out of a person. This is not to say I feel like a prophet right now. In fact, it's quite the opposite. The earthquake has shaken my sense of order. I feel like I have been operating out of a reality that more closely resembles a two-dimensional map of the world than the world itself: it works fine for the most part, but it distorts at the poles.

Alas, Greenland is not bigger than South America, and daily life does not always make sense. Random odds carry a casual sort of eminence in this world, and the situations into which you place yourself only regulate your life as is allowed by those situations that place themselves into you. This is easy to forget—unless you regularly have opportunities to look into the eyes of people whose homes have just been destroyed in the span of 30 seconds.

That I was in Los Angeles eight days ago is an accident. I only stopped there because Michele Poulos—a girl I met at a party in Oregon two years ago—offered to let me stay at her parents' place while I was passing through on my way from Seattle to New Orleans. Since I am always up for a chance to sleep someplace other than my van, I took her up on the offer.

I have since forgotten what I was dreaming about at 4:30 that morning. I do, however, recall being suddenly awake at 4:31, the lamp above the bed clanging and smacking into the wall, my bed bouncing like it was skittering down a rock-strewn hill. I heard an explosion, and the room was filled with a harsh blue light, illuminating a desk, which galloped like a rigid horse away from the wall, the drawers sliding open and regurgitating their contents onto the floor.

Confused and bewildered, I grabbed hold of my mattress and held on as the house bashed and thundered against itself. Something broke free from the wall and landed across my back. For an odd moment, I thought reality had given out on me, that I would have to cope for the rest of my life in a world shaking itself apart. I tried to wriggle deeper into bed, as if the covers would protect me if the house collapsed. Pillow over my head, I waited for the ceiling to crash down. Then—suddenly—abrupt, exhausted stillness. After a couple moments of eerie quiet, I cautiously rolled over to inspect the room. A framed painting slid off my back and thumped onto the floor.

What I did next was the first of the mild absurdities marking my post-earthquake experience. Lamp swinging above; floor littered with books, clothes, broken wall-hangings; bathroom mirror exploded into a glitter of shards across the carpet; cracks drunkenly zagging the wall from floor to ceiling; I lay back down and tried to sleep. Perhaps I assumed all earthquakes were like this, and that everyone put off cleanup until daylight.

Michele's mother burst in with a flashlight and told me to go down to the ground floor. I put on my shoes and ran down the stairs, where, huddled in the doorjamb, we weathered a sudden series of aftershocks. We waited out the lulls between tremors in tense silence. Everything seemed so melodramatic and improbable, I half-expected Mrs. Poulos to break into song—as if I had somehow entered an absurdist off-Broadway stage production of my own life.

We eventually met Dr. Poulos in the kitchen and sat through the uncertain calm of the predawn morning, grouped around the radio like a post-apocalyptic campfire ring. The safety procedure information crackling from the radio sounded sterile and serenely creepy. I imagined the worst, reviving long-latent post-nuclear war survivalist fantasies wherein I wander for days and days through piles of smoking rubble. A live announcer came on after a while, but he mostly described the earthquake in terms of fault lines and tectonic plates. Seismology might be meaningful to some people, but to me, the aftershocks came on like the powerful anger of some irrational, obsolete earth-god.

Curious about the non-scientific extent of the quake—and somewhat uncomfortable sitting in a dim kitchen with these people I barely knew—I ventured outside at dawn to check out the damage and stock up on food and bottled water. Outside, Los Angeles was a full-sized facade of itself. Everything looked the same as before, but nothing functioned. Stoplights hung dead from their poles, brick fences slumped into yards like capsized stacks of dominoes, and workers were already out nailing plywood over shattered storefronts. Everyone I passed on the sidewalk peered around with stunned fascination, like they were walking through a museum. The air was warm, fragrant, and strangely quiet. I walked and stared for two hours but never found a functioning grocery store.

I returned to the Poulos house, where none of us knew what to do. We mostly just sat in the narcotic glow of the TV and waited for some feasible official interpretation of what had happened to us. Omniscience was in short supply. We watched helicopter footage of smoking buildings, listened to officials give tentative death-tallies, peered at hastily-assembled graphic maps of the metro area. Awkward and lost for words, TV reporters stood on street-corners making analogies about the Kennedy assassination. Seismic scientists squinted under bright lights and admitted their data was incomplete. Viewers called in and spoke in shaky voices about drinking water, electricity, missing pets, fear, and the Book of Revelation. By late afternoon I was pacing around in the Poulos basement, shooting a disjointed game of pool against myself. I could never finish without the balls getting jostled by aftershocks.

That evening—in a moment of paranoid boredom—I resolved to leave, to drive to the desert and check up on my friend Josh in Valencia. Against the advice of Dr. and Mrs. Poulos, I fired up my van and left Los Angeles.

I made it as far as the San Fernando valley before a row of orange cones sent me off I-405 into some of the worst-hit sections of

Northridge and Sylmar. Entire neighborhoods sat in a spooky, siege-like blackness as we crept through the epicenter war-zone. National Guardsmen in full combat regalia patrolled the streets, clutching M-16 rifles and eyeing license plates. Brick fences lay uniformly flattened. Water from broken mains rushed through the gutters. On Balboa Boulevard an office building had crumpled, crazily squashing out its own first floor. Gas-main fires had blackened and pocked stretches of ground like fiery acne on Northridge's face. Cops with flashlights waved me through dead-stoplight intersections.

I thought I might have a smooth, slow transit into Valencia—until a National Guardsman shined his flashlight into my face and told me the route to the Santa Clarita valley was closed. He waved me down another blackened street into a neighborhood full of cul-de-sacs where I wandered lost for an hour. Front yards in this neighborhood had become tent colonies, and residents sat in front of their ruined houses and stared blankly as I drove by. The whole neighborhood looked useless, like an oversized closet of broken toys. When I finally stopped and asked a woman for directions, she spoke in a tiny, ghost-like voice, as if she were saving her breath for fear of another jolt. The yard behind her was stacked with hastily-salvaged possessions, her house charred black at the windows.

Around midnight I made my way into Valencia and located Josh's apartment complex. I parked my van at the curb since all the gravel-topped carports sagged and wilted toward the ground, as if they had been roofed with bed-sheets.

Josh is a film student, and his living room was a mangled chaos of borrowed cameras, carts, electrical cords, capsized light-stands, notebooks, splintered wall-hangings, and furniture. His huge player piano was gouged into a wall across the room. Every time an aftershock hit, the apartment swayed around like a wooden box in the surf. I pushed aside some of the mess, spread out my sleeping bag, and slept amidst the disarray of the living room.

I stayed with Josh for nearly a week. We jokingly referred to each other as "victims" the whole time, and—in a way—I guess that's what we were. Josh is an Oregon native who looks like a TV sportscaster, talks like a diplomat, drinks a gallon of Coke a day, attends church regularly, and has the single-minded motivational skills of a cult-leader. Although the aftershocks continued at regular intervals throughout the week—and most of the apartment tenants abandoned their units for tent living at the Cal Arts campus—Josh somehow convinced me that there was no danger in immediately making his apartment livable again. As military helicopters thumped their way across the sky toward unseen duties, we threw open the doors to the unlighted apartment and went to work. We reorganized the film equipment and swept the floors, then rehung all the wall-hangings—most of which fell down again during the aftershocks. We tossed the broken kitchenware into the rubble piles in the parking lot. One room was littered shin-deep in film reels, antique projectors, screenplays, storyboards, still photos, an old Bolex camera, super-8 films, and various elements of a homemade film editing setup. We spent two days making sense of everything.

Even the most basic functions required creativity. To use the toilet, we had to bring pitchers of feathery green water up from the duck pond in the outside courtyard and pour them into the commode. Bottled water was nearly impossible to find, so we subsisted primarily on two cases of kiwi-lime soda donated by an aid station. For supper, we warmed up cans of Spaghetti-O's on my camp-stove. Josh immediately went to work on the problem of bathing. With all the meticulous detail of a Hollywood producer, he took to the mangled phone lines every morning trying to locate showers for the day. We traveled as far away as Palmdale in the pursuit of functional plumbing. Josh had run out of options by the third day, so he pulled out his file of acting portfolios and landed us showers at an aspiring actress's apartment in Burbank.

The direct route to Burbank had been rendered impassable, so we crept along desert back-roads amongst a huge snarl of LA-bound traffic. Despite the chaotic conditions, most people were remarkably patient and cheerful. At dead-stoplight intersections, drivers politely yielded to one another. At one point, where traffic was forced to a crawl by a narrow canyon road, a couple of kids went car-to-car selling cans of Pepsi for a dollar.

It took us so long to get into Burbank, we decided to stay in the LA area for the day and salvage the afternoon with some generic Hollywood tourism. We parked off Hollywood Boulevard and wandered around for a while, but nearly everything was shut down. Eventually we narrowed our agenda to finding a drink of water, but this proved fruitless as the entire LA tap-water supply had been declared unsafe. After a while we actually began to crave our kiwi-lime "victim soda." We went to Mann's Chinese Theater, hoping to get soft-drinks, but instead we got free tickets to a taping of the "Leeza Gibbons Show." Unfortunately, we got onto the wrong RTD bus on our way to the studio and ended up riding north to Van Nuys with a bus full of laborers headed home for the day. The earthquake had rendered the Hollywood landmarks irrelevant, and everyone stared out at the new attractions: boarded-over stores with "open" spray-painted onto the plywood, patrols of armed National Guardsmen, piles of rubble.

By the time we figured out we were not anywhere close to the "Leeza Gibbons Show," our bus had come to the end of its line and we had to catch another bus back to Hollywood. It was late when we arrived, and we decided to go to a Taco Bell drive-through for dinner. "Where the hell have you been?" the Taco Bell voicebox squawked when we asked for water with our food. "Don't you know there's been an earthquake?"

We didn't get water, but for some reason Taco Bell gave us nearly 50 packets of hot sauce. Stirred to callous absurdity by the events of the day, we drove through the snarled LA rush-hour traffic yelling at people out the window.

"Where the hell have you been?" we yelled at pedestrians. "Don't you know there's been an earthquake?" After this got tiresome, we changed our slogan to "Don't eat the fish!"

Perhaps not understanding us, perhaps identifying with our delirium, a surprising number of pedestrians yelled back or gave us the thumbs-up. Encouraged by the response, we continued into downtown LA for more sloganeering. In one particularly seedy neighborhood, I leaned out the window and asked a transvestite hustler what I could get for four packets of mild. He blew me a kiss with his extended middle finger.

We returned to the apartment that night and never did attempt another foray into Los Angeles. On our final afternoon in Valencia, we went down to the duck pond to loll in the sun and watch the mild aftershocks ripple the water. The management had prohibited wading, but three little Mexican boys made the most of the situation by skimming the water's edge for insects. Whenever one of the kids caught a bug, he would show it to his companions, then triumphantly squash it into the pavement. The mother—a slim, pretty girl who didn't look much older than me—sat stiffly in a metal folding chair nearby, never taking her eyes off the water. Whenever a tremor shook the pond into a cluster of little waves, she winced. Despite her children's small, gleeful victories over nature, I sensed it would be a while before she would trust the earth again.

Five days after arriving in the Santa Clarita valley, I did something few other people who had weathered the earthquake could do: I left and took my home with me.

Sitting here in this Joshua Tree desert, I look up at the hovering clouds and see something resembling a bull floating its way overhead. The bull drifts west, where the clouds have laced themselves together at the edge of the sky, dissolving the horizon into mystery. Not a mystery of the unknown but a mystery of the familiar, of places already traveled.

Reality resists triangulations and formulas. In the end, reality becomes a choice, a decision after the fact. I am tempted to add up the extremes of the earthquake—the dull horrors and the absurdities—and pass them off as cloud-like aberrations, manifestations of the surreal, melting clocks and fur-covered teacups in an otherwise ordered gallery. But then, surreality only occurs when we believe too much in reason and order, time and space, predictability and consistency. Civilization is surreal, not earthquakes. And when we derive too much meaning from the manifestations of civilization, we sometimes find ourselves in a meaningless world.

The olive-drab desert surrounding me now communicates the same idea. It vetoes the constructs and intrusions of man. There are no horrors or absurdities here because the desert does not allow us to fool ourselves in the first place. Perhaps, like Job in the Old Testament, we have missed the point. We have looked for answers and received only a reprimand. Unlike good or evil, randomness carries no antipode, only a blank expression.

Consequently, we discover the only way around randomness is to return full-circle into a world of oversized Greenlands, to ignore this blank expression as it ignores us. To live by faith. It makes for an odd compromise—this faith—and it requires we use it with caution, that we resist the urge to glance skyward and brazenly conclude clouds are bulls.

ANA DOINA

Earthquake

From April/May 2004

WHEN I WAS a little girl in Romania, visiting my father every other weekend and on vacations, I had to share a room with my brothers. The oldest, Ilie, five years my senior, used to tell us kids stories in the dark before going to sleep.

Thus I found out at an early age how the earth is round like a cabbage, how the monkeys at the zoo are actually our first cousins, how if I wanted to sing with the Beatles, all I had to do was talk with my tongue twisted inward and my mouth half closed, so I might realize that particular British accent. And if I wanted to be a hippie, I needed to let my hair grow unwashed, not cut my nails, and not wash my feet for a couple of weeks, and the same recipe would work for becoming a gypsy, too. Or if my dream was to be the first woman to conquer Mount Everest, I had better start my training with climbing on the walls of tall buildings while holding my breath.

One night during a winter vacation, our cousin Avia, with whom I shared my birthday, was with us. When we were together, my brothers and I, we liked to test each other's limits, each other's strength. How far could we stand verbal or visual images of life's vicissitudes before starting to cry, before crumbling under the weight of fright or disgust? But we became inspired master-artisans at this game when a cousin or a friend was around, and Avia was always a perfect companion, getting into the game, inventing new challenges. After all, she was the one who introduced the fly-in-the-soup game, to see if Ilie would still eat the soup after a couple of flies were thrown in among the noodles.

We girls were about eight, Ilie 13, and the baby, Florin, was three years old when one night, with parents gone to a party and Tanti Ana, our Hungarian nanny, in the next room watching a sad Russian war movie, the four of us stood in the dark near the glistening Christmas tree, telling stories and laughing to camouflage our fright. We dared each other to come up with something scarier and scarier, while Tanti Ana's loud sobs and the heart-wrenching music of a *balalaika* filled the house.

Outside, the frozen bare branches of a wild-cherry tree chimed in the wind, sending darker-than-night shadows across the room, over our bodies, becoming part of our stories. Each one of us was trying to find out what scared the others the most. What was it that really put the fear of death into us? What image, what notion, what event would shake us and crush us? But none of us older kids would recognize anything as scary. We were tough.

Only Florin readily confessed that a wolf's cry in a winter forest was what scared him the most, although I don't think he had yet seen a forest or a wolf back then. Nevertheless, he got out of his crib and crawled around the room, howling with his three-year-old voice and coming to frighten and bite us.

We were roaring with laughter when suddenly Ilie shouted, "Stop! Stop!" and jumped to his feet. But I couldn't stop. From his bed Ilie threw a big pillow towards me, and a glorious pillow fight was just about to begin when Tanti Ana marched into the room, turned the lights on, and yelled in her broken Romanian, "You kids, devils, you make house shake. You go sleep now or cake no tomorrow."

Ilie and Avia looked at each other as if something only they knew or understood had happened. Florin was on all fours on the floor, still howling like a lonely wolf. I, up on my feet in the middle of the bed holding a pillow, burst into a cascade of laughter.

"It was an earthquake," Ilie said, and Avia nodded.

"It was not," I dissented, and they showed me the lamp still swinging above our heads.

"Earthquake, shmarquake," said Tanti Ana. "You kids shook house jumping. Go sleep," and she picked Florin up from the floor and placed him back in his crib.

Florin was asking again and again, "What's an earthquake? What's an earthquake?"

After Tanti Ana turned off the lights and the *balalaika* could be heard again through the walls, Ilie proclaimed, "It was a five on the Richter. Sure it was!"

"It was cool to feel the earth shake! Awesome!" said Avia.

I protested. It couldn't have been. I didn't feel anything, and the lamp? It must have just been hit by the pillow. There had been no earthquake! They declared me "insensitive" and explained to Florin what an earthquake was.

We were getting quiet. Soon I could hear my brothers' even breaths. Avia and I, awake long into the night, talked and giggled and finally admitted to each other what scared us the most. For her, airplane crashes. Her father was a pilot. For me, the possible death of my mother, and we both admitted we were afraid of war and the bomb.

Earthquakes? I couldn't feel them. The earth would move; some felt it, some not. I didn't.

For years Avia would call me after a short trembler, asking, "Did you feel it?" and I wouldn't have. "How could you not feel it?" she'd ask me, excited by the event, bewildered by my lack of registering it. I don't know. I just did not feel them. They were rare occurrences, small, not more than four to five degrees or so, only a few seconds. It could've been a truck on the road for all I knew, or a slammed door, and there were always slammed doors in my house. Growing up I had learned not to pay any attention to what made a house shake.

We all grew. Avia and I consoled each other through parents' divorces, new stepmothers, new stepfathers, high school, boys. We remained friends even through the biggest trials friendship could go through at that age: a boy she liked had a crush on me, and then she stole the only guy I had ever had a crush on. Through it all we laughed, danced and grew, and we loved each other dearly.

We were a lot alike, interested in people and books, trying our pen at writing poems and stories, but she was always prettier than I with her huge blue eyes and long, silky blond hair. She was always positive, self-confident, and witty, while I was pensive, insecure, and moody.

At the time, I was living with my mom in one of the tallest buildings in town, and Avia and I used to love watching the world from my bedroom window. From the 12th floor everyone looked like a small marionette, and we'd imagine their lives, their loves, just by how their sketched silhouettes moved and interacted with people and landscape. But most of all we loved to watch the sunset from my window. It was a breathtaking view of the eastern side of the town. Parks, lakes, large boulevards, old churches, marble buildings, and the old Triumphant Arch built after the first war, all bathed in the amber and crimson lights of a huge sun going down behind thick forests at the outskirts of town.

Somehow, in the last year of high school and the first few years of college, Avia and I grew apart, busy with admission exams, new friends, jobs. We'd talk sometimes, or meet by chance at parties or on the street, always promising we would again make time in our lives for each other, sometime soon.

After high school and during the first two years of college, I had a part-time job as a sound technician at the TV station, close by my mother's house. I had moved out to a small flat of my own in a different part of town by then, but still I spent a lot of time at my mom's.

One evening going home from work, I met Avia on the bus, and it was as if we had never been apart. She told me of her fiancé and her paintings—she was a very talented artist—and I told her about exams, work, the guy I was dating. Upon parting we promised to get together the following Friday. It was Monday night. She was very happy, and she couldn't wait to get together again and introduce to me her fiancé, so Friday at my house was to be it! I was already thinking of what to wear and what desserts to bake.

Usually on Tuesday after work I met with three friends for *profiterol,* my favorite dessert, at Casata, one of the city's most popular cafes, but somehow this one particular Tuesday all four of us were busy and had to take a rain check from our weekly ritual. So much the better, I thought. I had a lot to study for a midterm exam.

While studying in my room, I had the door to the balcony opened. It was an unusually warm, early March evening with a huge, full, ruby-red moon like a grapefruit. I was fascinated by this moon and could not keep my eyes on the notes or my thoughts on the simple Aristotelian logic, when all of a sudden a roaring noise came from the street, and the building started to shake violently.

"An earthquake!" I said out loud, almost amused, but then I saw how threatening and huge the wall unit in my room was. Full of books, it swayed and buckled right in front of me. I jumped on my bed and covered myself with the thick down comforter, pulling a pillow over my head, but not before I saw a century-old crystal vase I had from my grandfather fall to the floor and miraculously remain intact.

The building shook and shook and shook for what seemed an eternity. The lights stayed on for the better part of the earthquake, but eventually the entire town was plunged into the eerie redness of that moonlit night.

The morning of that same day, while at work at the TV station, I had watched a movie about the 1906 earthquake in San Francisco, doing some editing to it to make it fit for viewing. It was scheduled to show the following Friday. Now, all I could think of while my building shook was how San Francisco had been consumed by fire after the earthquake. I feared the same would happen to us. At one point I thought to go out of the building, but then I dismissed the idea, knowing that across from the exit there was an old school, and from its roof tiles would fall during even a simple storm.

When the shaking finally stopped, I could hear people screaming, sirens, and my neighbors, mostly old ladies and retired couples, coming out of their apartments, asking, "What happened? What happened?"

I put my coat on, took my purse. My hands were shaking, and a thousand thoughts were racing through my head: What about my mother's building? Should I report back to the station?

I picked up the crystal vase from the floor. The exquisite cuts caught and reflected a reddish glow. While it hadn't shattered, the vase was indeed cracked.

The air coming from outside was dusty, and in the distance I could see fire and smoke, and I could hear the loud noise of glass breaking, people screaming, honking horns, sirens, and more sirens. The night felt like an ultimatum. Ominous, tragic.

For a moment I thought not even to bother locking up the apartment, and then I thought to look for and take with me the deed to the house. Nothing made sense, my thoughts least of all.

My next-door neighbor, a very old lady for whom I'd sometimes bought milk or brought the newspaper, knocked on my door, crying. A few of the oldest neighbors, afraid or unable to go down the stairs and outside the building, were congregating in the hallway in front of my door, sharing impressions and fears. An old man, a war veteran, said the Russians had bombed us. "Nonsense!" I said, forgetting I should be respectful to my elders. "Nonsense! It was an earthquake."

"Really?!" a few old ladies said in disbelief. "How big?"

"Seven," I said. "Must have been seven," and for a moment I smiled in the dark. It really must have been seven. I had felt none of the ones before, the smaller ones.

When I left the building, I noticed the roof on the old school was intact. None of the tiles had fallen. The pharmacy at the corner had all the windows broken, and people were already inside, looting. Two trams were stuck on their tracks in the middle of an intersection, a third one was turned on its side alongside the boulevard crossing that part of town. There were no buses, no taxis, only cars driving haphazardly, many on the wrong side of the street.

I managed to stop a car and begged the driver, an older man, to take me towards my mother's part of town. He seemed to be going in that direction anyway. His wife was with him. She couldn't stop crying. The old man asked me to help her calm down. "She suffers with her heart," he said.

I asked her what she was doing right before the earthquake. "I was cooking," she said. "Chicken."

"And what kind of spices did you use?" I asked, while the old man drove through a town I could no longer recognize.

At times he had to go around large chunks of buildings piled up in the middle of the boulevard. Wires were everywhere. At Lizeanu, a major intersection a block away from where I lived, two buildings had collapsed, each ten stories high. Leveled. I knew that two of my schoolmates lived there. Other places were so thick with dust, the car's headlights were reflected back, blinding us. Driving past the emergency and trauma hospital, we had to brake suddenly when a naked woman holding a bulky blanket jumped in front of the car, crossing the street without paying attention to the chaotic traffic. "My

God," said the wife. "People have no shame nowadays." Then we saw the woman's huge, anguished eyes shine in the headlights, her mouth twisted as if she was moaning, and we noticed the young child she was holding wrapped in the blanket, bleeding from the head. The wife shrieked and crossed herself with wide gestures while the husband began to mumble something. "He's Jewish," the wife said almost apologetically. "He prays in Yiddish."

I started making a checklist in my mind of where my loved ones were, or where they could have been. Ilie was in a remote village, a young doctor. My dad was on a business trip in a town many miles away. Florin was in Canada. My mother, she could have been anywhere, home or elsewhere. I didn't know, but I knew wherever she was, she was worried about me, just as I was worried about her.

Normally the ride shouldn't have taken more than 15 minutes, but it took almost an hour to cross the town as we had to take back-roads, avoid fallen and falling debris, turn around from blocked streets, drive on sidewalks.

The old man dropped me off right in front of the station. The building was still standing. Some windows were even lit. I ran through the streets all the way to my mom's. A few blocks before I got there, I could see the dark silhouette of the building. Good, it was still up.

The entire neighborhood was quiet and didn't show any damage. I felt a bit safer there, but I realized no one in that part of town had any idea of what the rest of it looked like. You could hear laughter and jokes in the dark. I ran with tears streaming down my cheeks and yelled to those I could see, "Lizeanu is down! There are collapsed buildings all over town!"

"You're exaggerating," a few said. "Stop spreading rumors," said another.

In this part of town surrounded by parks, not even the sound of the sirens was heard. In front of my mom's building, a few neighbors were still outside. Poly, our housekeeper, was afraid to go back in and didn't like the idea of having to climb "all those damned stairs," since the elevator was not working anymore.

Mother was not there. She had not been home at the time of the earthquake.

The building didn't seem to have been damaged, but when she fled the apartment, Poly said, she had heard behind her a loud thump. The many bookshelves must have collapsed all over the house.

At one point the entrance doors to the building opened, and Nini, our next-door neighbor, a huge 27-year-old man, came out carrying on his back his just-as-huge, bedridden mother, while his tiny sister was tediously pulling and pushing a folded wheelchair down the last flight of stairs. Their father, a cardiac patient, had decided the chances of being killed by an aftershock were meager compared to the real chance of a heart attack brought on by going down and eventually back up the 12 stories. He remained in the candle-lit apartment, despite his family's pleas to come out.

Slowly, more people returned from downtown, all telling confusing stories. Among them was my mother, who had been visiting with some friends when the earthquake started, and had first run over to my place to see if I was okay. News of the destruction elsewhere was sifting into this surreally calm neighborhood.

Later that night I decided to go to the station after all, but once I got there they sent me home, asking me to be back early next morning.

All night long we tried to catch something on the radio. Our radio stations were mute for many hours, and then for another few hours there was only funeral music. We tried Budapest, Moscow, Prague, Free Europe, Paris, London. All said nothing about the earthquake, just their usual programming, music, news bulletins relating the local events of the day. Nobody knew something had happened to us, and we didn't know what we were facing. We could just as well have been wiped from the face of the earth, and no one would have even noticed, while our officials were drowning us in funeral marches.

Finally, around midnight, a commentator at some English-speaking radio post announced jokingly that for the last few hours only funeral marches had been broadcasted from Bucharest. He speculated that in the best Cold War tradition, that probably meant Ceausescu was dead. Shortly after, Free Europe interrupted their regular programming with a news bulletin announcing that a 50 second earthquake of 7.2 degrees on the Richter scale had been registered with an epicenter in the Vrancea Mountains. They said that no contact could be established with Bucharest. And then they prayed for us, wishing us luck and strength in the face of whatever it was we were facing.

By midnight the phone lines in some parts of town started to work, and a neighbor whose apartment was on the first floor let me call a few people to find out how they were doing. Most of them were all right, which made me think maybe things weren't as bad as they had first looked.

The idea of having to walk up all those stairs and the fear of aftershocks, not being able to assess in the dark the damage the building had sustained, kept us outside for a long time. But we were tired, worn out, and confused, and after a while Poly, Mother, and I decided to go spend the night at Aunt Lori's, a few blocks away from our place. Hers was a two-story villa, spacious and solidly built in the middle of a garden.

It had started to rain. I was lying on a velvet sofa trying to sleep, but each time I closed my eyes, I saw the face of that strange, naked woman. The terror in her eyes, her incomprehensible specter, her twisted mouth, the bundle she was holding.

Towards daybreak, the sky turned a milky color and the town was eerily quiet.

I went to work very early, six o'clock or so. A few cameramen and a news director were already there. They looked grim and tired. No cameraman wanted to take me on his team. "You're too young," "You kid, stay out of it!" "You're a girl—it's no sight for a girl," "Stay in the studio; you'll get to see enough," they said. Truth be told, I was afraid. My fear was nothing I could name, just anxiety. But there were not enough sound technicians, and I knew the equipment, so I ended up going anyway.

On any other early morning, the town would have been busy with people going to work, waiting for buses, buying bread, newspapers, flowers. The shops would be open, the street sweeper washing the sidewalks, garbage men collecting the garbage, their bulky trucks making traffic impossible. Not that day. Only peasants from the suburban villages were coming with their horse-drawn carriages, bringing produce to market and asking, "What the hell happened here?"

There were a few buildings down at the outskirts of town. One of the news teams was going there, while the rest of us were distributed through the town. Our van took the same route I had come by the night before. Some of the buildings were visibly shaken but still standing, while some I hadn't noticed the night before were down. Groups of men and women, exhausted, hurt, were pulling rubble out of the way. Some had kitchen knives in their hands, buckets, brooms, hammers, and they were desperately trying to find out if anyone caught under the heaps of wreckage was still alive.

Many of those pulling survivors out of the ruins had just walked out from underneath the crumbled walls themselves. Prepared? Back then, this was not even a concept. Faced with an emergency, one was left to one's lucky star or to prayers if there were any. Usually, when an emergency struck, families would help their own, and an informal network of friends and neighbors would form, eventually. But now we had all been hit at once.

In all the 27 years I had lived in that city, I knew of only one firehouse. It was a century-old historic building about four stories high, placed in what once was the middle of the old town. As there were very few if any wood structures left (most buildings were made of concrete, limestone, marble, steel, and glass), fires were unusual. I had only seen one fire there, the interior of a room burned. An ancient firetruck took its time coming to the rescue, but the fire never spread, and damage was minimal.

Each hospital had two, maybe three ambulances: white vans painted with a big red cross and a noisy siren on top of the cabin, carrying a driver and a nurse with a first aid kit, maybe.

The police were well-equipped and trained to suspect and fight a potentially angry population, but never to come to its rescue. Besides, we didn't trust them any more than they trusted us. There was a lot of animosity between ordinary citizens and officials, most of whom were out-of-towners brought in through political promotions from rural areas and who had a poor understanding of a large city's needs.

This was a city the size of Manhattan, maybe even larger, with a population of two million and growing. It was the capital, the largest city in the country. A vital center for the entire economy and administration of a European nation in the last quarter of the 20th century, and none of us knew what to do or where to turn.

If there were emergency plans or strategies to salvage the town in case of an emergency like war or foreign invasions, these certainly did not include coming to the aid of ordinary people. Police, medical, news and mass media personnel were always instructed to report to their work station as soon as possible in emergency situations, but most other people didn't know what to do.

After 30 years of being menaced and persecuted every time we had tried to associate—to form even innocent, non-political groups or clubs—after 30 years of distrusting the official unions and parties imposed on us by the communists, we were a population who was not only afraid but also too incompetent to put together the most rudimentary network to help us survive in an emergency, to help those who could have been saved.

The majority of adults had some military training, if only minimal, to prepare us for a street to street, house to house fight with the enemy. We all knew where to go get guns and ammunition. But buckets? Shovels? Ladders? Medical supplies? Food, water, or blankets?

In the large urban area, most of us lived in apartment buildings. We each had a bucket and a broom in the house, maybe hammers and screwdrivers. And although there had been other powerful earthquakes in the past, none had happened in recent times. The last one had taken place about 80 years prior, when the city was a fraction of its current size. Now we were two million people thrown in the midst of the most devastating disaster any of us had ever known. Not even the war had brought as much physical destruction to the city or its people as the earthquake of March 1977.

The center of the town was in ruins. Almost every street had two or three large buildings down, and those still standing were in a precarious state. On one main artery every fourth building was reduced to ruins or damaged so severely that passing by it was dangerous. My hometown looked as if it had been bombed. Driving through it, I couldn't help remembering the many people who lived there, the places I used to visit almost weekly: the French teacher's townhouse, a boy I had once dated, a party I had been at only two weeks before. The collections of books and records this one had, the photo albums I leafed through in that apartment, the silverware, the elegant porcelain china set this friend served tea in, right in this building at the seventh floor... Where was the seventh floor? Where were all those friends?

People walked aimlessly, mourning, crying, calling names of loved ones. Many children were lost and abandoned out on the street. There were scores of dogs and cats running from ruin to ruin. Building after building stood like broken teeth against a gray sky, and there was dust, dust everywhere, thick as winter fog.

Army units were trying to organize search and rescue teams out of the civilians. Men and women digging with their bare hands pulled survivors or dead out of unstable structures, all the while endangering their own lives. The smell was overwhelming: the stench of sewer, gas, diesel fumes, putrefaction, garbage, and smoldering fire was everywhere.

At what once was Casata, we stopped to film a medical team searching through crumbled walls. While I was placing the sound equipment on a heap of rubble, a strange object on the ground caught my eye. It looked like a dark leather glove, used, bulky. I was about to pick it up when a mean-looking nurse yelled at me, "Don't touch that!" I felt weak in my knees and almost fainted. "That is someone's hand," she said matter-of-factly, giving me a surgical mask and gloves. "If you're not here to help," she said, "get out of here quick. You're in the way."

Scattered around me I could now recognize body parts, fingers, chunks of arms, legs all over the place. I felt my heart sinking inside me, painfully, as if something that held it in place had ripped. Medics were separating the wounded from the dead; police were building barricades to keep looters out of stores and to shore up falling buildings. There was a desperate race against time to find the missing.

The morgue filled up first. At the entrance someone was giving out tickets to those standing in line on the street who were waiting for their turn to look for their loved ones. Inside, even the garden was filled with cadavers lying on the bare ground. Stretchers were needed for new transports, we were told. It's funny how the language cannot adapt to extreme tragic situations. "Transports." That is what those alive called those dead, as if they were lumber or some other everyday object.

Our team was out of place. I was ashamed to be doing what I was doing. A feeling of inappropriateness was present among us while moving wires and cameras, lights and microphones, setting up or looking for the proper "scene" for the next shot, saying "action" while those around us were dying or mourning or frantically working at saving a life. Usually a TV crew is boisterous, dynamic, whimsical, fun. Most of its members are creative individuals, smart, ready to outwit any situation, get the scoop, find the "special" angle and the best light, and have fun while doing it. Not this time. Not even the macabre jokes we had told each other when first leaving the station prepared us for what we had to film that day.

When they saw us, people came with questions about the rest of the town, about where to go for help, asking if we had seen this girl and that boy, showing us wallet pictures, begging to put the images of the missing on the news, hoping maybe someone would know something.

And then there were those who, after being pulled out alive and unhurt from under the steel and concrete that had fallen on top of them, walked through the streets for hours, dazed, stopping anyone who would listen to tell them their story. They seemed not quite sure if they were dreaming or if it had really happened. We interviewed a couple of them, as we interviewed doctors and army officers, policemen, and on-lookers.

With the radio and TV back on, an official communiqué finally came. We were under a "state of emergency." Aftershocks were possible and expected. Everyone was advised to go to his or her place of work or school and see what if any cleaning needed to be done. Water? Blankets? Only the next day the Red Cross started to distribute them. Help arrived from all over the world, but it took days. At first we were utterly alone and unprepared.

Some panicked and tried to take refuge in the forests at the outskirts of town or with relatives in nearby villages. An exodus of cars, motorcycles, and horse-drawn carriages filled with women, children, and household items inched its way towards the suburbs, creating difficulty for the incoming troops sent to help. The army, young kids mostly from other parts of the country, was coming to save us. They were armed with shovels, construction equipment, fresh barricades, and news of other towns just as badly hit as we were. By the afternoon some plan of recovery took shape, and most civilians were ordered out of the ruins, unless they were construction workers, structural engineers, nurses, or doctors.

We saw a lot of looting, too. The usual suspects, ruffian gypsies and trash, hooligans from the poor neighborhoods at the outskirts of town, but also people who would never, under normal circumstances, go take something that wasn't theirs. As if possessed by greed and an atavistic instinct, they would break into the most incredible places, taking things they had no need for ever in their lives. People who did not have kids stole baby clothes and toys, someone stole needles and thread, yet another stole pipes and a toilet top while his house lay in ruins, his entire family missing.

Any and all looters were to be shot on the spot. There were many rumors, but I don't know if anyone actually was shot. Looting is the most horrendous crime in times of disaster, and if I hadn't seen it with my own eyes, I would never have believed it, but looting is also a reaction to extreme psychological shock. In the days to come, the looting stopped, only to be replaced with break-ins by organized gangs who hit the houses of those who had fled.

After four gruesome hours that first day, my team went back to the station. My clothes were stained with dirt and blood. I was numb. I couldn't feel anything anymore. Couldn't cry, couldn't feel compassion or pity or even physical pain. Not right away. Back at the station I called my mom and found out our building was fine, didn't have any damage, but Aunt Lori's house, the spacious solid villa where we had spent the night, was all cracked and falling apart.

The only problem at my mom's: no door could be opened. In every room we had huge wall units overfilled with books, and all of them had fallen like dominoes, blocking the doors. By afternoon they got two of the doors out of their hinges, and the big cleanup began. Same with most of the neighbors. Everyone was cleaning up broken porcelain, glass, furniture.

Our part of town was so serene compared with what I had seen that day, it was as if I had stepped into a different life. People were making up jokes about "the big shaking." But by nightfall, with the phone service restored, we could hear wailing cries coming from other apartments. News of dead and missing relatives was coming through the restored wires. And my cousin Avia was one of the missing.

"She went to the movies with her fiancé last night, and no movie theatre had been affected, but she has not called or come by the house since, and she was not at the morgue or at any of the hospitals," her mom said in an even, almost quiet voice on the phone. Could she have been with me? Didn't we have plans to see each other that week?

"She'll come over on Friday," I said. "She promised."

"Please call me the moment she arrives," her mom said, although it was only Wednesday, early in the evening.

I crouched on the floor, suddenly feeling sick to my stomach and wildly hungry at the same time. The whole day I hadn't eaten anything. I took a big chunk of bread and chewed furiously, thinking how there had been miracles, people who walked out of the rubble alive and unharmed. In other places people had survived for days under ruins.

The next morning Avia's mother called to say she knew where Avia and her fiancé had been. A friend who was with them the night of the earthquake had come to tell her how the three of them had been siting at a table in his house when the building started to shake. He ran one way, calling them to follow him, but he couldn't tell if they did or did not. The building was down.

In town, hundreds of soldiers and volunteers were furiously working to pull out of the ruins those still alive, with many successes. Many, many incredible stories came out of the rubble for days. Many more tragic stories emerged, too. Entire families wiped out, or worse, only a mother or a father left alive for days under the ruins near the decaying bodies of their children. We lost many friends. A writer friend of the family and his wife died while his son and his fiancée escaped miraculously on the eve of what was supposed to be their wedding day. A child was born while his mother succumbed to her injuries.

At the site of the fallen buildings people kept vigil night and day, and every time a survivor was pulled out, cheers of joy and applause were heard, and we all hoped for one more, and one more, although it had been three days, and then four, and then seven.

When they finally found them, Avia and her fiancé were holding each other in a final embrace. A few hours later, a few feet below them, a young man was dug out alive. It was Friday.

The places that were not affected were back to as normal a life as they could be, and although traumatized and depressed, we were trying to put our lives together, to go on. There was a strange type of solace in the collectiveness of our grieving; there was some heroic stubbornness in the everyday task of surviving. Those who were to get married got married, because that was what those killed would have wanted them to do. Those who were to leave for vacations left for vacation, knowing none of those who died would have wanted them to do otherwise. Those who had planned to redecorate their houses rebuilt them instead, and architects were busy with planning new buildings where the leveled ones stood. The earthquake had killed many public figures and celebrities. A singer, a poet, a few writers, actors, movie and TV directors, cameramen. We were humming their songs, reciting their poems, quoting their lines, watching their movies, celebrating their lives, as if none of us was ready to let go, to lose them forever in the rubble. With the gas back we started baking the most sophisticated cakes and went shopping for Easter chocolates.

Flowers and candles, even priests and public prayers were seen on the streets in a town where any religious display was almost outlawed. There was hunger and thirst for life and for rituals. There was a stick-together and toughen-up, help-each-other and lend-a-hand spirit even between those who usually engaged in puny garden-variety feuds and jealousy, gossip and rivalries. We were all sharing our still-standing houses with those whose houses were condemned, and there was an increase in the number of weddings. About eight months after the earthquake, Avia's mother remarried after ten years of steadfast celibacy. She married a man she had met while they both were searching for loved ones. He and his little girl had survived while the mother had died under ruins.

But the grieving went on for years. In fact, it never stops. If I had only said Tuesday instead of Friday, if she had only gone directly to the movies. She was twenty-one.

NORMAN BALL

Dining on the Future:
An Inward-Out Exploration of
Cosmic Retribution, Alienation, and
Market Dynamics

From January/February 2009

FOR MANY YEARS the political shtick went something like this: by indulging in debt-fueled consumption today, we were mortgaging the futures of our children and grandchildren. Invariably we would cluck our tongues before heading off to explore the efficacies of an "interest-only, minimum-payment-option-enabled, negatively-amortizing, no-money-down, no-documentation, prepayment-penalizing, three-month LIBOR, 40-year adjustable-rate mortgage with a balloon." Actually this beast was a tongue-in-cheek construct that appeared recently on *MSN Money*. As we've learned, the truth was not a whole lot stranger than the fiction.

Stretching financial jargon to a sardonic extreme, we effectively discounted future cash-flows with cavalier abandon in order to plump up present value. This present value bias was due to an overweighting of the pronouns *me, myself* and *I*. Each of us was eating for three—and I have the obesity trend lines to prove it.

There is a corollary in the mythological record. When Tantalus was discovered serving his dismembered son Pelops to the gods, his punishment was an eternal lesson in need and unmet desire. Every time he reached for the fruit tree just above his head, the wind would sweep the branches out of reach. As he bent to drink from the neck-deep pool, the water would recede. There was nothing capricious about the Greeks' meting out of punishment. As Freytag's Pyramid elucidates (a derivation of Aristotle's six elements of tragedy), the rising action must be fully offset by the falling action before authentic resolution arrives; i.e., the nadir of the hangover must retrace the apogee of the party. Thus we should note (with appropriate gnashing teeth) that the fate reserved for a parent who robs his child to curry favor with the gods is about as steep and unforgiving a denouement as a triangle can allow. Talk about righteous right angles.

The current macroeconomic debate has swung decisively in recent weeks to a discussion of just how deep the ensuing recession—if not depression—will be. If one subscribes to the sublime wisdom of Greek mythology, the darker prognostications deserve our close attention.

At the risk of belaboring parental avarice, I am reminded also of Goya's Saturn, the very portrait of mindless consumption as he dines on his own child, one of whom it was prophesied would usurp him (as Zeus ultimately did). For the offense of cannibalistic infanticide, he languishes in chains beneath our feet.

Alas, there are many ways to eat a child, or certainly his future. But perhaps there is no better way to gauge a society's moral tenor than to examine the steps it takes to safeguard the welfare of future generations. For us, this is a very timely question as our society's future seems to have suddenly crashed into the present—and with a swift, retributive vengeance.

Watching the current turmoil in financial markets, it is clear to me we are now reaping what we have for so long sown: our profound crisis in values is finally reverberating outwards into the metrics of traditional asset valuations. The markets are not "broken" as some have alleged. On the contrary, they are flashing a deep-seated, existential crisis. What is a market after all but the expression of the personal, writ large in the aggregate? Like a bad horror film where every corridor seems to house a lurking monster, there is no safe harbor—no rest for the wicked, a tiresome moralist might say. Not stocks, not bonds, not commodities, not real estate. Perhaps the crisis lies not in the stars (or the plummeting charts) but in ourselves. We are speechless for want of value to impart. Like Tantalus, nothing bends to our reach. Like Saturn, the future has finally caught up to us.

In short, the dilemma is moral before it is financial. No vessel will accept our offerings until we ourselves know what it is exactly we wish to decant and why. The externalized receptacles of what we hold dear will continue to bedevil us until we can with assurance identify what it is we hold dear. Profound confusion cannot be warehoused. We stalk lightning with a bottle when we attempt to transact fear and loathing between similarly stricken parties.

I've decided Jesus's rage in the temple was not triggered by sanctimony or procedural offense. He knew that commerce was the ultimate substitution effect—for authentic self-listening. Lost souls gravitate toward the false-solidity of material possessions. Denial is the currency of the worldly realm within which the temple is our sole respite: a precious, trade-free zone where gnosis, inward-out knowledge, can be ushered forth unguardedly. Markets are all about studying the competition. Temples abet the process of knowing thyself.

It is to the starving man alone that Maslow's Hierarchy of Needs appears for what it is: a daunting edifice. Pitiable bottom-dweller though he may be, his starvation clarifies his vision. As for you and I, well, we need our Internet, we need our MTV, and yes, a little food would be nice, too. Sated by a lifetime of relative comfort, we inhabit a flatland fog of indistinction brought on by the fearsome efficiency of that needs-satisfaction (not to mention needs-creation) factory, the thoroughly-modern economy.

But what happens if the modern economy should irrevocably break down? The hierarchic structure of need would reassert with the onset of hunger (or an equally authentic unmet need such as inadequate shelter). Hunger reestablishes its primacy in short order. Alienation evaporates like a bourgeoisie daydream. My father, in periods of his life, knew hunger. I never have. To my son, a hunger pang is a sure sign something has gone horribly awry. Dinner is late! Am I a good father for barricading him from the sacred murmurs in his stomach? Faced, perhaps for the first time, with choosing between an Internet connection or a restocked pantry, our value-system would sharpen in short order. The availability of so many things for so long has dulled us to the exigencies of existence.

Moreover, a lifetime of comfort puts us at a tactical disadvantage to those who have negotiated the rigors of deprivation as a normal course. In this way, the poor stand to reinherit the earth. While our future lot may amount to a lengthy denouement punctuated by denial, anger, and finally—for those few who successfully navigate the Eye of the Needle—a rapprochement with the real. Indeed, the poor may be on their way to becoming comparatively less poor as a salutary wealth distribution effect ensues. Intrepid blogger London Banker says this:

> The crash of global financial markets therefore will have a disproportionate effect on the elites, impoverishing them to a far greater extent, although it will be felt throughout society as employment, pensions, investments and public services contract.

Though he may seem, on systematic grounds, a strange bedfellow, I am drawing closer to a Baudrillardian interpretation of the current value-confusion, particularly the interplay between his functional and exchange value processes. Our frenetic interrogation of exchange value mechanisms betrays a functional value crisis. How can we hope to enter a transactional dialogue if no one can explain the functional value of a Credit Default Swap (CDS)?

What's more, our alienation is so complete, we have lost sight of our needs. Or to couch this dilemma in John Kenneth Galbraith's terms (from *The Affluent Society,* 1958), we can no longer differentiate our psychological needs from our physiological ones. It's as though we've been blessed right into a gilded cage of profound incoherence. In the words of Columbia philosophy professor Douglas Kellner:

> ...Baudrillard also describes a situation where alienation is so total that it cannot be surpassed because "it is the very structure of market society" (1998: 190). His argument is that in a society where everything is a commodity that can be bought and sold, alienation is total. Indeed, the term "alienation" originally signified "to sale," and in a totally commodified society where everything is a commodity, alienation is ubiquitous. Moreover, Baudrillard posits "the end of transcendence" (a phrase borrowed from Marcuse) where individuals can neither perceive their own true needs or another way of life (1998: 190ff).

Alienation has become our edifice, God help us. We have arranged our society on the "foundation" of a $513 trillion derivatives complex. More insubstantial even than sand, this kingdom traverses the ether every second of every day just above our heads. In typical lopsided fashion, the ephemeralities of Wall Street threaten to devour the very real sweat and toil of Main Street.

Our foundation thus mortgaged to the clouds, the world has been turned on its head. Hubris has overwhelmed wisdom—for a time. However, as the great tragedians showed time and again, hubris never prevails. Unity of action now requires *lusis*, a great unraveling equal in measure to the remarkable ascent. Only after denouement can a fresh narrative arrive.

JULIA BRAUN KESSLER

Our Own Mid-Century Mannahatta

From April/May 2009

THERE WAS EXCITEMENT to be found in New York, but in The Bronx? For anyone growing up in the 1930s and '40s (especially for those of us from the boondocks of the City's boroughs), despite searches in every corner for any sign, it began to seem like we had exhausted every possibility.

We'd gone to school there, spent our young lives in what was a collection of neighborhoods with their characteristic main streets filled with milling open stalls of fruit, vegetables, of grocers, butchers, and fishmongers. We had stood in appetizer stores with their huge displays of pickle barrels and sauerkraut tubs. We'd eyed their luscious dried fruits and the salamis, bolognas hanging from above. We enjoyed the tang of their strong scents together with the constant and fierce exchanges of customers, harangues performed daily.

Yet all of it paled, those enterprises that once enticed us. As the growing children in our families, we'd been sent "down" from our small, upstairs apartments to shop for our Mammas—to fill their milk cans, for fresh bread, for peaches or apples as the seasons provided. Yet, entering into adolescence, we scorned these activities. Chores provided small diversion. There had to be more, and we set out to find it. Ours was *the* Metropolis. We were ready to venture into its great world.

Which meant Manhattan. Once a mere primitive Algonquin Indian isle, and one so notoriously undersold! Yet a century later it was to be Walt Whitman's own *Mannahatta*, his pet, a city of "open voices" and "manners free," seen and heard amid "hurried and sparkling waters." Still another 100 years later, into our own century, and it had become for us the very center of the world! A narrow strip of island where streets were filled with people and purpose. Among them, the preoccupied mover types, the exotics, travelers, foreigners, above all cosmopolitans. Their very look and dress was distinct from our too familiar Bronxites! And none of that resigned doggedness our own streets showed, that resignation to drudgery we watched in our parents' faces and among the shopkeepers of the boroughs heavily given over to long hours of daily labor. For us, for youth, the time had come to sample the cultural life of New York City and what it could hold.

With most of us on our measly school allowances, we had little means. But a nickel could get us on the subway, and we were free as birds to explore what was then a safe city. We made our way in bands of girls, eyes open to whichever notions a wider world offered. We knew Manhattan could provide us that edge, a would-be avant-garde consciousness, altogether unknown in the Bronx.

Some of us fancied dance, a realm just then beginning to grow "Modern." We sought whatever was emergent amongst the groups performing downtown. And we found inspiration, not among the world-class ballet companies often visiting, but in the new styles, many American and as yet unknown to the Old World.

Innovators like Martha Graham, Merce Cunningham, Doris Humphrey, Jose Limon, Katherine Dunham and Lester Horton were among the pioneers who themselves had been inspired by such initiators as Isadora Duncan, Ruth St. Denis, and Ted Shawn. We embraced their revolutionary ideas, their definitions of new forms of movement, their novel notions of dance. And instead of Petipa or Fokine, we had Balanchine and Agnes de Mille!

Such artists had no money to further their ideas as yet and few venues for performance space. Only a small, fanatically devotional audience assembled to attend them. Yet, they offered us moving bodies utterly distinct from the common classical chestnuts. We'd not seen it before. We, the "swing" generation, were enchanted by every twist and turn. We'd seen the movies, the tap-dancing, the ballroom and jazz halls. But those dancers brought us a dance language quite amazing and their very own. It defied earlier principles, invented new ones. Soon it was dubbed modern dance, or contemporary dance, and would-be jazz dance.

Mostly performed barefoot, Modern Dance was fluid and balletic enough, yet it was weighted to the earth while embodying the tricks and scenarios of the jazz story. While ballet offered romantic, 19th century royalty as themes or exotic fairy tales, including animals or flowers, the new dance was often naturalistic musical theater. Sometimes it consisted simply of everyday kinds of moves with a rhythmic flux of the torso. Arms and legs emphasized natural, mechanical, or animalistic motions, and the legs exaggerated the weight, grounding them to the earth.

Dancers then lived the impoverished artist's life, mainly in Greenwich Village, "downtown's downtown." This was a small venue, mostly buildings left over from the 18th century, ever lively, and a walking distance from Washington Square, which once served as the center of "Bohemian New York" in the 1920s.

On Seventh Avenue and Eighth Street sat an all night cafeteria, where a coffee came to five cents, and with it the chance to sit chatting with friends for leisurely hours and hours, even until dawn. Drunks, bums, office workers, students, and teachers arrived and departed. People came and went freely and safely—that is, when cruel winter nights allowed. Often enough, encountering friends in 10th Street bookstores or "store front" galleries took them to a quick retreat into the warmer atmosphere of such affordable diner evenings. How well I remember the exalted philosophical arguments that floated over the tables, those casual posturings of youth slouched around them, feet up on whatever empty chairs were around, coats tossed over those same chairs. And of course clouds of cigarette smoke drifting overhead.

So much "business" went on under those conditions. We girls not only gained a new freedom on our treks, but we encountered all types inaccessible to us in our uptown world, first of all to include available young men who read books. Those were hard to find among our starched Bronx schoolmates. We came upon them in Manhattan's off-beat locales: libraries, museums, at lectures, in concert halls, at dance performances.

And of course, they came in a variety of models: tall, short, skinny, plump, but mainly of the geeky variety or, as it was termed then, "gooky." Yes, that was a different sort of opportunity for us Bronx girls, a breakthrough, a different kind of encounter. It roused the newly-blossoming gushes of hormones of our adolescent years.

Riding the tedious subway treks, we would have provided ourselves with reading matter, some "literary" book currently engrossing us. Above ground once more, we walked about, taking care to keep its dust jacket visible enough for some curious boy to notice. It favored the possibility of lighting up a conversation of some potential.

In most cases that ploy suggested the "seriousness" essential to the inciting moment. It made things less frivolous, enhancing mere everyday flirtation. Those exchanges could be awkward, but nevertheless, once they got going, they could wind up in intense conversation. It might be about philosophy, history, even religion. Atheism loomed large for us young people in those Depression times.

In a way, the badinage legitimatized our posturing. No doubt the accidental acquaintances made at those meetings deviated from the "proper" introductions those still somewhat formal times required. Proper they should be, or so our parents kept reminding us. Naturally, our parents kept informing us adolescents that there were lots of strangers out there, the worrisome kind best avoided by girls. A meeting arranged through their friends or relatives—a complex ritual—was for them *the* rule to follow.

Even so, we found our own haphazard adventures exciting, certainly agreeable, if not always convenient or leisurely. And, after all, there was something of a thrill in all of it. When any of us got lucky and managed to make such an acquisition, the telephone calls that went round made for long talk. Details, details! *What's he like? Where's he from, which school?* Only later, there came, *Who were his folks?* Eventually, of course, the crucial question popped up, *Is he Jewish?* Yet enthusiasm—so infectious!—was not to be curbed. *He called! He asked for a date!* Even a visit to the neighborhood. A boy from another borough coming all that distant way on a Saturday afternoon! Casual exchanges they may have been, though still vivid in memory. So easy then, so much simpler than what was to follow during our college years.

There were myriad choices in our city. During those prewar days there was a stir in Manhattan regarding a place called the New School for Social Research. That too was down in the Village. We were awed by extraordinary names—all those talented foreigners who'd been gathered to teach there when the geniuses of Europe were being threatened by the Nazis and Fascists. We profited from their calamity. Rescued by a remarkable institution, they came and influenced our generation, particularly in Social Sciences.

The New School for Social Research had been founded by pacifists at Columbia University during the First World War. They were the Modernists who presented the new intellectual, political, and aesthetic views. At the New School early faculty had included eminent figures like Thorstein Veblen, John Dewey, Charles and Mary Beard along with Alvin Johnson, who was to become its president and spokesman during the chaos that erupted in the '30s in Europe.

From the start, these scholars maintained close ties with European colleagues and became conscious of the danger Hitler presented to democracy, even to civilization. Johnson wasted little time in soliciting support from the Rockefeller Foundation and other philanthropists who were ready to help.

Miraculously, they managed to provide the needed documents and the visas for those jobs the New School could offer. Nearly 200 scholars and artists and their families arrived in the New World.

Among them were the leading intelligentsia of Europe. Such an economist as Gerhard Colm or political scientist Arnold Brecht and sociologist Hans Speier, who subsequently served as advisor for the Roosevelt Administration. They had come to the United States through their offices. Freudians, Reichians, Horneyites, etc. There was Max Wertheimer, the psychologist who challenged the reigning theory of behaviorism and brought to our attention his concept of "Gestalt" and its cognitive psychology.

Also philosophers like Hans Jonas and Hannah Arendt, both of whom were soon to attract notice for their work and become world famous. There arrived Leo Strauss, whose political theory has continued to gather scores of students and loyal followers, year after year.

Others arrived carrying keys to new ways of conceiving social science—even now one wonders at how (or when) that advanced thought might have evolved on this continent had these men and women not fled their would-be murderers in time! Rescued by the New School intellectuals, not only did they live and benefit, the world has been privileged to profit from their accomplishments.

The New School was also dedicated to theater. Their recruiting of innovative stage artists was remarkable. To their credit, they made their contributions early to Modern departures from the traditional 19th century theater still playing everywhere.

Bertold Brecht, whose notions figure prominently even today in that flourishing art, was revolutionary in his approach even back in Germany. The Nazi regime was to attack him from its start. The sooner Brecht's sort departed Europe, the better for their safety, and it was the New School intellectuals who first recognized their plight.

What luck for us growing up then to be right there on that stirring scene. We certainly felt its excitement, and it stimulated our notions of what was new in "culture."

Together with such stirrings of internationalism, we had New York's heady offerings. Best were those delights the City held out for us in the arts and sciences. Weekends we went on our aimless excursions "downtown." We explored a museum like the Metropolitan, then free and open to anyone, and walked its endless galleries awed. Titian, Vermeer, El Greco, Cezanne, van Gogh, Manet, Turner, de La Tour—all montaged inside our heads. Untutored, we scarcely grasped how or where they'd been painted, all those exotic cities and countries, epochs upon epochs during which they had once lived.

It played as a hodgepodge of forms and figures to us in those days, and oh, how stimulating and glorious. Yes, and all right there inside the museum through which we strolled, though it was scarcely heated. Outside it was much colder, sleeting or snowing as we wandered those halls. Saturday and Sunday afternoons were a waking dream until we headed back to the Bronx, to home's mundane chores.

How vividly I can recall the Met's cavernous vaults and corridors, its basement galleries where Egyptian mummies slept stored. Nothing informative was laid out then; it was only the glass cases provided together with minimum signage, little labels telling where and when they had been excavated and whose expedition retrieved them. We moved with trepidation, pretending to study them, although in a trance of terror. Those impressions remain strong—it was a first encounter with death as something real but uncanny! To think that there was a people and a history older than we ever imagined. And, to climb up to other halls and find the models of Greek temples and their surroundings presenting what glories had once existed and remained through famine, disease, wars, and cataclysmic earthquakes. For us, such new perspectives! We were like moths flitting about for an hour in which civilizations were born only to fall to earth forever.

Still, being young, what we hankered for and sought was "the new" and "the revolutionary." Most eager were we to look to the future, to become a part of it, "agents of progress." And that goal was embodied in a new Museum of Modern Art, just then being constructed in Manhattan. We watched as the marvelous building came up at 53rd Street just off Fifth Avenue. We imagined radical change in art, a rainbow of hopes exciting our sleeping young souls.

With access to new works from Europe sailing in on dollars laid out by rich art lovers and philanthropists—people like the Rockefellers—all right there before us in New York City, the latest European creations of our century simply staggered us. We looked upon Kandinsky, Miro, Klee, Giacometti, Egon Schiele, Braque, Picasso, Dali, and many others. From an initial gift of eight prints and one drawing, the Museum of Modern Art's collection grew, until today it holds thousands of paintings, sculptures, drawings, prints, and photographs. Later, it integrated a movies division, archiving and presenting early European and American creations. No wonder 53rd Street was becoming our "in" place, a hangout and theater of dating for us adolescents.

Offering fresh prospects, encounters with novel artistic achievement, fine years they were. There we met "abstract" art. Perplexed, we wondered what those artists thought they were up to?

What rules were relevant? How many discussions, fuzzy theorizing about "the abstractionists," as though they were all alike. Among us arguments were lively; often enough they ended rancorous, all sneers and jeers about fakes and fraud. Silly it would seem today. Then, a life-and-death affair. Even then, though, we were two generations younger than Stieglitz and his O'Keefe. Who "got" Duchamp's "Nude Descending A Staircase," let alone his "Urinal"? Yet there's little doubt the new Museum was already a force downtown in the Village and Lower East Side tenement neighborhoods, wherever artists were struggling in still barely affordable lofts during the '30s and through the '40s.

Some came to notice celebrity with their move into the Solomon Guggenheim collection, which was once to be viewed in his millionaire's private quarters at the Plaza Hotel on Central Park. But as Guggenheim began to expand his collection and form his Foundation, he went public with the art of those who had struggled in poverty for years and years. At first, quarters were set up on the east side of 54th Street in a brownstone and named The Museum of Non-Objective Painting. Soon after came his niece Peggy's own gallery/museum on 57th Street, known then as the Art of This Century. And there she prospered five or more years with her discoveries, among them American painters like Robert Motherwell, Jackson Pollock, and Mark Rothko, formerly unseen beyond the confines of a Village or Lower East Side gallery. Their work was to revolutionize post-World War II art.

It wasn't until 1943 that Solomon Guggenheim commissioned Frank Lloyd Wright to design the extraordinary vortex of The Guggenheim Museum. The building didn't open until six months after the architect's death in 1959. Wright remarked controversially of his creation that it would remain after "the beards" had devastated mid-Manhattan.

What we saw during the '40s, however, was Peggy's burgeoning collection of Surrealists and Cubists. Though she chose to house her acquisitions at the Palazzo Venier dei Leoni on Venice's Grand Canal, her finds were carried in New York by her storefront gallery. There we had our early views. In any case, so many of her discoveries had originated on this side of the Atlantic and were exhibited *before* they went off on their travels.

There were other distractions to occupy us in those years. Like today's young activists, we fretted over the corruption we saw in the Big Apple, as it was later termed. In politics first, business, and that which was coming from intimates within our daily milieu—even among some of our own colleagues at school. We would look around at various groups, seeking out one of the organizations then current, which, oddly enough, was to be found in posh quarters of the Upper West Side, and whose arguments over culture and about politics were juicy and hot.

The Ethical Culture Society of New York was one venue where the view was taken that eternal dispute about religious and philosophical doctrine could distract people from the "real" goal of living ethically and "doing good." That message struck us and brought us awake. The Society had been founded back in 1862 by one Felix Adler, who considered himself a Transcendentalist.

His was a natively American notion. He followed Emerson and Thoreau. The Society's credo was "deed before creed." Such pragmatism appealed. We were so young, we floundered within the weighty yet vacuous theorizing of politics in those mid-century years.

We thought Ethical Culture broad enough to include all sorts of faiths, not just traditional religion. There were Buddhists and Taoists, an exotic bunch for those times. Early on, Adler boasted that "Ethical Culture is religious to those who are religiously minded, and merely ethical to those not so minded"; yet he also observed that religion, per se, given whatever dogma, does bind individuals and fosters "a sense of humility and gratitude." He argued his mode as pointing the way towards action that "transcends" merely personal interest. That message we welcomed for its inspiration.

So downtown we went expressly to find that purpose. We wanted to listen to those who came from all over the world, who spoke eloquently on purely ethical themes. Given our youthful hopes, our post-war dreams of vast possibility in the future—a life of utopian peace—Ethical Culture painted a glamorous portrait for humanity. It enlivened a sense of respect and dignity and taught these things sincerely. "Always act so as to elicit the best in others and thereby yourself," the lecturers told us. They imparted a sense of togetherness, an appreciation of how an individual could influence others, which suited our hopes for liberality of spirit. It encouraged an enthusiasm for life in these new times.

There seemed hardly any limit to the wonders we were finding in our City, even to discovering places new to us in our own borough. On the Northernmost edge of The Bronx, for instance, rose The Cloisters, a miraculous structure to eager minds. Stone by stone it had been brought from decayed old Europe, by the whim of some eccentric millionaire who determined to save its glory, providing a store of works of medieval history. To think of it, he had had transported the very structure to this remote corner of our Bronx!

And a short subway ride away was a little cottage tucked in a pocket-sized park off the Grand Concourse. There, in what we had once thought of as a short walkabout amidst greenery in spring and summer, were trees and shrubs and beaten-down lawn, where baby carriages were rocked by gossiping mothers. It had been the place Edgar Allan Poe had chosen for his remote hideaway a century ago. The Poe Cottage was still there, spare furniture, kitchen and wooden tools left as they had been when he wrote "The Raven."

But it was always back to Manhattan. We sought to keep it blanketed around us in the hours of solitary study. We headed downtown doggedly to find the bustle of the greater world. At the mansion that is now the Morgan Library at 38th Street and Madison Avenue, Pierpont Morgan had acquired in the 1890s an immense number of literary and historical manuscripts. Documents he bought before his death in 1913 became the source of a magnificent trove of drawings, letters, and manuscripts, including Isaac Newton, Voltaire, even Queen Elizabeth I. His was not only the original of John Milton's *Paradise Lost,* it was the one surviving copy, the centerpiece of his collection.

New York City in those decades was indeed a memorable theater: a life we played in and grew up with amidst such public luxuries. And for adolescents with high hopes and the most modest of means, given our over-worked immigrant parents, it was a paradise found. I look back at it as my gateway to a greater world through which I was privileged to walk, a paradise inevitably lost but never forgotten.

JOHN PALCEWSKI

Patroness of the Arts

From October/November 2000

ON MY FIRST morning in Manhattan during the winter of 1966, I bought a copy of *The New York Times* and sat on a stool in an Irish bar and grill near the YMCA on Lexington Avenue. I found a most interesting ad. A single room for a gentleman was available, on the Upper West Side, $7.00 per week.

I got on the Seventh Avenue IRT, rode uptown. Breathing hard, I knocked on the door of a brownstone on West 87th Street. The wrinkled, gray-haired landlady looked me over and invited me upstairs. The room was about ten feet wide and 15 feet long. A monk's cell, with a window on the end. A bed, a table, a chair. Bathroom with shower down the hall. Perfect.

In another room down the hall lived a Turk, a foreign-exchange film student at NYU. Yes, she said, the rent was $7.00, which would include her changing the sheet and pillowcase every week, but there was to be NO cooking in the room, and of course no noise, because she in her advanced age needed peace and quiet. I gave her a month in advance, plus a two-week security deposit.

I quickly found employment as a typist at Doubleday & Co., Inc., on Park Avenue between 47th and 48th Streets. A most genteel place with soft carpets, muted lighting, and an informality that initially made me feel welcome. I worked hard the first few months, filling in for absent secretaries, going from editor to editor, department to department, receiving excellent marks for my speedy and flawless typing. When I got to the Syndicate Department, my boss Sally liked my enthusiasm and productivity and made arrangements with personnel to get me full time work as her secretary.

Sally, recognizing my ability to improve her letters, gave me a shot at writing promotion copy for the serializations of Doubleday bestsellers the Syndicate Department was peddling to newspapers throughout the US. My first piece of professional writing was an upbeat blurb about a book by Dr. Norman Vincent Peale titled "Sin, Sex and Self Control." This self-righteous Christian preacher was wholly aghast and disturbed by the great sexual revolution sweeping not just New York and Los Angeles but the rest of the country in between. *Oh. My. God. Look at what these young people are DOING these days! It's utterly disgraceful!* I laughed as I typed.

I went on to write blurbs for other bestsellers by famous authors, like John Barth, whose *Giles Goat Boy* was raising the eyebrows of intellectual critics, not the least for its length. Barth's double-spaced typed manuscript was all of eight inches thick and weighed more than a sack of sugar.

On one of my inter-departmental secretarial assignments, I'd taken a seat at what I thought was a free desk when a guy came into the room in a rumpled white shirt and askew silk tie and demanded, in an imperious baritone, whether I had "ensconced" myself permanently at his desk. I made apologies and moved.

David's initial gruffness was replaced by a quick smile and explosive laugh, and soon we became friends. He had blond hair and a rough, pock-marked face strongly resembling the portraits I'd seen of

Beethoven. I told him so, and he was pleased because like me he loved the great composer's late quartets, the piano sonatas, and of course his Diabelli variations.

David was a researcher on a special company project and also a musician. He sang with the Bach Choir at the Presbyterian church up in New Haven, his home town. Most important, he was a Harvard graduate, Phi Beta Kappa. An intelligent and charismatic man, a most articulate man, whom I deeply admired.

And by that time I was deeply involved with Gabrielle. Oh, Gabrielle! I've tried many times over the years to write an honest story about her but never succeeded. There was just too much pain permanently attached to my experience with that strange, lovely woman. I was so angry at the way she treated me. And I felt deep guilt and regret for the way I ended up treating her.

If I could find her now, I'd tell her how deeply sorry I am.

The portable typewriter I'd used to write my debut novel's first chapter was a gift from Gabrielle. So were my new shoes. She'd laughed at the ones I'd come into town in and said of course they had to go. They were ones I'd stolen from Cowtown Bowling Palace in Ft. Worth and had painted with black liquid shoe polish. The red and green colors were not entirely masked. "Oh, yes," Gabrielle said. "Let's get rid of them." I could not walk the streets of Manhattan in those god-awful shoes.

Gabrielle was the breathtaking vision I saw just four days after my arrival in Manhattan. I'd walked in the wet snow from my room on West 87th Street all the way uptown to the Metropolitan Museum of Art, and there she was in a long tan coat and high leather boots, in the lobby at the information desk, gathering brochures of the various exhibits. On a wild impulse, I approached her.

"Would you care to join me?" I asked, smiling.

She turned, looked me up and down, grinned, and said, "Why not?"

She was from Stuttgart, recently arrived in New York, and was staying at the Plaza until she found an apartment. Gabrielle's hair was long and blond, her eyes light blue, and her nose was thin and flared nicely, like Marlene Deitrich's. Her English was excellent. She also spoke French and German.

This young woman was beautiful, sophisticated, and sexy. And I instantly wanted her, badly. She smiled when I rattled off what I knew of Degas, Van Gogh, Picasso, Hopper, as well as classical music and literature. It pleased her I was trying so hard. I probably could have saved myself all that effort. I believe she'd decided right off she'd take me as her lover, that very first moment in the lobby.

After an hour or so wandering the galleries, we walked in the slush down Fifth Avenue toward the Plaza. She locked arms with me and listened to me talk about the novel I was writing. I was sober that afternoon, but my head was swimming. How was it possible I was in the greatest city in the world with such a beautiful woman at my side? How had that come to pass?

Gabrielle said, "Why don't we go into that restaurant and have a bite?" It was French, very ritzy.

My face flushed. "I don't have any money," I said.

She laughed. "Don't worry! I shall buy you dinner. You must eat. You must take care of yourself."

I replied that being a starving artist was exactly what I'd always dreamed about becoming, since I was a boy.

"Nonsense," she said. "You do not need to starve to be an artist."

Three days later, in her small room at the Plaza, she whispered, "I must submit to you." But when I tried to pull off her sweater, she resisted. I stopped. "What's the matter?" she said. "Have you lost interest?"

So I resumed, and she resisted. It became a vigorous wrestling match. But gradually off came her sweater and her black-laced bra. Her breasts were perfectly formed. Smooth, white, so soft, with small nipples. Her trousers were dark corduroy. I fumbled for the top button, but there was no button. A safety pin was all that stood in my way. That gleaming safety pin holding her trousers together at the top was, and inexplicably remains, a most poignant image to me.

Sex with Gabrielle was the most intense I'd ever experienced. In bed naked, a flush would spread over her cheeks and neck, and her eyes would glisten, and she'd grasp me and draw me into her. It was impossible not to be swept into a sexual frenzy by the sight and feel of her pale, utterly perfect body.

"Why do men always come so quickly?" she once asked after a violent but enormously satisfying encounter.

"Because you are so beautiful, so incredibly erotic," I replied, running my fingers gently down her flat, moist belly.

"Excellent answer," she said, smiling. "Now do it again. *Macht schnell!*"

A week after the consummation of our relationship, she bought me a beautiful portable Royal typewriter in a green metal carrying case, several boxes of high-quality 25 lb. bond paper, and a new pair of shoes. I told her I would pay her back someday. She told me don't worry, forget it, she'd always wanted to emulate a great 18th century Russian noblewoman. Princess Yekaterina Romanovna Dashkova, friend of Catherine the Great. A patroness of the arts.

Meanwhile, she said, she had some important news for me. Which was that Lloyd, a wealthy older man she had recently met, had today offered her a proposition.

I blinked. A proposition?

"Yes," she said. "He wishes that I become his mistress. He will provide a lovely apartment right off Fifth Avenue in the upper 60s, and will pay all the bills, and expect to see me once, twice a week. I'll be free the rest of the time to do as I please."

I stared at her. She was relating this happily, as if she were a nine-year-old at her birthday party, opening a gaudily wrapped package.

"This will be perfect for us," she said. "We can continue as lovers, and I won't have to worry about living expenses." She saw the look of disgust twisting my face.

"What's the matter?" she said.

"Tell me," I said in a low, angry voice, "what would be the difference between that arrangement and prostitution?"

Her face hardened. "How can you say that to me?"

"You'd be trading sex for money."

"Not quite," she said.

"What in hell do you mean, not quite?"

"At his age he isn't capable of having sex. He would just want to..."

"What?"

"Give me oral sex."

I shook my head. "That's just about the same thing."

"So you are saying that if I agree to this I'm no better than a whore."

"What do you call trading your body for money?"

"So you don't want me to do this."

"I can't tell you what to do."

"But you are against it."

"What do you think?"

I didn't call her for a week, and finally she called me to say she had finally decided to turn Lloyd down. So, she said, why don't you come over and we can pick up where we left off? She didn't mention the "proposition" again.

Of course I had to introduce Gabrielle to David. I wanted him to see the kind of woman I was able to attract. I wanted—actually I needed—to show her off because I secretly was jealous of his wealthy New Haven family and his degree from Harvard, a great contrast to my impoverished background and lack of degree.

I invited him to Gabrielle's apartment. She looked great in a thin, black, clinging blouse and trouser combination. She brought drinks and joined our conversation. It didn't go well.

Somehow the topic of the German language came up, and she got out her dictionary. She handed him the book and, bending over his shoulder, translated from the preface.

"Excuse me," David said gruffly, "but I can read German."

She frowned at his rudeness.

Ignoring her, David turned the pages until he came to a chart depicting language origins. Suddenly he laughed out loud, an explosive laugh, his trademark.

"HA!"

"What do you find so amusing?" Gabrielle asked.

He laughed again. "Look," he pointed. "It says Indo-Germanic."

"So what is wrong with that?"

"It's typical German arrogance," he said. "Don't you realize that it's actually Indo-European?"

Gabrielle's cheeks flushed. They argued loudly for a while and eventually quieted down, but the evening was ruined.

Afterward at work I asked him what he thought of her. He didn't hesitate. "She's a fruitcake," he said. "Absolutely insane."

When he said that, I thought he was jealous.

A few weeks later I was sitting in my jockey shorts in Gabrielle's apartment, reading some galleys I'd brought from work, bare feet up on a stool. I heard the elevator open down the hall and the familiar sound of her voice. I thought she was speaking to a neighbor. Her keys rattled in the door, and she pushed it open.

She saw me, and I was about to say hi, but she quickly closed the door. A murmur of a man's voice. And then her loud voice. "Oh, MERDE!"

After a few seconds the door flew open again, and she entered. Following her, carrying a brown grocery sack with a phallic rod of French bread sticking up out of it, was a balding man in an open overcoat and a plaid muffler.

I sat motionless and stared.

The man put the bulky grocery bag on the counter. He was probably 40 or 45, and chunky. His eyes were droopy sad, like a basset hound's. He saw me and half smiled, as if he'd expected something like this.

He turned to Gabrielle. "You have company," he said quietly. "So I'll see you later."

"Don't be ridiculous," Gabrielle said. "Stay. Allow me to introduce you to my friend. John, this is Harold. Harold, John."

But Harold was having none of it. He cleared his throat. "No, I'm going." He headed for the door, but stopped and turned.

"Let me give you some friendly advice, John," he said.

I looked at him. He wasn't mocking me, he was serious.

"Don't ever believe a word this woman says."

And then he left.

I expected Gabrielle to be nervous and apologetic, but she wasn't. She began unloading the grocery sack. The bread. Two-inch-thick t-bones. A bundle of fresh asparagus. A net bag full of potatoes. Two bottles of champagne.

I remained seated, paralyzed, my heart thumping. What should I say? What should I do? I had no idea.

"We might as well eat this stuff," she said. "You're hungry, aren't you?"

Harold was a spur of the moment thing, she explained later that evening after we had finished the meal. Harold was in a most unhappy marriage, but his wife refused to give him a divorce. She wouldn't have invited him were it not for the fact that he held a most important position at the United Nations. He was high up in the personnel department, in charge of hiring all the language interpreters. Which was what she wanted very much to do. And most important, she had to find a job soon. Why? Because her money was running out.

"And why shouldn't I look out for myself?" she shouted. "I can't expect much from you along those lines, after all."

She was right. What right had I to complain? She was, from the beginning, very generous to me, and I had very little to give her in return. She couldn't keep helping me indefinitely.

"And by the way," she said. "You should have called to let me know you were coming. You might have spared yourself some embarrassment."

"But you gave me a key, for Christ's sake," I said.

"Nevertheless," she said, "next time call."

One evening she stood naked, talking in French, on the phone. I thought of climbing out of bed, going over there, bending her over, and taking her from behind as she carried on her ever-so-cheerful conversation. Her caller—whoever in hell he was—would hear a grunt or two from her, that's for sure.

She pranced back to the bed. "My friend says there's a most interesting party going on right now, and I'm invited."

"Excellent," I said. "I hope you have a wonderful time."

"I want you to come with me. There will be some important people there."

I didn't want to go. But I did.

It was awful. She had every man in that Third Avenue penthouse captivated, and they circled her like a pack of sniffing jackals. At one point she came up to me and nodded toward a dark-skinned guy in a tuxedo, who stood expectantly beside her. "Darling, would you please give Pablo my telephone number? I don't remember it because I never call myself."

She had a twinkle in her eye. Pablo insouciantly reached into his jacket pocket and pulled out an elegant leather-covered notebook and a huge Mont Blanc. I recited the number, and he wrote it down. "*Agradecimentos muito,*" he said.

Back at her apartment that night, she was insatiable. Her drawing all that attention at the party had turned her on. Perhaps those handsome, elegant men told her exactly what they'd do to her if they ever got her in a dark, private place. She pulled me to bed, and she insisted I do precisely what she said. She wanted to make this last for hours, and it was absolutely essential I obey her every command. "*Verstehen sie?*" she said. "You must NOT come right away. You must hold back."

I nodded.

"Concentrate," she whispered hoarsely.

Four hours later, still before dawn, I felt her nudging my arm. She was gazing at me. "Are you awake?" she whispered.

"Yes," I replied.

"Listen," she said. "No matter what happens to us, no matter whoever else we might end up with, I will always be ready to make love with you. Just call me, and I'll come to you. Do you understand?"

I nodded. "Yes. I understand."

"You are a perfect lover, John," she smiled. "I'm yours forever, whenever you want me."

Three weeks later we were lying in bed, naked, as usual. I had my hands clasped behind my neck. My heart was still pounding from what we'd just done. "I have to tell you something," she said softly.

"What?" I said.

"Tomorrow morning I am going to Mexico," she said.

I blinked. "With whom?" I asked.

"A friend."

"How long will you be gone?"

"Three weeks, perhaps more, perhaps less. We're driving down."

"What's his name?"

"Giancarlo. He's just a friend. We will have separate rooms."

"Separate rooms?"

"Yes. I said he's just a friend. I don't intend to go to bed with him."

"Oh, no? You expect me to believe that?"

"Yes," she said. "Because it's the truth. I've always wanted to see the rest of this country. And Mexico."

"And you'll do anything to get what you want."

"Don't be rude. And besides, where have YOU ever taken me? Answer me that. You can't even afford to take me to a concert, or a movie. I didn't come to America to spend all my days and nights in a dreadfully tiny apartment like this."

I sat up in the bed. Her light blue eyes didn't blink. I raised my hand and struck her, very hard, on the side of her face. A bright red trickle of blood came from her flared nose and dripped on the front of her cotton nightshirt. Bright red spots that soaked quickly into the delicate embroidered yellow flowers. She reached for the tissue box. I felt like hitting her again, but the sight of her blood brought a serious lump to my throat. I wanted to cry. I wanted to kill her. Or myself.

"While I'm gone, will you check my mail for me?" she asked, pressing the wadded tissue under her nose. "I'll leave you a key to the box."

"Check your mail? Are you serious?"

"Yes, of course I'm serious. I want you to forward my father's letters."

"I can't believe this."

"Please?"

While she was in Mexico, I went to her apartment every day to check the mail. Letters came addressed to her from Stuttgart. German postage stamps. A return address in heavy, black block letters. Herr

Dieter F. Hoffman. Also letters came addressed to me. One each day. Envelopes filled with dozens of pages of thin paper with the imprint of close lines of script written with a ball point pen. Tiny letters, straight blue lines, a meticulous script. From those light, crinkly pages came a scent of lavender.

She wrote about the long trip from New York, the drive south toward Florida, and then west through Georgia, Mississippi, Louisiana, Texas. I scanned the lines, not allowing myself to hear the sounds or to see the landscape she enthusiastically described. No, all I could think of was the guy who was driving the car. What's-his-name. The guy who was just a friend. Giancarlo. Who had agreed, like an idiot, to have separate rooms. I could think only of them together, having dinner at hotels, all those long, intimate conversations.

That's all I allowed myself to see. I hurried through the lines of poetry she'd written for me, full of bright desert images of baked red sandstone and shimmering orange sunsets and saguaro and prickly pear and barrel cacti and speckled green lizards standing motionless then vanishing. I would not allow her naïve, sentimental lyricism to soften the hardness forming inside me. I bundled her father's letters into a large envelope and sent it to Mexico City's Hotel Marquis Reforma, which she said was located on the famous Paseo de la Reforma, overlooking Chapultepec Park. And that was all.

When she returned from her international jaunt, she insisted I come over. When I arrived, she asked, "So why did you not write to me?" Which led to a loud argument.

I told her, "You betrayed me. You were disloyal. Unfaithful. That's why."

She looked surprised. "How can you accuse me of these things?" she said. She was perfectly serious. She believed what she was saying. She insisted she had not gone to bed with Giancarlo, that she had been faithful throughout.

"Each night I wrote to you," she said, "alone, yes, alone—in my room. Betrayal? I have never betrayed you. I have been totally honest with you, every step of the way."

I told her that there were just too many other men in her life.

"Oh?" she said. "And what about you?"

"Me?"

"I seem to recall that you have a wife down in Texas."

"Yes," I shouted. "And that's the point. She's 1,500 miles away down in Fort Worth, whereas the men in YOUR life are only a few blocks away."

She repeated she had never cheated on me. And so on, back and forth, shouting at each other, until I just ran out of gas. I stood while she sat on the sofa bed, and I suddenly felt battered and exhausted. Finally I told her, quietly, and I meant it, "I'm sorry, but I can't do this anymore. I just can't. I've had enough."

And I walked out.

Three weeks went by. I was beginning to think I was going to make it okay, when the phone rang.

"You've got to help me," she said.

I closed my eyes and shook my head. Jesus. It just never ends. "What exactly do you want?" I said.

"I am broke," she said. "Totally broke. I don't have money even to buy dinner."

"What about your benefactor Lloyd? Or Giancarlo. Whatever happened to them?"

There was a long silence. "Just tell me, John, if you will help me. Yes or no."

"I don't have much," I said, which was the truth.

"Bring me whatever you can spare. Tonight, if you can."

"The bank is closed, it'll have to be a check," I said.

"Thank you," she said. "I really appreciate it."

The next day at work, I very calmly and deliberately called my bank and asked how one went about stopping payment on a recently written check. A check I had written. Yes, just last night. I wish to stop payment on it. Well, the clerk said, just stop by and fill out a form.

Which I did. I wanted to hurt Gabrielle as much as she'd hurt me. It made me sick and angry to think of her with Lloyd, and then with Harold, the guy with the grocery sack, and then Pablo with his Mont Blanc, and then the big cross-country expedition with Giancarlo. Maybe there were more men she hadn't bothered to tell me about. So god-damn it to hell, I would pay her back. Big time.

Between and even during relationships over the decades, I've recalled how it was being with Gabrielle. Her esthetic and erotic perfection, the look and feel of her smooth nakedness, the most delicate sweep of her blond pubic hair, the flush of her cheeks, her grasping me, urging me. These images have remained with me all my life.

And yet despite that I have, until now, avoided recalling the look on her face in a chance encounter in Greenwich Village just a few weeks after I stopped payment on that check. She was wearing the black silk blouse and trouser combination she'd worn when she met David, and her hair was pulled back in a pony tail.

She saw me. She looked tired. In her pale blue eyes I saw not anger, but acute disappointment. My embarrassment was excruciating. How could I have been such a disgusting, ungrateful shit?

V.K. REITER

Living/Tango

From April/May 2015

I HAD BEEN working at the main New York City library for two years, doing research for a novel. The studious atmosphere in the Rose Reading Room, the easy access to historical material, books, and documents I ordered up from the stacks as well as from other libraries around the country were so conducive to my work that at times I fantasized taking over a corner in some hidden area of the vast building, bringing in a cot and a toaster oven to sustain me. When I first began working in the library, I had often been irritated at having to wait an hour or so for a particular book to be retrieved from the depths of its prodigious collection. Then, as time passed, the week or two wait for documents to arrive from other libraries taught me patience, and I began to appreciate the short interludes before some military history or memoir appeared, using the time to search out other documents, to ask a librarian for information, or to visit the ladies' room. To my dismay the library had rid itself of its traditional card catalogs, so one could no longer flip through the many drawers in which cards were bunched together according to subject matter and the splendid Dewey decimal system. I had often found interesting juxtapositions there, connections I had never considered, titles and notations providing new thoughts, new imaginings, new possibilities. The computerized catalog was less congenial, subjects being arranged in what I considered a poorer system than the one I had successfully navigated in the past.

At last, after more than two years of research, I felt I had assimilated enough information, enough history, enough social detail and arcana, at least for the moment, to begin writing, and so I announced to my husband I would no longer be spending time at the library but would be working in the small office in our apartment. "You must be relieved," he said, "not having to take the bus every morning and coming back during rush hour." He seemed glad I would be home, fully concentrated on writing, but from past experience, I wondered how long it would be before he would begin telephoning in the middle of the day to mention some domestic or social matter needing my attention.

I set to work. My main character appeared almost effortlessly, as if speaking to me, through me, and so it went for three exhausting, exhilarating chapters. I knew that while such exhilaration feels wonderful, it cannot be trusted, and inevitably, anything that gave me such facile joy would need to be rethought and rewritten many times.

One day, while walking to the post office, I felt faint. The next day, I became faint again, and the next. "Maybe it's my heart," I thought since the moments of feeling faint were accompanied by palpitations. I went to a cardiologist and had the appropriate tests. "Your heart's fine," he said. The next day I went to my internist and had what seemed like every blood test in existence, so many that the results would not be available for two weeks.

That weekend I received a call from the West Coast. My mother, who was 96, was in the hospital. I had known she was slowly failing but was not truly prepared for the inevitable. Setting aside the moments of feeling faint, that evening I was on a plane to Los Angeles. "She's dying," the attending physician said as he led me to her bed. "It'll be a day or two."

My mother's body was visibly diminished, her skin thinned and paper white. Then she opened her eyes, saw me, and tried to sit up. "I want to eat something, little daughter," she said, in Russian. "I want yogurt."

I fed her. The next day, holding her hands, which were cold when I had always known them warm, I could feel she was at the last of her strength.

"The end of the week," I told the physician.

"I think it'll be sooner than that," he said.

"Her generation's the strongest there ever was," I insisted. "She'll give herself a few more days."

Telephoning my husband in New York, I asked him to come to Los Angeles. My husband is steadfast in moments of stress or whenever I find myself in unusual or worrisome situations. I had learned to trust he would always come through whenever I, or close friends or relatives, were in difficulty. When problems were manageable, we tended to spare each other knowledge of them until they were solved. So I had said nothing about feeling faint and of the tests that had been done, not wishing to burden him with a problem that might not exist. Both he and I had had unfortunate first marriages; both of us remained jealous of our independence, taking for granted our ability to cope. I had not wanted to marry again, but he had cajoled me into giving it a try for a month or so, saying that, if I did not like the arrangement, the marriage could be annulled. For over 30 years we had been married on a month-to-month basis. On occasion it would occur to me that he had been extremely clever.

My mother died on Sunday morning. The funeral was on Monday. Just before the burial, a mortuary attendant opened the coffin lid and asked me to identify her, which I did, touching her icy cheek and hands before placing a few family photographs alongside her body as well as the last lemons from the ancient tree in her garden. The tree had long refused to die, each year producing a handful of fruit as if to demonstrate its determination. She was buried in the grave alongside my father. My husband recited the prayer for the dead.

After that we went back to her house, where I gathered the trust and estate documents she and I had organized years earlier when such matters had become increasingly wearing and confusing to her. Freed of responsibility for herself, she had handed me her checkbook, so that I might pay her bills, see to her taxes, and keep track of her savings, the latter of which had dwindled considerably since, over the last several years, she had needed live-in care.

In the next few days, I saw to all the legalities, and we began emptying out the trash, donating what could easily be donated to charity. That done, my husband returned to New York. From the time of my arrival in Los Angeles, through the days when my mother was actively dying, through the funeral, the legalities, I had never once felt faint.

With my husband gone, I opened my mother's long-abandoned workroom, where for decades she had earned a living sewing draperies and pillows and bedspreads for a decorator service. She had always made her own clothes: floral blouses and bright-colored dresses, a flamboyance left over from her early theater days in the old country. Perhaps it was that unending flamboyance that caused me to wear nothing but neutral colors, enlivened only by a scarf tied about my neck or shoulders in the complex French manner, or a piece or two of discreet jewelry.

I brought what remained of the workroom contents into the house: bolts of cloth, vintage Italian hat bodies in fine straw or silky felt from her days as a milliner, the many worn, wood blocking forms she had used for shaping hats, and cartons filled with old dress patterns.

Friends sent me two young costume designers who came, leafed through the fabrics, hat bodies, blocking forms and patterns, and eagerly bought up what my mother had held on to for years: In her 80s she was still saying she would resume designing and sewing when she felt stronger.

I ordered her grave marker. And then I grew faint again.

Leaving most of the chores undone, I closed up the house, gave my best friend a set of keys but no explanation for my sudden departure, and flew home. There had been no time to grieve.

"Hold my calls," my internist told his staff, then took me into his office and closed the door. I had known him a long time and had never seen him so pale or so agitated. "You probably have leukemia," he said, "chronic myelogenous leukemia."

Half an hour later I was in an oncologist's office undergoing a bone-marrow biopsy. Afterwards, the oncologist explained I was feeling faint because my white blood cell count was dangerously high. He gave me a prescription for drugs that, he said, would bring the white cells under control.

"What next?" I asked.

"You start treatment."

"What are my chances?"

"I think it's CML. If it is, we have a couple of treatments available or maybe a bone marrow transplant, if we can find a donor. Do you have siblings?" I shook my head. "I have to be frank with you," he said, "there's usually not a great outcome: three, four, five years." My mind went numb.

I brought the prescriptions to a friend's pharmacy and realized I was short of cash, but he, seeing which drugs I had been prescribed, told me to forget it.

Then I went home and waited for my husband. When he arrived, it took me an hour before I was able to tell him I was ill. We spent the evening and the next few days being alternately devastated or paralyzed, my husband repeatedly asking me to tell him exactly what the oncologist had said until I could no longer answer him but merely shake my head, and at last, retreat to my office. In my disarray, I put the printed-out pages of the novel's first chapters into a manila folder, which I placed in the bottom drawer of one of my file cabinets, far back behind all my accumulated research material.

The novel I had been writing with such determination and joy, in which I had invested so much time, thought, effort, and emotion, had disappeared, no longer existing except as a faint memory of something set aside.

At the time, my husband was a department manager at the local Veterans Administration Hospital. He had graduated university with a degree in pharmacy, had run several chains of pharmacies, and as a result knew a good number of doctors in New York City. Over the next several days he made many phone calls and finally found a hematologic oncologist who appeared to be universally respected by his peers. The man's office was two blocks from our apartment.

We sat watching nervously as the new oncologist read through the laboratory results and reports from the other two doctors. "I think I'd better do a bone marrow biopsy," he said.

"I just had one."

"I'd rather do my own," he insisted.

A bone marrow biopsy is the sort of procedure doctors call "uncomfortable." I lay myself belly-down on an examining table, and a certain amount of lidocaine was injected painfully into the skin and muscle over my iliac arch. Then the doctor pushed a sharp device through the skin and muscle, drilling it into the bone until the tip reached my marrow. The device in place, he aspirated several vials of bone marrow. The sensation was one of something fundamental to my very existence being sucked out of me. The aspiration finished, the doctor chipped off a small piece of bone that was also to be biopsied.

After that, I turned over on my back and lay still for a half hour, applying pressure to the wound. Having experienced two bone marrow biopsies within three weeks, I now knew that the difficulty of the experience depended on the doctor's lightness or heaviness of hand. The pain from this second biopsy lasted almost a week, and I was grateful for painkillers. In the year and a half to come, I would have seven bone marrow biopsies in that same office.

At our next appointment, the doctor told me he would be treating me with PegIntron, a slow-release form of interferon, a chemical that, he assured me, exists naturally in the body and was the latest, most effective treatment for CML. This sounded anodyne and reassuring. But the treatment could not begin until the drugs I was taking had lowered my white blood count sufficiently. We were in early October, and he estimated this would take until mid-November.

"I'm feeling a little better," I said. I had been taking the medication for two weeks and could already sense a difference since I rarely felt faint. I could feel my strength returning, and with it an instinctive desire to travel. "I'd like to go to Paris, if I can."

"Why?"

"To visit friends."

He thought about it for a while and then said, "If you're really feeling better, go to Paris. There shouldn't be any problem as long as you take the medication every day."

This was not the first time in our marriage my husband thought me crazy, yet he had never interfered nor stood in my way once he was convinced I was serious about what I planned to do. Over the years we had built our partnership, each of us making accommodations in order to live our life together, accommodations that would not offend our sense of ourselves or threaten our marriage. After so many years we truly knew what manner of acceptance was necessary, and what we could offer, in order to oblige each other's needs and ambitions. So it was that I had often traveled on my own, as had my husband, remaining out of touch for days or weeks and, upon returning, feeling truly content to be home again. Now, even though this particular situation was not the usual sort, he seemed to understand my desire to be elsewhere, saying merely, "Do you really think you ought to leave New York?" What he did not tell me then was that, having learned all he could about CML and the other forms of adult leukemia, he knew that if I was to be treated with interferon, which cured only a small percentage of patients, I would be betting my life on bad odds.

I went to Paris and saw friends and acquaintances who had made the city an enchantment for me when I lived there, as well as two former lovers with whom I had remained friends: one, an editor and translator who always telephoned me on my birthday and, from time to time, would ask for my help with American locutions or social usage in the novels he was translating; the other who often sent me stories he had written and was gracefully welcoming when I reciprocated. To my mind, I was saying goodbye to them all.

On my last night there, which was the night when the *Beaujolais nouveau* arrives in the city and restaurants are filled with people and music plays everywhere in an annual celebration of life and wine and everything that is good, friends took me to dinner and, in the middle of the meal, one said, "You're not looking well."

"I have leukemia," I said. "This may be the last time I come to Paris." They embraced me and said affectionate things and then ordered another bottle of Muscadet and another two-dozen Belon oysters, which I love but perhaps are not a good thing to eat if your immune system may not be up to par.

The bistro's owner had hired a band to play and sing throughout the evening. The musicians were French but sang Eagles' songs in accented English, and every fourth number seemed to be "Hotel California." I sipped Muscadet and sang along with them even as the feeling of dread I had temporarily been able to ignore returned, as intense as ever.

A week after I returned home, the PegIntron treatment began. On the evening following that first injection, I rose from the bed, vomited and, still standing, blacked out. The next day my husband told me he had waited for the vomiting to stop, undressed me, washed my body, changed the bed linens, and cleaned the bedroom carpet. I was mortified, not only at my thorough loss of control when my body reacted to the chemical, but that he had been forced to deal with the mess. Luckily, that first violent reaction to the drug did not occur again although, far from being anodyne, it almost immediately rendered me unable to move. In the coming months I would scarcely leave our apartment, and then only to go to the doctor's office for the weekly injection. Barely able to eat, I lost weight. I lost hair. I lost the ability to read, the most serious of my losses at that point, as books had been the center of my life since childhood. The drug's assault on my very being left no room for fear, but at the time, I would not have been able to recognize nor put a name to that emotion. My true self had disappeared, leaving me capable of nothing but the determination to endure. There were brief moments when I recognized anger in myself, and despair, with an occasional rare oasis of tentative hope. But the one, unending constant was overwhelming illness and fatigue. Since the doctor had decreed PegIntron was the newest, best treatment for CML, I found myself not only too weakened but too dependent, or perhaps too intimidated, to question his expertise.

As devastating as this was for me, it was unbearable for my husband. Each morning he would leave for work and return in the evening knowing he would find a speechless skeleton in place of his wife, a person he would have to care for, no matter his own fatigue. How he bore it, I do not know. I do know that about three months into the treatment, unable to shop or prepare meals, I managed to focus just long enough to find a cook to come in twice a week. As she had recently begun training to become a chef, her fee was minimal. She proved to be a fair enough cook, although not in a style we were used to. My husband said nothing, but I could tell from his determination to get through the meal, his posture at table, and the way he finished dinner in 15 minutes, that he was unhappy, although he never complained. His attempts to make me eat something, anything, inevitably ended in failure as, to please him, I would stagger to the table and take a few bites from the small salad plate with its scant serving of food, its size plainly meant not to be intimidating; or, if I was too weak to leave the bed, from the saucer he would bring to the bedroom, knowing I would almost always turn away. I have no memory of what I did manage to eat all that year. I do know at the end, I had lost so much weight, the one pair of French-made suede jeans I kept packed away, a souvenir of my long-ago life in Paris, fit me again.

The weeks cycled by: injection on Monday, nausea and annihilating weakness through Saturday, Sunday in something like recuperation, and then Monday again.

Stubborn in his belief that fresh air was a necessity, my husband insisted on walking me around the block every Sunday so I could breathe something other than the atmosphere of the sickroom. He would take my arm, and we would move very slowly, each step an effort until inevitably I would say, "I'm going to faint. Don't try to pick me up." And I would fall, most often on a side street, remaining on the ground until my mind cleared. Habit having drained him of embarrassment, my husband would stand over me and wait until I raised my arm so he could help me up, after which we would return to our apartment and I would go back to bed until our next outing.

The day came when I was convinced I was being poisoned, that the interferon was quite possibly killing me. One afternoon, alone, my husband at work, I somehow managed to take a taxi the two blocks to the doctor's office and staggered toward it, holding on to the wall leading to his door. An EKG showed no indication my heart had been damaged by the medication, and so I was sent home without a word to acknowledge I felt in danger from the drug and barely alive. That was the only time I cried.

A year went by. The bone marrow biopsies showed the leukemia had not improved, and so one day the doctor decided to stop the treatment. Within two weeks I began to feel better, but the next step, he told me, was to try an older, more primitive combination of chemicals that in the past had worked on a small percentage of patients.

Determined to enjoy the respite, I asked him to wait until after the New Year.

The next week my husband learned a second-stage trial of a promising new leukemia drug was being offered. He made inquiries and was bluntly told that, given my situation, I had nothing to lose. To our consternation, my oncologist had not mentioned the new drug to me, nor that he was supervising a portion of the trial, even though I was a perfect subject, the trial having been designed specifically for those whose treatment with interferon had been a failure.

Through colleagues, my husband had me volunteer for the trial, and I was accepted. A few days later I was informed that the cohort in which I had been enrolled was already complete and so I would not receive the drug. In despair, knowing I would refuse the more primitive chemical treatment I had been offered, I turned numb again, unwilling to accept I was going to die even before I actually reached that stage. Unknown to me, my husband spoke to my doctor. I do not know what was said, but the result of that conversation was that the doctor immediately pressed my case with the pharmaceutical company while my husband telephoned everyone he knew who might help overturn their decision. Whatever arguments they used, a few days later I was reintegrated into the cohort from which I had been expelled. My husband's determination saved my life.

In February, I began taking the drug, then called STI-571, which underlined its experimental nature. The side-effects were immediate: nausea from the drug itself, which was corrosive to the esophagus, excruciating cramps in my legs, feet, and hands that came in the night and brought me awake, crying out; periorbital edema causing the flesh around my eyes to swell until my face looked like a frog's; the melanin leaching out of my skin until I resembled a wraith; occasional bleeding in the whites of my eyes; and then, very soon, weight gain around my midsection that distorted my body into something I did not recognize. The doctor informed me these side effects were usual. I would have to bear them or, if they proved too difficult, simply give up despite the hope the drug would work for me. Treating the nausea and pain in my esophagus with what my husband called a "PPI," and I being too ill to even want a translation, rendered the other problems somewhat easier to tolerate. My husband's suggestion that the nausea and burning sensation might be alleviated in this way had taken a while to be approved.

Of all the side effects, one of the worst was being awakened several times during the night by ferocious leg and hand cramps. Remembering what I'd done in my teenage years to reduce menstrual cramps, I began taking calcium, which proved helpful for a short time. My husband came up with a new medicine designed to treat leg cramps and bad circulation. Although unfamiliar with that particular drug, the doctor wrote the prescription. It worked for me. Slowly, the side effects began to abate, although they never completely disappeared. My face and body would be forever changed.

I stopped looking in the mirror.

In anticipation of the quarterly bone marrow biopsies demanded by the trial, I searched out and found a hypnotist who was attached to the Sloan-Kettering Cancer Center and came highly recommended. Years earlier, facing serious surgery, a hypnotist had taught me a method for controlling post-operative pain. Her guidance had served me well, especially since that hospital's nursing staff proved to be both curious and cooperative. Unfortunately, she had died, and so in attempting to retrieve the discipline, I was forced to teach the new hypnotist the vocabulary and images I had used so successfully in the past. Even though he obviously felt awkward about a few of the techniques, he appeared willing to try, and so, with each of us guiding the other, I managed to reach, and sustain, something near the deep concentration I had known before. In late April, I informed the doctor, who was still performing the bone marrow biopsies, what I needed in order to retain that state. In early May, I lay down on the table and took myself away from the moment. The doctor came into the examining room and loudly said, "So she's hypnotized or what?" My focus was destroyed. Sitting up, I ordered him to leave the room. His nurse, who had cooperatively remained silent as I concentrated on the smallest details in the bare landscape of the Mojave Desert, was appalled. Whether it was at his behavior or mine, I do not know. In a panic, she said, "Doctor has another patient after you."

"He can come back after he's seen that patient, but tell him not to say a word. He's blasted my concentration to hell, and I'll have to try to get it back." A half hour later the doctor returned, but I had not been able to regain the depth of focus needed and could hear the instruments clinking as they were picked up and laid down again, could feel the burn of the lidocaine as it was injected, the pressure of the trocar and cannula and the aspiration that followed.

The results of the biopsy showed there was some improvement. By August, after another biopsy, there was scant sign of the leukemia. I was not cured, but the expression of the disease had been blocked, and it now became a matter of waiting to see how long this would last. I suppose the lack of certainty might have caused me to live tentatively, or to worry the disease would outwit the medication and cause a relapse. But, without consciously deciding to do so, I simply ignored those possibilities, living as if this reprieve would continue and that the leukemia would remain at bay, becoming merely a situation to be managed.

My husband was hugely relieved: evidently the months of waiting for me to live or die had worn him down more than I had been able to recognize. Now, I watched as he began to feel our lives were returning to normal. I watched his anxiety lessen, watched as he became less centered on my illness, but I could also sense his wariness, his fear the leukemia might reappear and there would be no other miracle available. Still, he very soon became the man to whom I had been married for so many years, no longer careful in our exchanges, once again giving free rein to his normal moments of grouchiness or teasing, again recounting his workday and the situations in which he found himself, or the doings of the people around him. And we were beginning to have our conversations again, one of the things we had both lost during the time of leukemia.

We were living a semblance of normality, but I was aware the person I had been, before becoming ill, was not back. I suppose my husband knew it, too, yet neither of us spoke of it. We merely carried on, waiting for me to return to normal.

Having been in bed for almost a year and a half, I had lost muscle mass and stamina. Slowly, I began to move around the apartment. Slowly, I began to put order into our household, which had become chaotic while I was ill. My brain was still not functioning normally, although I was aware of what needed doing and could do it. One morning, I absent-mindedly picked up a book on the history of New York City in the late 19th century, and opening it discovered I could read again, which was an enormous gift as I had thought my mind had gone forever. The cook was back at school, and I was preparing simple meals from the groceries my husband brought in, although the effort usually exhausted me.

I have never liked exercise, have always avoided gyms, hating the promiscuity and other people's sweat, abhorring the jargon. I do not like wearing shorts and a tee-shirt in front of others, although in earlier years I had happily worn a bikini. I do not like being one of a crowd, hopping around or grunting or running to nowhere. Yet it was obvious I needed to regain my former energy and strength, if I could.

There was a building nearby I had often passed without paying it any particular attention, only vaguely aware its second floor held a dance studio. I had never danced, not even as a teenager nor socially as an adult, perhaps scared off by my brief experience of ballet class, at the age of six, that had immediately left me with ankles aching so badly I was unable to climb stairs. For me, dancing had always been something nice enough to watch but nothing I would ever choose to do. Yet one day I entered the building and, relieved there was an elevator, rode up one floor. Inside the bare, mirrored studio, three couples were practicing ballroom dancing. To my unaccustomed eye, their movements appeared strenuous. After a while, the studio manager asked if I was interested in lessons, and I said I might be but I had been ill, had never danced in my life, and was so out of shape I could barely walk.

"No problem," he said. "Whoever's teaching you can stop when you have to, and you can sit down until you're ready to go again." Then he quoted prices.

Along with her house, my mother had left me what remained of her savings. To my surprise, I found myself signing up for a month's worth of dance instruction, renewable at the same rate. "What do you think?" I asked my husband.

"Whatever you want," he said.

The next Tuesday I met my instructor, a pale blond, lanky Bulgarian, formerly that nation's national ballroom champion, who like many other Central European ballroom dancers had made New

York his new home. I explained my situation. "We know about it," he said. "Is no problem." And he put one arm around my waist, held my right arm out to the side, and said, "Right leg, step back. Left leg, step back. Right leg, step right, left leg together. Then reverse, forward."

I tried to follow his instructions, and soon we were moving in a sketchy foxtrot, although it was actually more like walking. Two minutes later, I had to sit down. After a while I got up, and we walked some more. The studio was filled with loud, recorded music that changed every five minutes or so, at one point a waltz, the next minutes the rumba or some other form of Latin dance. The couples on the floor continued rehearsing whichever form of dance they wished, ignoring the music until the moment it shifted to the one of their choice, so that at times a couple might be dancing salsa to the strains of a bolero, or the quick-step to the sound of a waltz. It seemed there was a confusing disconnect in this, but it was all so new to me, it would take weeks before I came to understand how the dancers managed it.

"How was it?" my husband asked.

"We walked to music," I replied.

"Is this actually exercise?" he asked.

"No, thank God," I said.

A few days later I returned to the studio, and we walked again. Soon, Stanislav taught me a variation on the basic step, and we did that twice a week for another two weeks, pausing frequently so I could catch my breath.

In the second month he taught me the steps for the rumba and the cha-cha-cha. By now I was able to move for perhaps five minutes between pauses. A month later, we attempted the waltz, which in its Viennese version is taxing for even the healthiest person. Through all this Stanislav was infinitely patient, and when I came to think of it later, I realized it could not have been easy for him to accommodate not only my awkwardness but the number of times I was forced to rest.

Still, in a while, I could manage about six or seven minutes of rumba or foxtrot before I had to stop, and soon after I was moving long enough to raise a sweat. This regimen lasted nearly six months until I was dancing for the full 55-minute lesson, pausing now and then for a swallow of water before starting up again. I had even become invested enough in the lessons to buy a pair of black rehearsal shoes that matched my dance costume of lightweight black sweatpants and a black top. The dance shoes made things far easier as they held my feet properly and their thin suede soles allowed me to feel the floor.

My oncologist had passed me on to one of the other doctors taking part in the study, and every three months she would perform a bone marrow biopsy. She had a light hand, yet I would still concentrate and try to take myself away, prefacing each biopsy by saying I would be timing her. Within the year, the entire biopsy, from lidocaine injection to "all done," rarely lasted longer than eight minutes, although I still needed pills for the pain afterward. And it would take a month before we received the results, which inevitably showed the leukemia was being held at bay.

One day, Stanislav was gone, having disappeared into the professional ballroom dance circuit. Feeling stronger now, I was reluctant to give up the lessons that had come to punctuate my week and had increased my stamina. When I told my husband I would have to find a new instructor, he simply nodded, having grown used to the idea that an hour, every Tuesday and Friday afternoon, was now devoted to dance lessons. Plainly, he considered those lessons a personal matter, and so he had never questioned me about them, nor about the person of the dance instructor, showing only mild interest when I first reported the man was Bulgarian, was a dance champion, and, now, that he was gone.

At that time, many New York dance studios offered a free or low-price trial lesson as a come-on to new students. I made the rounds of studios in Manhattan, dancing for a half-hour with a variety of teachers, and at last came upon a place in Chelsea where the try-out instructor was a Utah boy with a sunny disposition and Broadway ambitions. This time I said nothing about leukemia. In a few lessons he straightened out some of my more awkward movements and attacked my guarded posture, the result of all those months of illness, but I was still doing simple fox-trot/cha-cha/rumba/waltz with a daring few minutes of basic swing dancing to finish the session. My physical strength had vastly improved, but I was becoming bored since it was always the same predictable dances, the same sorts of steps performed more surely now, with less hesitation, yet I had not become enamored of dancing and was considering giving it up.

One day, looking through a window into a smaller, private dance studio, I watched a couple dancing the tango. It was not the flashy, faux-sensual performance tango seen in movies or on the stage; this was an intense, highly technical, personal dialogue of a dance. The instructor, a short, dark-haired man, noticed me watching, looked hard at me, then went back to the lesson he was giving. When it was finished, he came over. "I'm Rodriguez," he said. His accent was pure Brooklyn, and he had a smart-ass air about him. "You want to learn tango?"

"I don't know," I said. "I've never tried it."

"Come on, I got a half hour before my next class." He led me into the largest studio, where other couples were practicing their particular dances to the usual variety of music.

The tango stance is not like that of competitive ballroom dancing where, when entering the dance, the body is held somewhat in opposition to the partner's and the center of the torso acts as a fulcrum for the movements of the dance, all of which are highly choreographed. In salon tango, which is what Rodriguez taught, the bodies are tilted slightly forward and held fairly close, uncomfortably and inappropriately close, to my mind then, so that one may sense where the leading partner is about to move. A variety of step combinations must be learned, along with the body cues indicating which step will be done next, and once these have been mastered, the dance should become an improvisation.

Rodriguez and I moved slowly, carefully for a while, I keeping my distance, reluctant to bring my changed, thickened and ungainly body close to his. There was something disturbing about this, not only the physical proximity, but the fact that, ideally, the partners share an improvised dialogue demanding the closest attention and receptivity. When the half hour ended, I was upset, the first time I had felt any deep emotion other than anger and despair and then relief when I realized I was not going to die. I spent the evening thinking through, analyzing, my reaction: here was something completely alien to my life and somehow so threatening in what it might require of me that I was truly reluctant to continue. Yet I felt attracted to its complexities, its difficulties, and what I sensed were its demands, which I had recognized even from that brief lesson.

The next day I canceled the ballroom lessons and started to learn tango with Rodriguez.

We began with the proper way to enter into the dance and the basic figures. I was still not moving freely, but Rodriguez taught me to take long steps backward, and when prompted, to cross my left foot over my right after the fifth beat. He led by a subtle tilt of his shoulders or weight shifts that, over time, became easier and easier to recognize. All this was performed to the demanding tango rhythm, regardless of the music being played. Soon, Rodriguez taught me *ochos,* forward or backward figure eights where the follower crosses in front of the leader, smoothly pivots on one foot, and then crosses again in the opposite direction. The forward *ocho* is fairly simple, but the backward *ocho* demands perfect balance. My body's center of gravity had changed, my muscle control was questionable, and I struggled to accommodate its new reality. After two weeks of doing *ochos,* Rodriguez showed me the *molinete,* in which the follower circles around the leader in a series of varied but clearly defined steps. I had been vaguely aware my short-term memory had been damaged by my illness and the drugs, but my inability to learn new steps quickly and to link them together brought that awareness into focus and caused me great frustration. I had trouble remembering the pattern of certain steps and grew increasingly anguished as I failed to immediately assimilate what Rodriguez was trying to teach me.

At every lesson I felt I was moving with all the grace of an elephant, trudging through the hour rather than dancing, and after about 20 minutes, I would find myself sweating, water pouring out of my pores as if I'd run a mile. I began bringing two towels to class along with two pints of water I would finish before the hour was over.

One afternoon, halfway through another session of heavy treading and missed signals, Rodriguez, who early on I'd learned was far more clever than his patter might indicate, said, "So is this the first thing in your whole life you haven't been able to learn in three days?" Startled by his perception, I merely shook my head.

I had been studying the other dancers in the studio, watching them rehearse new step combinations, new variations, new choreography for their next competitions, and I quickly became aware that, despite its reputation as a dance of seduction or of the establishment of power by one partner over the other, tango was actually a matter of technique and athleticism rather than sensuality. Often working with a dance coach, a couple rehearsed their steps and figures but also the gestures, postures, and facial expressions that, on stage or in competition, would indicate the expected eroticism. The only struggle for power I ever saw was once when two men were dancing together. Having established the basic pattern of steps they meant to perform, they began to challenge each other with variations within the established figures, breaking the agreed-upon pattern by introducing new steps or movements. It reminded me of the challenges one hears in jazz, when one musician riffs on the tonal and rhythmic patterns being played, and another musician takes up the challenge with an answering riff of his own.

I was running out of tango money. Telephoning my best friend in Los Angeles, I said, "Can you find someone to rent the house?" She said she would try, and then a few days later called to say that not only was the house still filled with my mother's things, it was also filthy from two years of neglect and, too, the interior was sad and unattractive. "Can you find someone to move everything to storage?" I asked, "and someone to spruce up the place?"

Several days later she reported she had emptied the house and was now volunteering to redo its interior. She had been my best friend since childhood, but what she was offering was beyond friendship and something near to sainthood.

"Send me some money," she said, "and I'll probably need more before it's finished."

Putting the tango lessons on hold, I withdrew money from the savings account I had sworn never to touch except in the gravest emergency and sent it to her. A while later she reported that when the old carpeting inside the house had been pulled up, they had uncovered an intact, red oak floor. And when the ugly mantelpiece was removed, she discovered it had been hiding an Art Deco fireplace. From time to time she would report on the appearance of painters and plasterers, plumbers, tile-setters, and other craftsmen. From time to time she asked for more money. Fourteen thousand dollars later, the house was done and put up for rent. A week later she reported that I had tenants, and that she was sending me the first month's rent check along with the security deposit.

I signed up for three months' worth of tango lessons.

"Glad you're back," Rodriguez said. "Where'd you go?"

"To find money," I said.

Now there came weeks when I struggled with posture, with holding what he called "the frame," with arm and head position and smoothness of movement. Rodriguez often came to the studio by bike, riding from his home in Brooklyn, over the Brooklyn Bridge and through the Manhattan traffic. He would arrive damp with sweat from his exertions, change into his dance shoes, and immediately begin the lesson. Since I always sweated my way through a lesson, I said nothing, taking it as only fair.

Rodriguez and his wife were sharing care of their newborn son, and one day, unable to find a sitter, he brought the infant to the studio, carrying him in a sling across his chest. The boy was fidgety, whimpering when Rodriguez set him down in an infant car seat. Picking the baby up again, Rodriguez replaced him in the sling across his chest, saying, "Will this bother you?"

"No problem," I said, even though I was skeptical about his parenting technique and worried we might crush the infant while we danced. For the next quarter of an hour, we danced with the baby nestled between us, our bodies adjusting to his presence, carefully keeping the exact distance to accommodate him. Strangely, this exercise in infant care taught me more about "holding the frame" than anything Rodriguez had ever been able to explain or show me.

After this there were many times when, impatient, I presumed what the next step would be and was inevitably wrong. There were times when I hit a plateau and was convinced I would never get past it, would never improve, would never dance tango well. The constant repetition of the exact same steps and figures reminded me of the endless violin finger exercises I'd done as a child, attempting to master the techniques that would eventually, I was told, allow me to produce real music.

One day, dancing in a small private studio, there came a moment when, while doing a series of steps we had done 100 times before, the tango dialogue was suddenly there, unexpected, unhesitating. The connection was so intense—and so delicate—I actually managed to say nothing.

Now I began hearing tango wherever I went: in advertising music, in movie scores, in jazz, in short passages within popular songs. Although puzzled and often irritated by my single-minded pursuit of the dance, my husband eventually gave me a CD, *The Soul of Tango,* performed by the cellist Yo-Yo Ma. Most of the pieces were classics of the tango repertoire, but in others, the tango rhythm was often bent or extended or disappeared. I brought the CD to the dance studio, and we began using it at the end of the hour's lesson—a small lagniappe, a promise of the possibilities inherent in tango when the body remembers what it is supposed to do. This music was tantalizing in what it offered, the tempo and beat of the dance being set loose, leaving even more room for improvisation.

All through those months, Rodriguez had been urging me to come to the studio's tango evenings, but I had absolutely no desire to do so. I had not undertaken all this in order to take part in social dancing, or worse, make a spectacle of myself. Some instinct had told me learning tango would not only serve to retrieve my strength but would help me adapt to the transformation of my body. Most important, it would prove I was still able to gain control over something complex and foreign to me after having lost control of my life.

When it was offered, I now felt strong enough to take on a consulting job at a language institute. I had known the owner for years, the work was both interesting and demanding, and I was being paid enough to establish a balance between the money coming in and going out. After several weeks of seeing me leave the office early twice a week, the owner asked where I was going, and I told him. "Tango?" he said. "I danced tango in Vienna, when I was young." I had known him as a master teacher, had known details of his courageous and daring wartime activities, had known something of his personal life and a great deal about his business struggles, and it never would have occurred to me that this profoundly serious man had, at one time, danced tango. A few weeks later he handed me a bonus check, insisting it be used only for tango lessons.

The next year, on a visit to Los Angeles, I went to meet my tenants but actually to see what my best friend had done to the house. She had accomplished wonders, the house now so attractive that for a moment I considered whether my husband and I might leave New York and live there, a notion immediately abandoned when I remembered he was a hard-core New Yorker and I had become one, too. Afterward, I went to check on my mother's things being held in storage but gave up after only an hour of opening and closing cartons: Obviously, I was not yet ready to face all that packed-up memory and grief.

A day or so later I learned friends of friends were studying tango with a Buenos Aires *tanguero* who came to their home to teach them. They invited me to take part in a lesson, and so I went, although with some trepidation since I had never danced with anyone except Rodriguez.

Jorge was tall, had long hair tied in a ponytail, spoke an approximation of English, and had brought his own tango music with him. When it was my turn to dance, it was immediately obvious his style of tango was different from the one I had learned from Rodriguez. And it was also apparent I had been pampered, since Jorge made no concessions except those one makes when first dancing with a new partner.

Soon he was leading step combinations Rodriguez had not taught me, taking it for granted I knew them or would learn them easily. I did not, but then, suddenly, I was able to assimilate what he was showing me. At the time, Rodriguez had begun teaching me *ganchos,* those fast leg hooks that are so spectacular when done onstage. Now Jorge began leading *ganchos,* but I had not yet learned the body cues for the various sorts of hooks and kicks, and he had to show them to me: a pressure of thigh against knee or against thigh demanding an immediate reaction, one leg hooking backward or forward or around the partner's leg, or between his legs and then often across one's own leg again in a sort of mirrored reflex finishing the movement before one is led into the next variation. Too, Jorge's version of the *molinete* was slightly different than the one I had learned in New York, and so we walked through it slowly four or five times before I managed it almost correctly. To my surprise, it took me just five minutes of repetition to adopt his style. We then worked through an entire tango, and I found myself following him almost unerringly since the figures he was leading were neither the most complex nor the most demanding. Perhaps he, too, was pampering me.

I returned to New York, to weeks of work and tango. A year passed before my next visit to Los Angeles. Telephoning Jorge in advance, I asked for a lesson every morning of my stay there. My best friend moved all her living room furniture back against the walls and lent me the bare floor for the week. On the fifth morning, she stayed to watch, and at the end of the lesson, Jorge transformed its last few minutes into a performance, ending in a classic tango pose. I managed to follow him with no hesitation—and a tentative feeling of elation. My friend applauded; we bowed.

Following this, Jorge invited me to visit a tango club, and now, perhaps more accustomed to my new body, or far enough from home to feel safe looking ridiculous, I agreed to meet him there. My friend came along for moral support; Jorge brought his fiancée, a German geologist he was teaching to tango.

The four of us sat at a table for two and ordered soft drinks and water. There was no live orchestra, only a CD player and several speakers hanging against the walls. Most of the dancers were either beginners or had reached an intermediate level of proficiency. Jorge and I walked onto the floor, and he began leading me double-time, so that we were moving faster than anyone else: It felt as if he could not bear being surrounded by tentative, amateurish dancers.

"Slow down," I said, and he did. We danced several times during the evening, and suddenly the Yo-Yo Ma recording was being played. There were only a few couples on the floor. I asked Jorge to dance it with me.

"It is not tango rhythm," he said.

"It is, but you have to find it and improvise as it comes." He obliged me, leading with his usual authority, although I could sense he was uncomfortable with music unfamiliar to him. Perhaps it was his discomfort, or my familiarity with the tango music being played, but for the first time, I felt I was truly dancing, moving smoothly, strongly, intensely attentive, and not merely performing an exercise in technique. The sensation was so new and so exhilarating, I did not want it to end. But of course it did, and we sat down again. Leaning over the table, Jorge said, quietly, that he liked my style in dancing tango.

It had never occurred to me I might have a style.

Back in New York, Rodriguez seemed surprised at the manner in which I followed him. I did not mention I had been dancing with another partner. It was plain he hadn't expected any changes in my dancing other than the new figures he might teach me. And so, perhaps to test me, he began showing me how to perform adornments, small steps that one or the other partner adds to the figure being danced: one foot tracing circles on the floor; a series of quick toe taps; a short caress of a foot against the partner's leg. Whenever one dancer offers such ornamentation, the other always pauses for that moment, giving the partner freedom and space to make a declaration in movement, quiet, contemplative or assertive, or as a challenging personal statement within the dialogue of the dance. After a time, I found myself daring to offer such steps, not waiting for Rodriguez to call for them, either with spoken suggestions or body cues. Soon, I found I was capable of performing those adornments whenever appropriate, of being able to take advantage of the natural pauses between figures, or to cause them. My pleasure in all this was less a matter of performing the adornments but the feeling that, despite the changes in my body that had rendered it awkward and foreign to me, I had come to accept those changes and for the most part, ignore them. On the street, I was able to walk quickly again, to stride, to rush, and best of all, to ignore the differences between what had been and what was.

Soon, Rodriguez announced he and his wife were leaving the city and moving to Saratoga, which, he told me, had become a center for ballroom dancing. Surprised by his announcement, I congratulated him on what no doubt was a well-considered move for his family. And as I dried my body and changed into street clothes, I realized I no longer needed tango.

The studio was preparing a farewell evening of ballroom and tango dancing in the Rodriguezes' honor, and he telephoned to invite me to attend. It was evident he did not expect I would since I had always refused his invitations.

"Of course," I said. "I wouldn't miss it."

The evening began with a series of performances by the studio's teachers and students, each preceded by a small speech of thanks and wishes for the Rodríguezes' future success. Toward the end of these ceremonies, Rodriguez and his wife took the floor and danced an elaborate, highly choreographed tango: for the first time I saw how serious a competitor he was, something I had never realized since I had known him only as an instructor. I left the studio shortly after his performance, well in advance of the buffet, the wine-bottles being opened and poured, and before general dancing began, stopping only to shake Rodriguez's hand and thank him for his unfailing patience, generosity, and cleverness while teaching me. At this, he put his arms around me and kissed me on both cheeks, a gesture he had never made before. I reciprocated in kind, just as one finally bids farewell to a favorite teacher or a friend.

Tango is no longer a part of my daily life. It is my husband who often notices advertisements for recitals and theatrical productions offered by touring tango companies and asks if I would care to attend, but I thank him for the suggestion and refuse, reluctant to spend an evening watching what I know will be theatrical and over-blown: tango as gymnastic, Broadway-ish exhibitions rather than a personal dialogue. Whenever I hear tango music being played, I usually ignore it, but if at that moment it speaks to me, I may take out the Yo-Yo Ma tango CD and listen as the music conjures up the steps, the figures, the adornments, while my mind dances.

IKHIDE IKHELOA

Life in America: Cow Foot by Candlelight

From October/November 2005

For you Uche, wherever you are...

I AM THINKING of going home to Nigeria to visit my papa, Chief Papalolo of Nigeria. I miss the old man very much. America has been very good to me, and I can't complain. I learnt all my bourgeoisie *ajebutter* habits here, you know, like using fork and knife to eat ice cream, cleaning my *ajekpako* peasant lips with paper napkins, stuff like that! Before America, my foray into the rich man's world consisted of occasional trips to supermarkets like Leventis and Kingsway to munch on "sangwages," "scottish egg," and, eh, "meat pipe" washed down with *odeku*, Guinness Stout. How many of you remember those days? Let's form a mailing list! But I miss Papalolo very much.

About my dad, Papalolo. I am the son of a man whose education never went beyond Standard Six, which was the height of primary school in those days. Like all our fathers, he was always first in his class (there were apparently no dunces back then). But my father never went beyond Standard Six. A bright man, nonetheless, who was fond of talking wistfully about an illustrious education interrupted by a marriage (to my mother, Mamalolo) and the birth of Babatunde (me!). Why Babatunde? Well, I was born somewhere in Lagos three weeks after the death of my grandfather. And our Yoruba neighbors promptly nicknamed me Babatunde ("the old man is back!") to my father's disgust. He had heard a vicious rumor I was so named because I looked like an old man with wrinkled skin and sad eyes sunken into a cow's head. But Allah is great; I turned out to be handsome. More on that later...

In the early '50s, my father was fond of taking me to the wharf to watch the traditional dancers and masquerades welcome the new African *oyinbo* white men and women, the new Nigerian intellectuals arriving in the big ships after sojourning in England. In those days nobody went to America (except the great Chief Nnamdi Azikiwe). Everybody went to England, where they visited Trafalgar Square and took grainy black and white pictures of themselves in winter clothes with thousands of plump pigeons doing the unthinkable all over their heads and other body parts. They came back home to Africa with something called the Golden Fleece. Papalolo would watch with envy the arrival of these Nigerian graduates, the Tokunbos whom Chinua Achebe talked about in his books *No Longer at Ease* and *A Man of the People*. These tattooed Nigerians would step gingerly into the steamy tropical sun wearing thick winter coats and hand gloves. They would fan their sweating faces with a *London Daily* and exclaim in their British-Nigerian accent, "Eet is rada het!"

And Papalolo would turn to me and say with extreme bitterness, "Son-of-your-mother! If not for YOU and YOUR mother, I would have been one of them!"

I have such fond memories. When last I visited Nigeria 20 years ago, it was with great excitement. I was going back to the Festac pepper soup joints, to all my friends—maybe they were still sitting on crates of Gulder beer just the way I left them. Ah, to taste Gulder beer again! I love America, but eh, American beer leaves a lot to be desired. I was going back to my girlfriend, the one who swore at the airport in Nigeria she would wait for me, no problem. I was going back to her, and we would buy piping hot plates of rice from Mamaput the fleet-footed food vendor on two wheels (her own two feet!), and we would dine on cow foot by candlelight while listening to the joyous music of Rex Lawson, Chris Okotie, and Jide Obi... just like the white man taught me. Boy was she going to be proud! And you thought African men aren't romantic! This man is one exception to that unfortunate generalization. By the way, there are more men like me where I came from. Nine of us, if you are interested. Be warned: IF you do not possess a green card or your citizenship papers, do not even think of responding to this solicitation. I shall call Homeland Security on you. Love has its limits!

On landing at Murtala Muhammed Airport, there was a slight problem. Actually, there were quite a few slight problems. The air-conditioning wasn't working, and the luggage chute was now being operated by manual labor in the shape of several skinny guys. Something about a late arriving spare part. But I found the immigration officials to be exceedingly kind and helpful. They offered to relieve me of all and any electronics equipment in my suitcase, plus all unnecessary American dollars on my person. They seemed crestfallen I had none of the above. One of them asked me after an exhaustive and disappointing search of my suitcase revealed it was filled with old underwear and books: "Oga, are you sure you are coming from America?" I could hear his colleagues muttering under their breath: "Nor be di better America dis one go!"

As I say, I miss my father Papalolo. The last time I visited him, things didn't go very well. I neglected to bring him the VCR and Mercedes Benz [v-boot] I had promised him. My father found this lapse in judgment extremely distressing. He made a point of taking me around the village to see other proud papalolos who had color pictures of their sons and daughters abroad posing by Mercedes Benzes they would be shipping home as soon as they could take a lunch break from their jobs as CEOs of McDonald's corporation. Until then, I didn't know McDonald's had so many Nigerian-American CEOs! Allah be praised!

I will also point out that at the time of my visit home, it was fashionable to fry one's hair to a greasy mess and speak double negatives, as in, "Sheeet men! I ain't gonna do no sheeet!"

When I left to visit Nigeria, I had only been in America ten years, and so I hadn't acquired the accent expected of a Nigerian-American. As for my hair, even in those days I had so little hair left, I was afraid if I fried it, I would go bald! So I went home nappy and with my original Nigerian accent. This, too, was a major disappointment—and a source of embarrassment—to my dad.

Whenever Papalolo needs to tell me something important, he interrupts my sleep at 3:00 in the morning. This he accomplishes by coming into my room armed with a lantern and nothing really important to say. Why does he do this? I don't know. I suspect he picked up this habit from reading Chinua Achebe's books, where the heroes are fond of waking up their sons to tell them things like, "He who swallows an udala seed will pay in the latrine!"

So this morning, he woke me up with his lantern. "My son," he began, gritting his teeth, "people are talking!"

"Talking about what? Who are these people?" I was clearly irritated at being interrupted from my beauty sleep.

"People are talking," he repeated, ignoring my scholarly inquiry even as he was intent on telling me the answer. "They are saying you don't look like someone who really went to America! You did not fry your hair, and you do not begin and end your sentences with 'men'!

"Son-of-your-mother, tell me, is it true what Akpeteshie our village drunk is saying about you? Have you been hiding somewhere in

Nigeria all these years? Akpeteshie says his brother Saturday once spied you in Sokoto!"

So, if you are thinking of going home to Nigeria soon, your first challenge is to find a travel agent who won't take your money in return for not giving you an air ticket. Good luck! By all means necessary, get rid of that Nigerian accent. Next, you must find a barber who will give you the latest haircut in the 'hood. Also have both your ears pierced (why pierce just one?). Kmart has some good earrings on sale. It helps also if your brother or sister waiting for you at the airport is "immigration" or an interloper posing as one. And please, whatever you do, when you get home, begin your sentence with "yeah" and end it with "man!" They like that! As for a Mercedes Benz with a DVD player in its trunk, do not even THINK of leaving America without one!

Oh, about my girlfriend... she was waiting for me alright... with eight children and a hefty husband named Johnbull!

ANDIE MILLER

Reflections on Glass

From October/November 2005

IN 1998, DANIEL Auster, the son of author Paul Auster, then 20 years old, was sentenced to five years probation in the Manhattan Supreme Court after pleading guilty to stealing $3,000 from the body of murdered drug-dealer Angel Melendez. The Reuters report stated the facts, but what happened on the night of the killing is much murkier. Melendez was killed by New York "club kid" Michael Alig, who then cut up his body. And though Daniel was never implicated in the murder, he admitted to being in the apartment while it took place.

The movie of Michael Alig's clubbing years, *Party Monster,* starring Macaulay Culkin in the title role, has done the festival circuits. But Culkin, the angel-faced star of movies like *Home Alone, Home Alone 2,* and *Getting Even With Dad,* bears as much resemblance to the character as does Charlize Theron to Aileen Wuornos. Facts are generally far less aesthetically pleasing than fiction.

The "better together" recommendations at Amazon for *Party Monster* suggest it should be purchased with *That Was Then, This is*

Now, S. E. Hinton's 1971 American classic about WASP vs. Hispanic teen gangs, written by and for teenagers. The movie stars Emilio Estevez.

Susan Hinton's books were my favorites as an adolescent, even as a South African. How much it had to do with a romantic idea of children living without parents and eating chocolate cake for breakfast, I can't say. But I can still recall the opening line of her first book, *The Outsiders*: "When I stepped out into the bright sunlight, from the darkness of the movie house, all I had on my mind was Paul Newman and a ride home." At least I think that's how it went.

In Paul Auster's first novella, *City of Glass,* part of the 1985 *New York Trilogy*, his detective, Daniel Quinn, is so confounded by the case he is investigating—of a young man having been imprisoned in a room by his father as a boy, and now afraid his father is going to kill him—that he seeks out the help of an author called Paul Auster (mistaking him for a detective of the same name).

Whether this is the same Paul Auster who is writing the novel, we are not sure. Though he borrows from the genre of detective fiction, the search in his writing is invariably the search for self. And he says wryly, "I grope my way forward in darkness as I'm doing it."

While Quinn and Auster are in conversation, Auster's little son Daniel arrives home with his stepmother. Paul introduces the two: "'Daniel, this is Daniel.' The boy bursts out laughing and says, 'Everybody's Daniel!'"

Maybe so. Maybe there's a cautionary tale in this story for us all. After all, how well do we really know anybody? Even those closest to us.

"Sometimes the same people, sometimes different ones," says Auggie Wren, the storyteller in Auster's screenplay, *Smoke,* who photographs the same spot for "4,000 straight days in all kinds of weather... And sometimes the different ones become the same, and the same ones disappear. The earth revolves around the sun, and every day the light from the sun hits the earth at a different angle." Daniel Auster had a small role in the 1995 movie (he was the "book thief"), though he went on to become a photographer by profession.

In Auster's first book, published in 1982, *The Invention of Solitude*—this one not fiction, but a two-part memoir of his father's death (*Book 1 - Portrait of an Invisible Man*) and his meditations on becoming a father to Daniel (*Book 2 - The Book of Memory*)—Auster goes on a journey of discovery of his own father, Samuel, who had been a remote enigma throughout Auster's life. Only in the process of writing this book did he unravel the mystery of what had shaped his father and made him who he was.

When Samuel was just seven years old, "on 23 January 1919, precisely 60 years before my father died," Paul writes, "his mother shot and killed his father in the kitchen of their house." She was found not guilty of murder on the grounds of mental instability, but the family (she and five children) spent the rest of their lives in poverty, constantly moving. So when Samuel grew up, he spent most of his life in denial of and oblivious to what was going on around him. Auster describes his experience of his father:

> For 15 years he had lived alone. Doggedly, opaquely, as if immune to the world. He did not seem to be a man occupying space, but rather a block of impenetrable space in the form of a man. The world bounced off him, shattered against him, at times adhered to him—but it never got through.

So much so that once, after Paul and his sister and parents had moved, his father—who regularly took a nap before dinner—mistakenly drove to his old house and slept surrounded by the new owner's things without even noticing he was in the wrong house. Auster writes:

> Even today, it still makes me laugh. And yet, for all that, I cannot help regarding it as a pathetic story. It is one thing for a man to drive to his old house by mistake, but it is quite another, I think,

for him not to notice that anything has changed inside it... For as long as he lived, he was somewhere else, between here and there. But never really here. And never really there... And if the mind is unable to respond to the physical evidence, what will it do when confronted with the emotional evidence.

Auster's father was no more emotionally conscious than he was physically, and Paul describes the first meeting between grandfather and grandson:

Daniel was just two weeks old when he first laid eyes on him. [He] pulled up in his car, saw my wife putting the baby into the carriage for a nap, and walked over to say hello. He poked his head into the carriage for a tenth of a second, straightened up and said to her, "A beautiful baby. Good luck with it," and then proceeded to walk into the house.

While he was writing *The Book of Memory,* and reflecting on having himself become a father, Auster was also translating Stéphane Mallarmé's *A Tomb for Anatole,* about the death of Mallarmé's young son. These fragments that "aspire to the condition of poetry," Auster describes as "anguished and moving material for me."

> you can, with your little
> hands, drag me
> into the grave—you
> have the right—
> —I
> who follow you, I
> let myself go—
> —but if you
> wish, the two
> of us, let us make...

an alliance
a hymen, superb
—and the life
remaining in me
I will use for—

Auster, whose body of work revolves around coincidences—"the rhythms and rhymes in the world" and "the music of chance" (the title of one of his books)—comments on the fact that looking at photographs of Mallarmé's son Anatole, and his own son Daniel "at that age, when they were very small, they could have been twin brothers."

Of Mallarmé, Auster says he "was able to transform more thoroughly than any other writer, the real into the imaginary, and to blur the distinction between the two."

Auster himself, of course, is a master of the blurring of fact and fiction. So is his wife, novelist Siri Hustvedt. In her most recent novel, *What I Loved* (that took her six years to write), she explores the effects of a troubled child, a pathological liar, on those around him. At once chastised for exploiting her stepson by thinly disguising the story of the Angel Melendez murder in the book, and then defended, because after all it is fiction, both ends of the spectrum of argument seem to be missing the point. More important are the issues she's exploring, and the way she does it. Interviewer Michael Silverblatt puts his finger on it. It's "the interpenetrations of actual actions and literary ones" that are so remarkable, he thinks. What he describes as "the enjambment of fiction and reality."

This interpenetration that happens between fact and fiction in style extends also to what she is exploring in the book, Hustvedt explains:

I'm very interested in the idea of our openness, and the fact that people really are created through each other in some important way. It starts in childhood, the intimacy that we have with our parents, maybe most particularly with our mother, or whomever is taking care of us in the beginning. And that intimacy is a kind of interpenetration of character, and that's how we develop. It goes on in life in friendships as well... Any ordinary conversation between people, there's that space where the language is taking place... Dialogue is something rather magical. The words are going into us, and coming out of us.

And this permeability seems to be heightened in art, she says.

Art, it seems to me, is probably the place where private life meets the culture in some way. With art we have the strange experience of looking at another person's inner life and unconscious through the vocabulary of the culture. Whether it's a written work of art, or a painting, art always borrows from history. It is never created in total isolation, never in a vacuum. You use an artistic vocabulary that you've inherited, from art history.

No doubt this borrowing from history extends to each other's personal histories, too.

The illusion of separateness and creation in isolation is what Auster was also exploring in *The Invention of Solitude*. The path of the solitary artist alone in a room is an alter ego he has explored in his fiction, as well. He muses from time to time, with wry alarm, on who he might have become had he not met Hustvedt.

But the echoes in their work extend beyond just thematic and stylistic dimensions. They extend even to the characters in their books. When she is asked about similarities in their writing and whether she is influenced by Auster's work, she suggests that "partly it is due to a shared world. After all we've been together for 21 years. Inevitably there are overlaps." At the same time, she reminds us, "what people often don't realize is that he's done some borrowing from me too."

In Auster's book *Leviathan*, one of his characters is a woman called Iris. Many people notice this is Siri "in the mirror," as she puts it. But not as many are aware that Iris is a character of Siri's creation, from her first book, *The Blindfold*. Auster asked if his main character could marry Hustvedt's main character, and she "thought that was a lovely thing, because Iris was left hanging at the end of the first novel. And I thought it was very nice that she ended up married to Peter Aaron, and doing rather well." Peter Aaron of course shares Auster's initials and is a semi-autobiographical character.

But life isn't as neatly tied up as fiction, and Michael Silverblatt wonders if perhaps our culture is encouraging its children to become pathological in order to imitate art. "When you talk about diseases generated by the culture, one of these diseases it seems to me has become the interest in the extreme case, the lurid case, the case that verges on poetry." Is pathology then the culture's self-fulfilled prophecy? Hustvedt takes a more practical view:

> I think that the human organism requires certain things in order to do very well. And it seems that some kind of consistent early nurture is really important. And I think that is the thing that to a large degree determines human health. At the same time, it's mysterious. If you read different case studies, you will not be able to find an honest psychiatrist who will tell you that you can predict. You can put two cases side by side, two children who have had very tough childhoods, and they will grow up to be two quite different people. What the factors are remain mysterious. Obviously personal history is very important, one's personal emotional history. But also one's genetic make-up. You know your nerves, the way you're strung. All of this goes together to make a human being.

Auster's first wife and Daniel's mother, writer and academic Lydia Davis, is quiet on the subject. After her divorce from Auster, Daniel moved between her and his father, and one can't help wondering about her thoughts of her child. Writer Amy Fusselman says of her:

> Lydia Davis is ferocious. When I attended her reading in NYC recently, and heard her read the piece about the old dictionary and her son, I was struck again by how that piece is one of the most fearless bits of writing I've ever read. It was all the more powerful to hear her read it in her own, soft voice.

In the piece to which she refers, a short story called "The Dictionary," from Davis's collection *Samuel Johnson Is Indignant* (2001), "a scholar measures her questionable child-rearing against how well she cares for a rare, antique book, and achieves a realization about how she could better treat her young son."

Davis specializes in short-short stories (sometimes referred to as "flash fiction"). In conversation with her, Michael Silverblatt observes, "I sense in your work an almost inhuman perfectionism." What is it that she is most sensitive to in her writing, he asks?

"Well, taking away excess, the sentence that's one too many. Dullness. Something that's too commonplace." She recalls learning to read. "I loved learning the words 'look' and 'see': 'Run, Jane, run. See Jane run.' It was so clear and easy and unconfusing and neat."

She cites Grace Paley as an example of the "compression" she admires. But has a sense of humor about herself and adds that, unlike Paley, she struggles to write slang. "I can't deal easily with casual writing. I wrote a story in slang, but to do it I had to go to a slang dictionary."

When she reads the story in question, "The Meeting," aloud, it reflects a similar sense of humor to Paley's, too. Though she cites Russell Edson as one of her earliest influences. "His subjects were from some deep psychic space that most of us don't want to touch. Family stuff. Crude, difficult family stuff." Her story "In A House Besieged" (in full):

In a house besieged lived a man and a woman. From where they cowered in the kitchen the man and woman heard small explosions. "The wind," said the woman. "Hunters," said the man. "The rain," said the woman. "The army," said the man. The woman wanted to go home, but she was already home, there in the middle of the country in a house besieged.

And from "The Professor":

All I wanted to do was go out into the middle of the desert, as far away as possible from everything I had known all my life, and from the university where I was teaching and the towns and the city near it with all the intelligent people who lived and worked in them, writing down their ideas in notebooks and on computers in their offices and their studies at home and taking notes from difficult books. I wanted to leave all this and go out into the middle of the desert and run a motel by myself with a little boy, and have a worn-out cowboy come along, a worn-out middle-aged cowboy, alcoholic if necessary, and marry him. I thought I knew of a little boy I could take with me...The fact is that if an alcoholic cowboy came into my life in any important way I would probably criticize him to death for his drinking until he walked out on me.

She characterizes her writing as "a philosophical investigation of the relationship between imagination and reality, as well as an exploration of one's perceptions of one's identity and the subjective nature of the truth."

Davis went into the family profession, as both her parents were writers, though "it wasn't an entirely happy fate," she says. Music was her first love. But what does her son Daniel feel about being surrounded by literary celebrity?

Photographer Ned Schenk of Pavement Studios recalls introducing himself to "a cool tattooed kid on Avenue B after taking his portrait:

"By the way, my name's Ned." The kid replies "Hi, I'm Daniel Auster." My response, "That's interesting, I'm reading a book by Paul Auster; he's one of by favorite authors..." Daniel grins and says "Yeah, I know him; that's my dad." A few days later I read in the Village Voice that Daniel would be testifying as a witness in the Peter Gatien ecstasy drug ring trial, and that he was apparently the teenage kid who was passed out in the apartment during the infamous Disco Bloodbath clubland murder of Angel Melendez by Michael Alig.

In 1979, Auster concluded his *Portrait of an Invisible Man,* his portrait of his father, with these words:

> Past two in the morning. An overflowing ashtray, an empty coffee cup, and the cold of early spring. An image of Daniel now, as he lies upstairs in his crib asleep. To end with this.

> To wonder what he will make of these pages when he is old enough to read them.

> And the image of his sweet and ferocious little body, as he lies upstairs in his crib asleep. To end with this.

It was these words that touched me, and made me curious to investigate what had become of this little boy. Now I am filled with a profound sense of sadness.

In Hustvedt's book, *What I Loved,* the father of the troubled boy dies of a broken heart. But this is fiction. Auster is as productive as ever, still averaging a book every 18 months. Of his most recent book, *Oracle Night, Guardian* critic Sean O'Hagan says its "noir shadings... and shockingly violent interludes... are indicative of a late style that is both darker than the Auster of old, and somehow more life affirming. They speak of endurance, survival, reinvention; the trajectory that one does not give up, follows loss, attends to the grieving process."

"Every life is inexplicable," says Auster's narrator in *The Locked Room*, the final novella in *The New York Trilogy:*

> No matter how many facts are told, no matter how many details given, the essential thing resists telling... We all want to be told stories... We imagine the real story inside the words, and to do this we substitute ourselves for the person in the story, pretending that we can understand him because we understand ourselves. This is a deception.

Recently Auster has had little to say publicly about his son. He says only that he "is currently finding himself—ask me again in a couple of years."

THOMAS LARSON

A Few Photographs of Molested Children

From April/May 2003

IN SAN DIEGO where I'm a contributing writer to a weekly feature newspaper, I decide to profile the world of pedophiles and child molesters—those who prey on strangers (the youth group volunteer or coach who puts himself in contact with young boys and girls; the maker and sender of kiddie porn on the Internet) and those who prey on children within families (dads, grandpas, uncles, brothers who have opportunities to molest children that are difficult to detect). To begin, I contact the man responsible for prosecuting child porn manufacturers and distributors in San Diego, deputy district attorney Jeff Dort. We meet in his office on the 12th floor of the Hall of Justice, a cubicle crammed with computers, stockpiled videotapes, pamphlets, files, and shelves of binders in which he is accumulating evidence for several cases. Dort is stocky, solid, news-anchor handsome. His suit, tie, and white shirt are the crisper side of new. Make no mistake, though; he's a seasoned prosecutor, having spent three years working on the third strike of "three-strike" cases. Newly reassigned to ICAC (Internet Crimes Against Children), Dort describes molesters he's caught and tried, among them Mac David Cochran, who videotaped himself forcing sex upon his nine-year-old daughter and posted the tape on a web site. Thanks to Dort's prosecution, Cochran is serving 114 years in prison. Dort says one of the myths that helps him do his job is that pornographers think they are being private online. They aren't, and he won't give away any of his or the FBI's methods of electronic tracing.

"So, you're writing about children and sex offenders?" He's a man who, I sense, has found some means of distancing himself from the perpetrators' lies and the victims' trauma. "I'll tell you what I tell families of the victims: 'Don't even try to understand how these people are put together.'"

We talk for a while, not only about Cochran and other "scumbags" he's prosecuted, but about the exponential growth of child pornography on the Internet, the fact that he commonly sees confiscated hard drives with up to 100,000 images of kiddie porn.

"Really," I say, "that many." I've never seen any kiddie porn.

"Oh, yes. There's multiple cases I have sitting here," and he retrieves one three-ring evidence binder, photographs he's collecting, investigations he's building, against those who traffic in child pornography. I move my chair next to his and, like a hand dealt in poker, the thick tome opens to a picture in a plastic sleeve: "This is very typical. These are very similar to other stuff I have—just thousands of pictures, books and books and books of this." Dort is paging; I'm trying not to stare, aware I need to control my reaction as he goes. He is my subject, I think.

"This little girl right here, she's obviously under eighteen. Kids and mom, maybe?" There it is: The mother, in lingerie, is posing, readying (I assume) to have sex with her kids, a boy and a girl. The boy is an adolescent, maybe 12; the girl is younger. Dort said "little girl" with anguish in his voice, a vestigial *Oh, No*. He said "kids and mom" as though here's an activity that "moms" like to do with the "kids."

Despite knowing it can be found at any of several million web sites and (so far) having resisted my (what?) journalistic duty to look, there is something dumbfounding about seeing grown-ups forcing sex on kids. At once Dort lets each image linger long enough to imprint upon me. Then he flips through a new batch of pictures, quickly, like he's looking through an L. L. Bean catalog for a pair of snow boots he forgot to mark. "Just by looking at this," another paused-at image, "you can tell that's a little girl. You have no idea where this is, how this is happening." This folder he's compiled (he won't tell me how he is getting these images, but I know he's "posing" as an interested party so he can receive them) from a man whose computer is DSL-downloading the pictures day and night. "There are images in here that are probably not illegal." He pages. "That one is not illegal. Now that one's okay." It's a woman, a young woman, an older adolescent girl? I'm not sure.

"What do you mean 'Okay'?" I ask.

"I mean the girl looks to me like she's at or above the age of consent. Whether we like it or not, an 18-year-old is old enough. According to the law." He pages: "Now she's obviously underage." He pages: "Now she's clearly underage."

What am I seeing? The sex? The image? The children? Girls we've guessed to be "old enough"?

At first glance, the sex act with adult and child seems bizarrely consensual. The figures seem to be participating with one another, equally. No one is crying out stop, no one appealing to the camera for help. The print has a grainy texture, and its sepia-like color (French postcard brown?) adds something dirty and staged. One image Dort pauses on is unmistakably lurid, and I squint at it in disgust. The photo is shot from behind and above the head of a grown man who has his upper body on a bed, his legs are spread-open and his feet are on the floor. Between his legs a girl—Dort says, "maybe seven? maybe five? maybe four? I don't know"—has her mouth on his penis. The man's legs easily enwrap the upper half of the girl's body. When I say "has her mouth," that is accurate, as if to say that's all the reality there is: This one moment, nothing before or after. One can imagine the girl's head in motion or the man's thrusts. But the photo resists that. Here I stumble out the words, "The look on her face is so—"

"Innocent," Dort completes the sentence. "She doesn't know what's happening," he says. "See what I mean?" But, I think to myself, it's not innocent; it's knowing, almost canny. In the photo, the girl's eyes are dumb, caught in half-lash: unposed, compliant, not resistant, stuck. There's a mask of "I know what's expected of me."

Later, at home, I find I can't let go of my participation with this image. How I completed it by viewing it, for one. "Has her mouth on his penis." Or is it, "Has his penis in her mouth?" No. Who's the agent? Mouth on, versus penis in, reveals conflicting agents. But I saw it the first way, not the second. It seems as though she is active, he passive; she the siren, he the prop. The truth is, I saw it from the girl's viewpoint, the recipient, for that's the design. The photo gives her agency, which makes it seem like the girl is in charge. The image—not the reality, I assume—contains as much of her doing the act as it shows the act being done to her.

Back with Dort, his hand a biologist's searching for a different specimen in the tank, he flips the big binder to yet another image. Here the camera peers down from the rapist's shoulder (like a devil on his shoulder, telling the man in the photo to go at her), and the penis is halfway in a very young girl's vagina. Dort says, "You can tell this is a child. Look how small her body is, and look how large he is." Later, (I've begun crisscrossing between then and now), I recall the Polaroid-like border background of black around the body images, that shame-filling darkness to which the manufacturers are drawn. And how quickly I see darkness as shameful before I can stop and say that, too, is what the pornographers want me to see. I recall the alienlike contrast between grown and undeveloped bodies, group scenes, those of an "implied" family having sex (it's okay; it's sanctioned by the family) that with clothes on might be a pillow fight on the bed. I recall the hammer-handle penises in every shot, arousal within the image to tempt arousal without.

Dort says, shutting the folder, the book-closing evaporative sound of *deal with it*, "I was thinking I wasn't going to show these pictures to you, but you need to see them so you can put some sort of connection to it." I say that I understand why he might be reluctant but I'm glad he did. And I am glad. "Now," I say, "I know what we're talking about."

But months later, hoping my brief sojourn would help me understand what I saw that day, I still don't know what we're talking about.

Writing the article hasn't helped. I chose not to include descriptions of the graphic images of child molestation because those images were not germane to the piece. I concentrated on the testimony of district attorneys, psychologists, sociologists, a radio talk-show host / anti-molester vigilante, and a 35-year-old man who described the aftermath of having been molested for five years as a young child by his father. The story developed little from what *I* had learned. I kept it away, in the experiences of others. Where Dort said it ought to remain. Objectivity: journalism's guard rail to protect the reporter, should he swerve. Despite publication and 30 letters the article generates from victims and pedophiles alike, my conscience is unrelenting:

> You haven't really reported it, haven't begun to report honestly what it is you are looking at, what your exposé kept hidden even as you thought you were uncovering it, and you may unconsciously be helping to keep the sexual abuse of children covered up despite your effort to be informative and provocative.

At first Dort said neither parent-victims nor anyone else should try to understand it. This was his desire speaking: to protect people from imagining and seeing what we commonly call the "unspeakable cruelty" of a sex crime against a child. But I believe once we classify the cruelty as "unspeakable," aren't we saying we refuse to understand the nature of molestation, risking even more isolation (and, ironically, more freedom) for the perpetrators? And then, after reflection, I thought Dort's second challenge contradicted the first. Having shown me several images, he said—again desiring to be helpful, perhaps feeling my shock—that I might put some sort of connection to it. It's this, more than anything, that troubles me. How do we, how do I, "connect to" something I've never seen, never imagined, without engaging some part of myself? And, once engaged, what can that part of me say about how and why molestation remains hidden in our culture?

I was not aroused when I saw images of adults forcing sex upon children. To be flummoxed and fascinated was mental arousal only. Viewing the images in their moment versus mine sets up an interplay between observer and observed full of conundrums. For one, these hidden photos have value as unseen icons. Anyone who looks and lingers demagnetizes the lure of their hiddenness. But once viewed, the lure doesn't evaporate. It is displaced from the object and lodged in the viewer's sensibility, exerting an extraordinary transformation: my response becomes the object, not the image. The image—and the action of having looked—"implicates" the observer.

John Berger, writing about images of war in his essay "Photographs of Agony," has expressed a similar crossing-over from image to beholder:

> It is generally assumed that [the war photograph's] purpose is to awaken concern. The most extreme examples... show moments of agony in order to extort the maximum concern. Such moments, whether photographed or not, are discontinuous with all other

moments. They exist by themselves. But the reader who has been arrested by the photograph may tend to feel this discontinuity as his own personal moral inadequacy. And as soon as this happens even his sense of shock is dispersed: his own moral inadequacy may now shock him as much as the crimes being committed in the war.

Transfer this to the images I saw. There is the crime and damage of the molestation itself, then there is the "crime" of "moral inadequacy" in me the viewer, occasioned by the image itself. As Berger suggests, focusing on the moral inadequacy of the looker is unfair to the victim, for it removes the crime of its power and raises (attempts to raise) our reaction to a level equal to the crime itself. So I'm damned from the outset—how dare I measure my reaction against what I'm witnessing?

Any response to molestation is a byproduct to what we might call molestation's "clear and present danger." We know pedophilia is wrong; adults abuse children and destroy their lives; the story has been told forcefully in such memoirs as *Half the House* by Richard Hoffman and *My Father's House* by Sylvia Fraser. Thus, we need not overanalyze what its images represent. If we are curious about representation, then this reflects individual differences and is not part of a social code telling us molestation is wrong. By recalling how I sentenced the girl's agency in the image—*has her mouth on his penis*— I am responding to my not knowing the right or accepted way to feel about this image. Though some might call this, *What don't you understand about rape?*

Despite their availability on the Internet these days, such images are not called up by most people. The pictures and stories of child sexual abuse remain in their shoe boxes, receive scant coverage. "It's like, how do you expose it?" another district attorney who prosecutes molesters told me:

The problem is, if you run a front-page article with all the pictures, showing people what's really out there, you couldn't do it. You couldn't publish the photographs. The public—I don't want to say the public doesn't want to know, but where can they go to read it? If I have kids, how do I go home and sit there with my paper and read this. And if I don't have kids, I'm 18 to 35, I don't care. It's so annoying, so distasteful, that even reading it for information's sake, people can feel as if they're condoning it or being a part of it.

Here may be the skin of the body I want to inspect. Why does mere looking feel like we're condoning it? Will the act depicted—some pervert's "desire" seen—rub off, embed itself in our psyches, if we linger on the image? And, if it's clear what it depicts is wrong, why must the depiction be kept from us? Or, better, why do we, especially non-child-molesting men, agree so readily (secretly responding with revulsion and fascination as I did) that we should not look?

At first blush, the depiction of sex seems a welcome problem for men. Most men are aroused by pornography, have grown accustomed to the visual stimulations of the R- and the X-rated. Men are raised in a culture where they expect buxom bikini-ed babes in their ads and their movies, while producers and babes gladly accommodate those desires. Imprinted thus, men learn that seeing is wanting and wanting consumes them. There is, of course, an imaginative leap made from sexual ideation via the tantalizing visuals to the sex act itself. But when the accustomed-to images get mixed in with those that depict children—a ten-year-old in a bra and panties, for example—the effect can destabilize any looker because he may without knowing it feel the twinge of excitement he felt with the adult image.

How does looking equate with condoning? When Jeff Dort said a few images of adolescent girls were okay (even by the limit of law), I balked. Was I, as he paged through the binder, supposed to look at the "barely legal" sexed-up girls and see their potential for arousal as okay, and then feel sickened by images of kids with penises lying on their faces? (I kept quiet in my non-responses, which may have seemed, to

Dort, like a brooding inquisitiveness in those images.) My sense is now, there was something dirty about it all. The depictions of the "young" were "soiled" in proximity to those of the "too young." Had I felt any desire for those girls in the "okay" images alongside the "not okay," I would have felt ashamed, unclean. But wait! How can I be so sure of my response when I have never seen such images before? I'm glad I was not aroused, though part of my worry was that, suddenly shown the smut, I might be. Something stopped me from making a connection between looking and being a part of what I saw.

Joyce Carol Oates's *Blonde* is the fictionalized portrait of the harrowing change of Norma Jeane Baker into Marilyn Monroe. The novel's best part is the story of her adolescent years. At the hands and with the lusts of attending males—among them an English teacher, a detective, and her first husband whom she married at 16—her sexuality was teased out of (and projected into) her early on. Post-pubescent, her vitality, her vulnerability, were thoroughly sexualized: calendar girl, screen siren, man-craving vamp, by extension, things many men hoped were latent in every woman. The source of her famed attractiveness is an edge that existed and was nurtured between her adolescent and adult personas. Even Marilyn herself toyed with this edge. She was beautiful not because she was a sexually free woman. She was beautiful because she pretended to be stirred by men's desire, by playing both sides of waywardness, the vixen adolescent, the vixen adult. Men would choose which one they fancied.

I think I sensed tension between looking at and condoning what I saw in Dort's binders as an awareness of this edge, which operates between adult and adolescent, but here is costumed, as it were, between adolescent and child. Consider a woman in sexual pose who puts her hair in pigtails to replicate a farm girl. Consider an adolescent girl in pigtails. Then consider a child, forced into sexual pose, with the same pigtails. The child's actual innocence mixes with the mock innocence of her "older self." And it is mockery, feigning the "real," that elicits desire. She is not what she seems to be; therefore, she is desirous. Mockery-as-desire is especially suited to the molester's ego.

Here's how. That sexual "stirring" of desire—pigtails, lingerie, make-up—may be but is usually not in the girl herself. (Marilyn did have some of it, even at sixteen.) The molester believes, though, that the girl or the child he is attracted to possesses only a sexual identity. How often do the police officer and the psychologist hear from the perpetrator the counter-charge, *She came on to me.* The older the girl or boy, the more the molester might, in his mind, think she or he is exhibiting adult-like traits making his advances welcome. But the prey's age is not a factor; the perpetrator has merely justified his advances. The molester who believes he is come on to has simply recast the sexual plot, matching his desire to the edge between adult and child bodies. The consequences of such behavior can be mystifying. Not only does the molester say the child is responsible for drawing him in, but he accuses the makers of such images (as seen on film or as part of young female bodies) of pandering to his lust even as he watches those images. He thinks himself twice-wronged by child and image. (Despite knowing, as some molesters do, that it is wrong and he is ashamed to desire children, the desire for contact drives him unmercifully.) Moreover, since the menstruating girl can be seen as biological fulfillment—she has attracted the man because our co-reproductive natures command us to hurry mating—then the molester is also not (or certainly less) responsible for his actions: He is simply furthering evolution's scheme.

Along this edge the contemporary theater of adult sexual stimulation "strays" into kiddie porn—and, surprise! it's the molester's design. Molesters use the adult motifs of pornography to catch all lookers in the act, to make us think we're equal to them on some leveled field. When those pigtailed images play the edge, a few men, maybe one in 100, who can't control their responses, will cave. To promote the best defense, it is easier to deny all men access to child porn than it is to risk unleashing the urges of those few. Thus, the square-chinned, thick-necked district attorneys, the psychologists, judges, newspaper editors, religious leaders, lawmakers—all forbidding entry.

And that, paradoxically, is the very thing molesters live for: forbidden entry.

The forbidden brings up perhaps the deepest element associated with these images, the taboo. I want to say several things about taboo and the sexual abuse of children. The first should be obvious by now. To protect children, our society stamps kiddie porn taboo. Keep the visuals away, and you're all right. Look at it, and you're soiled. Not looking, though, has jurisdiction over everyone but the molester. The taboo funnels him to the sacred. Even in JPEG collections of 100,000 images, each one is a shrine. A second thing to say is that the taboo works on us, the non-molesters, with an arcane agency. It seems we have so fully closeted as taboo the adult perversion of forcing sex on children and its images that we don't even know what we're not seeing and why we're not seeing it.

In *Totem and Taboo,* Freud cites the work of the late-19th century experimental psychologist Wilhelm Wundt. Wundt wrote that taboos are "the oldest unwritten code of law of humanity," classifying them sacred or profane. Taboos inhere in people or objects from which we feel inspired awe or aversion. Awe, like the power of a volcano or the ritual of a priest, is the sacred or mysterious taboo; one is forbidden to go near. Aversion, like the prohibition of handling food after one has handled the dead, describes the profane or unclean taboo, what's called a negative taboo. At bottom is "the fear of the effect of demonic powers." Those people or objects infected by a demon might, in turn, infect anyone who breaks the taboo, i.e., comes in contact with person or object. Freud, summarizing Wundt, writes, "Some persons and objects possess a dangerous power which is transmitted by contact with the object so charged, almost like a contagion. The most peculiar part of it," he continues, "is that any one who has violated such a prohibition assumes the nature of the forbidden object as if he had absorbed the whole dangerous charge."

Wundt also wrote that taboos strike us as "anything which for any reason arouses dread or is mysterious." Thus, with the images in Dort's office, I dreaded to look at that which (at once) had kindled a mystery. Awe, it should be clear by now, is not sexual arousal. I was separating the untouchable mystery of taboo from the twin untouchables of image and molester. I hadn't realized that inside me, in the non-molesting, non-aroused man, I could still be affected—"the dread of contact," Freud calls it—by that which seemed to be gunning for me. "The fact that a taboo is transmissible," Freud writes, "has surely given rise to the effort of removing it through expiatory ceremonies." Like a very long hot bath, the means some of us use to expiate our bodies' uncleanliness is to assay, to discover how it has affected us. In a world where journalists work without "acts of penance and ceremonies of purification," the reporter must minister to himself.

Freud also includes this quotation from Wundt: "The violation of a taboo makes the offender himself taboo." Makes him—he who has looked—unclean, infected, dangerous, outcast. If I linger on images of child molestation and consider too closely the industry of its purveyors, I risk not only being debased but also, with no ritual to oust the debaser who has gotten under my skin (that may be grandiose, but it feels accurate), being contaminated permanently. An example of this occurs in prisons where molesters are often segregated and abused. Or, in Jeffrey Dahmer's case, some are beaten to death, so afraid are the other prisoners of contracting his disease.

This, then, is the taboo's gambit. It insists I pretend to know what I'm not seeing, insists I can't and shouldn't know why I'm not seeing it—in order to protect me. It's there, it's working, it's in place for a purpose. How good that the psyche continues to shield us! As the burka fundamentalist Islamic women wear bars the man's curiosity and (thus) tempts him to remove it, so does the taboo bar and tempt an "interest" in sex with children. It reminds us that any desire for infection is equal to the certainty of infection. The taboo's multiple personality, what Freud calls its "ambivalence," is more solidly friend than enemy.

A question arises, which neither Freud nor Wundt consider: does an urge to molest exist in all people or only in a few? The answer is, it's an unanswerable question because the taboo's nature, in lieu of scientific evidence, is no different from our own. Taboos, Freud notes, connect us to the mystery of our origins. The indeterminacy of those origins suggests we may never know whether any individual is predisposed to fondle children. But we can recognize that the taboo and the thing we shouldn't see place molester and non-molester in the same enclosure. Besides, we can neither cure the molester of his desire to have sex with children nor (as yet) turn off the genetic switch for that desire. But we can manage his illness and our part in his illness if we get over our "failure to understand it," where it refers not so much to the disease but to our role in pathologizing the disease.

How do we help pathologize his disease, feed his penchant? Despite the molester's sought-after isolation, our "dread of contact" pushes him farther away. (In one sense, Megan's Law, the sex offender registration statute, isolates pedophiles as much as it exposes them, for the shame of identification makes molesters hide themselves more than they ever have.) I would argue that this dread is, in terms of perpetuating molestation, as potent a force as the molester's act. The molester has us right where he wants us once we categorize him king of the perverts. Expelling from our midst anyone who's that dirty gives him the separation necessary to hide the act even from himself. Such is the intrinsic shame of our sexual natures: we will nurture any taboo that walls in sexual feelings for children. It is yet another way we fit our species for survival, though it is not clear, given the extent of our sexual proclivities, what we are surviving as.

Maybe I'm beginning to grasp just how deeply unknown child molestation is as well as its ability to hide itself within and from men, within and from families, within and from the media and society. And maybe this need to understand began, inadvertently, in the scripts of my choirboy youth. No parent, no grandparent, no teacher, no adult ever that I recall looked at me salaciously, touched me inappropriately when I was a child. I trusted adults. Was I trusting because I was spared the wantonness of some adults in a small 1950s Wisconsin town whose moral script was never to present molestation in image, idea, or fact? They sent Mr. Wilson away because he didn't like children. Was Mr. Wilson actually lurking in the neighborhood? Could I not see him because I had no warning or sense (as women do instinctively) of his lurk? I grew up with the decree that to keep molestation at bay an unexamined male psyche was much more effective than an examined one.

But all that's changed. Today the disordered male psyche (not all of it is disordered with sex) is everywhere: absent fathers, adolescent men, militia groups, youth gangs, gangsta rap, bullies and shooters in high schools, child rapists displaying their crimes on the Internet, suicide bombers. (Dare we also mention the cultural terrorists in America, the adult male producers of extreme sports, violent movies, and video games, or those coaches, in corporations, on football fields, in military groups, who rationalize the good tuning boys and men must receive from unquestioned rituals of male bonding?)

It's a recursive nightmare—the male psyche ebbs and flows from ordered to disordered thinking, and it is this vacillation that censors (and in some cases attracts) our views about, and the images of, adults and children and sex. What trumps the male psyche is the male who can't or doesn't know that the problem of child molestation is in his psyche. Knowing that doesn't make a man a child molester. The man, alas, doesn't know this distinction because his culture won't tell him, won't implant the seed because to preserve itself the images and some collective responsibility for child molestation must be kept away from him.

One young woman told me a remarkable story about the proximity, real and imagined, of child molesters among us. When she discovered her landlord was a convicted child molester who had done the deed and the time 12 years before (so the California Sex Offender CD-ROM informed her), she told her boyfriend she was afraid and wanted to move. Her boyfriend said the guy was no threat because he'd paid his debt and, besides, his crime was just a one-time shot. For her these were twin insults, and they propelled her out of the apartment complex and away from her boyfriend. She also said her boyfriend's inability to connect to her wariness as a woman around violent men lay in his maleness, which, without damning all men, we might also call his brutishness. She didn't want to be around a man who couldn't subdue the brute, a man who was ignorant of his fuses and couldn't configure the wiring to disarm himself. On some level, are all men unconscious brutes, biological explosives? Because a majority of men are insensible to their sexual behaviors, should the gender be governed by laws whose creation and administration are deferred to women? There's nothing easy about this. It's difficult to argue for reason and compassion for men and not discount that their maleness exists one salacious touch away from violating an innocent.

ROBERT WALSH

The Bazaar Side of Catholicism

From October/November 2002

THE BEAUTY OF the Catholic Church is it is opportunistic,
knowing a good idea when it sees one. I learned this early on during
one Sunday afternoon at the St. Pius Bazaar.

Bazaars were just one of the many ways my parish sheared the flock
for some spare wool. "Passing the hat" is something every parish learns
to master. You can't get two Catholics together without one of them
passing the hat for the church secretary's new air conditioner. The
best example of Catholic opportunism is the contribution envelopes
the archdiocese made for kids. Every year, we were given a box of
color-coded envelopes with blanks for our names and the size of our
donation to the church. They were bright pastel colors, designed to
make giving up the money in your piggy bank "fun."

The envelopes were grouped by week, and each month had its own
color. This made it simple for the young Christian stewards to keep
track of their contributions to the glory of Rome. Usually, the parents
of the congregation would slip their kids a dollar or two to throw in
the envelope and get it over with. My parents, unfortunately, believed

their children should learn the joys of coming up with this money on their own. We got 25 cents a week in allowance for doing our weekly chores, and that sum wasn't even listed on the envelope; it started at 50 cents.

I was working like a child in a South American Nike plant to scrounge up enough money for the collection, mostly because I was under the mistaken impression I could buy my salvation. This impression was never corrected by the folks at CCD, even if it was never actually *stated*. I soon learned the best way to handle this situation was to give them what they really *wanted*. After all, it said in the Bible that it would be easier for a camel to pass through the eye of a needle than for a rich man to enter the gates of Heaven. Therefore, I took to giving them the gift of prayer.

Because each kid was expected to place the envelope in the basket him or herself, I had certain freedoms I could use to my advantage. For instance, the envelopes did not have our names on them. This anonymity allowed me greater flexibility to contribute to the church. While my brother Tom simply sealed empty envelopes and threw them in the basket, I was afraid God might strike me dead for doing it. So, while waiting to see if my brother got struck down, I came up with a better idea. I signed my envelopes, "Richard Stanton," and wrote left-handed to throw off the dogs. I took to writing short, inspirational notes and placing them in the envelope. I started off small: "This paper is good for ten prayers for the faithful of the church." Soon, as I realized this practice was not causing the priests to start an investigation, I became more generous. "This paper represents a life given to Jesus." "Forty Hail Mary's and 50 Our Fathers will be offered up, in your name, to the poor souls in Purgatory." "My contribution this week is to pull a pagan into the ways of the Church." Father Skull would collect the donations from the baskets in the back, and when our eyes would meet, I would offer him a smile. "Got you covered, Father," I'd think to myself, "I'm prayin' for ya."

The church always put on two bazaars a year, the big, bi-annual moneymakers. In reality, they were giant garage sales with all proceeds going to the parish. People would clean all the junk out of their garages and try to sell that junk to someone else in the parish. Basically, it was an insulated economy of crap moving around the congregation. The next day you'd see someone at school with your "I Love Fairfield Soccer" shirt on, or someone would come up to you and say, "Hey! That's my Nerf football!" Mothers were famous for packing up items they decided their kids wouldn't miss and selling them at the bazaar.

The week before the bazaar, the church bulletin would announce that all items offered for sale at the bazaar should be dropped off behind the parking lot. The advantage of this system was that no one's name was on the items, so some parishioners (my dad included) were shameless about what they stuck the bazaar with. You see, after the bazaar, anything not sold would have to be given to Goodwill or taken to the dump. One year my dad had me help him drop off an old mattress, several broken lamps, and a broken stove we had kept in our basement for years. We dropped it off in the middle of the night. "Why not wait until tomorrow?" I asked, only to be told he wasn't *asking* me to help him, he was *telling* me. "Why are we driving in with the car lights off?" I asked, but he ignored me. "Should we leave a note so they know that this stuff is from us?" I asked, looking at the notes on the other items. "Get in the car quickly before someone else drives up," was all he said.

The day of the bazaar, I noticed our contributions were not on display. I could only assume someone had snatched them up as soon as they were put out. The women of the parish hovered over tables of homemade deserts while the men huddled around the grills cooking for the barbecue. We learned quite a few new words from these men as they burned their hands or dropped a burger on the ground. They cooked like the descendants of a carpenter.

There were only a few lame game tables set up for the kids of the church. "Fish Jonah out of the Whale's Mouth!" shouted one sign next to a wading pool. It featured a stick with a piece of string and a magnet attached to it. You had to pick up a cardboard Jonah out of the pool without picking up any of the surrounding fish (all of them had magnets on the back). I think the game should actually have been called "Stick Magnet," with a sign that read, "Who knew a stick and string could be so much darned fun?" We would have responded better to "Sacrifice Jonah to the Whale!"

Most of the games had the same prize: goldfish. Catholics, I have learned over the years, are very big into the whole fish thing. The apostles were fishermen, the sign for Jesus is a fish, and we can only have fish on Fridays. Therefore, for some reason every prize at church socials involves see-through plastic bags of sickly goldfish that will die inside of a week. I even stopped naming mine because it was easier to flush Number 17 down the toilet than it was to flush "Lester." Knock over the bottles, get a fish. Toss the ring on the bottle, get a fish. Win the egg toss, get a fish. By the end of the bazaar, simply walking near a prize stand and breathing would win you a fish.

As the bazaar drew to a close, you could see the adults manning the prize tables getting antsy. The adults knew that if they didn't unload all of these fish soon, they'd have to find something to do with them. I had once asked Father Skull why we couldn't win scorpions instead, and he had made me say five Our Fathers right on the spot. "Jesus didn't perform a miracle on scorpions and bread while up on the Mount," he said. I took this as a sign to be grateful Jesus had not performed any miracles on the human brain, otherwise we'd all be cannibals. Father Skull never liked to get into these religious discussions, which I found ironic considering his choice of profession.

The currency of the bazaar was those small colored tickets (pastel, of course) with the numbers on the side. They used the tickets for the games, food, and raffling off goldfish. My bothers and sisters and I had to buy our own tickets. My mom would ask us, "Who do I look like, Monny Mintmore?" whenever we begged for tickets. One year my brother worked a raffle for school and had left several spools of colored tickets in his room. I took a handful of each color to the bazaar and ended up living it up like the Pope in Rome. Still, there weren't many places to actually spend your money.

The only "game" I really liked was the Secret Pocket Lady. Secret Pocket Lady walked around the bazaar grounds with a monstrous, billowing skirt with about 100 pockets sewn all over it. You would give the woman a ticket and pull out a secret treasure from whatever pocket you chose. I used to let my hands wander over the pockets ever so slightly, checking for bulk or shape. "Don't smear that chocolate all over Secret Pocket Lady's dress, honey," said the woman trapped inside the gigantic grab bag. It was the only time you could properly feel a woman up on church grounds without fear of excommunication, so I took full advantage. There is, after all, something magical about a grown woman asking a boy to put his hands in her skirt. Add the element of paying her for the privilege, and the church was practically training us to solicit prostitution!

"Okay, time to pick now! I've got other girls and boys to see," snapped the Secret Pocket Lady. She was a smoker, and she'd "rest" every 15 minutes and light up behind the jungle gym. I summoned all my powers of intuition for this one, because this was my last ticket. I always saved Secret Pocket Lady for last because it was like gambling; if you pulled out a great prize right away, you'd keep on playing. You ended up blowing all your tickets on a bunch of pastel Holy Cards, plastic mirrors, and chocolate rosaries. I knew they always saved a few great prizes for the end: baseball card packages, watches, transistor radios. However, because it was late in the day, I wouldn't be surprised if they had tried to sneak some goldfish in those pockets.

"You want me to pick for you?" interrupted the Secret Pocket Lady. I could see her hands were shaking, and that if I waited any longer, she'd light my head on fire and inhale me. At this moment Father Skull sauntered by and addressed the situation. "If I were you," he said quietly, bending down to look deeply into my eyes, "I would pick from one of these here." He was pointing to three pockets: one off to the side of her leg, one directly over her crotch, and one right over her shoes. "I seem to remember that we put special prizes into those pockets!" Father Skull loaded up the Secret Pocket Lady every half hour or so.

I knew the Secret Pocket Lady hated it when you dug your hand into the pocket over her crotch, kind of *leaning* into it to really dig down deep. I was too young to appreciate the sexual undertones at work here, but I loved the effect. "Hey, hey... *whoa*!" shrieked the Secret Pocket Lady as I performed the operation, "Jesus, kid, you fit your whole arm in there?"

I pulled it out quickly when I felt it was an envelope. There were a few money envelopes found in those pockets that very day containing five-dollar bills, and rumor had it there was a ten-dollar envelope still hiding in the pockets of her skirt somewhere. The Secret Pocket Lady stamped off, probably worried I still had another ticket on me. She was headed back to the jungle gym, pulling her cigarettes out of one of those pockets and lighting one. Wow, I thought, staring wistfully at the explosion of smoke she was now emitting, why couldn't I have found that one?

I returned to the task at hand and ripped the envelope open as quickly as I could. Inside was a piece of green paper upon which was inscribed, "Forty Hail Mary's and 50 Our Fathers will be offered up, in your name, to the poor souls in Purgatory." The note was in my handwriting. I looked up to see Father Skull staring at me as he filled the popcorn machine. He was smiling.

PIERS MICHAEL SMITH

Death Camp Tours

From January/February 2011

OUR TRAIN WAS nearly empty. So was the landscape. Stooks, each a frail shivering X, one or two houses with tomato-strewn gardens, hillsides like arboretums run wild, a river proceeding in slow crashes through woods. At one point, the river flattened out and lost its banks, becoming a field of wet stones; this scene was overlooked by an abandoned Grimm's fairy-tale cottage, onto which sunlight fell in clean shafts like helicopter search-lights. We entered a region of raggle-taggle hedges and broken fences. Just below, in a paddock of mucky yellow plants, I saw a small deer, then another one, or the ripple of stems it left behind.

The train had to skirt the Tatras, and the shade and blowing lacy-curtain mists briefly chilled us. A long wait at the frontier station of Plavec-Muszyna beside rows of freight cars and rusty track. A woman in a dark blue uniform came and giggled over our passports. Then the train appeared to reverse indefinitely. "Are we going back into Slovakia?" But the view turned into reassuring tilled fields and gabled houses, washing somersaulting in the breeze like headless gymnasts.

We passed a low-lying industrial town with its own smog-line (stretched out to one side like a wind-sock), a new motorway whose traffic easily outpaced us, young head-tossing poplars. Krakow announced itself with familiar baroque graffiti—3D loops in red with black outlines, English obscenities. We walked up a concrete slope past a man asleep with his trousers around his knees, the folds of his smooth waxy buttocks.

When I first saw it, on a list of recommendations posted by HotelsPoland.com, I was tickled by the name Atrium. It looked ineptly chosen or wackily metonymic. (Who would name their child after a body part?) Later, when I looked it up, I found that the laugh was on me. An atrium is an open space. It signifies a court or courtyard. The original Latin refers to the central hall of a Roman house. As hall, court, or courtyard, then, it could connote meeting, or the area in which meeting takes place—civil, polite, a moment of fearful reconnoiter before the tribalism and intimacy of the handshake, the kiss. The term can also designate the portico in front of churches. As such, it names a threshold, an interstitial movement (timeless, empty, raincoat-musty) before the tonic of worship or the neck-cricking labor of saying "wow."

Illuminated green and bronze at night like an Art Deco casino, the hotel aimed to cash in on the region's booming tourist trade. There wasn't much of a lobby, just a couch, racks of brochures, a cramped desk, two buzzing PCs, and a single steely-eyed concierge who moved his guests around like chips, pressing guides and itineraries onto them, offering direct transport to "the most attractive destinations in southern Poland." These included the palace at Lancut, the medieval town of Wroclaw, and the salt-mine at Wieliczka, where, 100 meters underground, a ramp had been constructed to enable the then local celebrity, Karol Joseph Wojtyla, his Popemobile and waving arm, to glide down to a cathedral carved out of salt-crystals. The transport service could also take guests to the State Museum, 60 clicks away at Auschwitz-Birkenhau.

Mostly the hotel, like the city, was looking for immediate returns. Our fellow guests were groups of elderly Europeans (Italian, Spanish, French). There were some middle-aged couples, but no young people. Like Las Vegas, prototype and presiding genius of the modern Grand Tour (the New World now modeling for the Old), Krakow was not a young person's holiday destination. The city attracted people with leisurely needs and longer memories. These, by a calculated if incalculably discreet set of nudges (the racks of brochures, the sharp-suited elbow-taking concierge), were being steered towards the Old Town's collection of Dark Age, Renaissance, and Austro-Hungarian Imperial memorabilia. As if these had just as much claim on our attention spans, if not more so, as any museum at Auschwitz-Birkenhau, or inversely, as if the latter could now be merged in the touring-mind with other quirks of our serio-comic history of the world in ten and a half chapters.

The Atrium's brochure-map showed the hotel (arrowed in red) just a few blocks down from Grand Square, site of the 14th century Cloth Hall (billed as "the world's oldest shopping mall") and the Basilica of the Virgin Mary. I didn't know this at the time, but the latter contains a 15th century, 48-foot high altarpiece depicting the Virgin's "quietus" amidst melancholy admiring apostles. I also didn't know that from the Basilica's turrets, a trumpet sounds every hour, always ending in strangled mid-note ("*Ooo—urghh!*"), in surreal commemoration of an 1,100-year-old flukish Tartar arrow. Although there were no directions, the map encouraged guests to walk the "Royal Road" to the square and down the main drag, Grodzka, to Wawel Castle, where centuries of Polish kings lay massively entombed. From thence, they might skip across the tram-lines into the old Jewish Quarter in the district of Kazimierz (where, presumably, one could find wizened "*Oy-vey!*" exclaiming shopkeepers and male chorus-lines

in elflocks, clogs, and black stockings). They might also walk beside
what remained of the Old Town's walls, posing with some handy
picturesque local before such postcard settings as the Barbikan,
Florian Gate, and the Slowacki Theatre. Leonardo da Vinci's *Lady
with an Ermine* could be viewed at the Czartoryskich Museum. For
the high cultural renegade—or truly tourism-challenged—there were
also 300-year-old mummies in a crypt and a stuffed ice-age rhinoceros
exhibited beside its own tongue and windpipe. A thumbnail picture
column to the right of the map anticipated the bare eye's gasp and
satisfaction.

Krakow, then, was "historic"—a site, a shrine, a monument, an
immovable feast—representing itself in its hotel brochures, street
signs, and caffeine-fuelled breakfast chatter as a blast from the past, a
UNESCO World Heritage destination, newly brought out of Cold
War mothballs and tarted up with Hot Peace pennants, with blinged,
naughty-badged, fake-tattooed, S&M-bracelleted and dog-collared
players strolling in national dress, café-cultured and Euro-currencied.
Yet if the Grand Square looked like any other European tourist town-
centre—that of Bruges, say, or Florence or Prague—with the same
clop of horse-drawn carriages (pork-pie hatted and whip-wielding
coachmen and straight-ahead-staring, curiously stricken passengers),
flower stalls, animated clocks, soft-spoken men with cameras ("photo,
my friend?"), and shops selling leather wallets and glassware, at the
same time an atmosphere of solemnity and what I can only call
shyness seemed to muffle even the clatter of cutlery in the open-air
restaurants. The waitresses seemed afraid to take down orders.

Some places have an atmosphere, an aura, which is more vague and
yet more pressing than an association, which cannot be seen or
photographed, and yet which hangs over the name, long before (and
long after) the actual physical world, the phenomenal outrage,
impresses itself on the senses. Associations are easier to identify, file,
and forget about because they are personal and temporary, prone to

aging and refurbishment. They don't testify to anything much outside of our own vigilant self-inspection. This is why they're a little errant and anarchic. For me, the word "Krakow" had nothing to do with Tartar arrows or kingly tombs. It came with cold and jagged edges, stiff blue fingers, gritty black bread, potatoes hard as stones, an exotic balding boy called Budzik whom I went to school with, the stink of crushed pears, bloody sausages, Joseph Conrad and (for some reason, wholly unclear to me) Flavius Mithridates, the awful seriousness of biography, romantic agony. An aura cannot be smelt or objectified in that way. It does not work on the imagination, nor does it allegorize the past. It is out there—outside the head, that is, and its endless ramifying evasions—hidden from sight yet palpable, and always growing but incredibly slowly, accumulating through time like a stalactite. No amount of digital technology, gloss, or depth of field can snap that away.

August 28th. We followed a sort of after-the-match crowd up Stawkowska, through a bottleneck of trees, cyclists, and taxis, coming across weirdly staggering men, seemingly unconnected but identical in their sweetish vinegary odors and dodgem-car collisions. It was as if some extremist religio-political group had just released a disabling gas into the atmosphere. I saw one man in a filthy parka petrify, foot suspended over a kerb, fuddled eyes searching as kids on bikes came swish-swooping through the trees. Another man latched onto us, crossing the street when we did ("don't look at him, don't make eye-contact"), perhaps using us as markers, buoys in the tossing sea of his recklessly pursued faith. Then, just ahead, two nuns, in freshly laundered habits and veils (that singed damp smell), linked arms and burst into peels of laughter. "It's okay. Drunks and nuns. This is a Catholic country."

On the square, an old woman in stylish peasant rags made only token passes with her roses and blue-seamed palm. A rambling speech, her eyes already drifting elsewhere. All along Grodzka—like one of

Giorgio de Chirico's experiments in perspective—silver-painted street performers were posed in attitudes of unrelenting monstration, eyelid paint peeling over an eye, a wasp perched on an ice-blue chin, an ankle with a birthmark showing through its icing-sugar glaze. A brass band in funny hats and red neckerchiefs was making trial pee-parps under an arch. A bored girl gave out flyers, not even looking round, hand held out as though testing for rain. A Viggo Mortensen lookalike in a leather singlet (my daughter: "Is that a Polish hottie?") and bovver boots strode with gimlet-eyed purpose down the street into a New Mexico sunset. Despite the sense of remission, despite the hard-working waiters with their billowing ice-skater tou-tous, despite the steaming coffee and urinous smell of bison-grass vodka, something else kept moving in the shadows or darting in the corner of one's eye like that little red-caped figure in the movie *Don't Look Now*.

In Kazimeircz, tour groups in cargo trousers and tee-shirts (still bearing the creases of packing and cargo-hold compression), were trooping along the cobbles, stopping to stare up at a piece of featureless wall, gathering (faces fussy with hard-working attention) at an Old Curiosity Shop-type window, while a woman with a checkered flag harangued them in Italian, French or Spanish. The speechifying was stupefying and hard to follow, so we wandered off into a nearby square. With its broken paving-stones, rainbow gutters and mean stalls, the place looked run-down, an area of neglect, still shivering and hugging its sides in Cold War misery, awaiting its turn at the new-minted tubular steel and under floor-heated soup-stall of modernity. We scanned the walls for tour-arrows and "you-are-here" maps. Down one street, other visitors were flicking through their Fodor guides, ears twitching, nervous as antelopes. Behind them, a synagogue—the Isaak Synagoga, the plaque said—looked misplaced, or pushed into a corner. A crane and bulldozer shook their booties nearby; something else motorized thudded invisibly inside a tent of dust. Snatches of catchy pop (Beyoncé and Sean Paul) came from a window. "Baby boy you stay on my mind / Fulfill my *fanta-seees*." Two women, emerging from the synagogue, wore the exhausted expressions of clubbers heading home.

Inside, a hectoring man was making sure each male visitor put on a tiny, feather-light yarmulke. We stepped into a bare cell-like space. No altar or tabernacle. A TV set to one side. Ranks of pews with scattered congregation. Silent flickering black-and-white images of men, women, and children gathering, dispersing, climbing into trucks, laying down parcels, picking them up, staring about, gathering, dispersing, climbing into trucks, laying down parcels, picking them up, staring about—a Nazi Schutzstaffel (SS) officer repeatedly swinging round, glancing at the camera. *Photo, my friend?*

Meditative as our companions, we thought: What time is it? Isn't it time to go? After the decent interval—always after the decent interval—we rose, moving on into the next room, which had been made into a makeshift gallery with freestanding screens of photographs, stills from the film. I had to keep my fingers perched on my head to hold the yarmulke in place. Hesitating, an old man looked back at an old woman ("Do we go this way? Is it permitted?"), bringing to the exhibition the pathos of a quieter, more humdrum, more conscionable kind of obedience. In another room, off to the left, in darkness, lit only by another ordinary TV, we could sit through it once again, could regard with wary eyes the same play of light and shadow, the same Schutzstaffel glance, and begin to worry once more about the time. There is nothing scandalous in this worrying. How do you understand what you're doing, what you're seeing, where you're at, if you don't know how to worry? Worry is what reminds you that you're alive, that you didn't have to go through that... No, that's not it.

Walter Benjamin, burrower among books and ideological meadows, gives the word "aura" an ever more fragile etymology, an almost nostalgic vanishing point. A work of art, he says, has (or had) an aura when it is (or was) original, authentic and unrepeatable (and therefore authoritative), testifying only to itself or, at most, to its passage through different settings and ownerships, from the seclusion of the cave or oratory to the public gallery. It loses its ritualized purgative magic as pure image, pure hymn, when it testifies to what is other than itself; in the age of mechanical reproduction, it undergoes a process of withering. This process, Benjamin says, has significance outside the realm of art. (All that once spoke so effortlessly of tradition, the unique, the authoritative—be they artworks, buildings, monuments, great speeches, constitutional acts—vanish into their copies.) For Benjamin, who had yet to flee Germany, the withering began to happen in the mid-1930s, with the increased accessibility of the photographic print and the moving picture.

The worry comes from what is posterior to the event, not to the event itself, to smaller everyday urgencies. My daughter's feeling of faintness is caused by lack of sleep, not by the repeated impact of transportation and genocide. My irritableness comes from having to lean awkwardly against a wall—because the rear seats are all taken, and you cannot sit at the front for fear of blocking out the screen, for fear of obtruding your brash 21st century back between the sacramental violence and the mute arithmetic of witness. Courtesy takes different forms. Is reverence so different from terror? But that is not the point; the point is the rascally persistence of consciousness, of the happening present and its little delinquencies. (This man who hunts under his chair for a dropped yarmulke, that woman who thinks she's trampled someone's foot, and apologizes to the dark, are also worriers.) And these demands, which are the body's indifference or resistance to the gravity of testimony, will always dog our steps, signal from the corner of our ever-widening eyes.

We got lost looking for further signs of the ghetto, fetching up at a cathedral where TV crews were stringing cables up and arranging studio-lights on the steps. When we went back up the street, we found another TV crew and a group of well-lit men in shiny suits, gelled hair, and diamond ear-studs. Perhaps it was a wedding, a movie, or the visit of a political dignitary or mafia boss. Whatever it was, it seemed appropriate. Our lives are televisual, are they not? We all have our 15 minutes, do we not? That night, we sat in my room watching the Athens Olympics' 4X100 meters final getting ready. My hopes (and fears) were pinned on Maurice Greene—all ludic strut and exaggerated hip-swing, the neurotic machismo of that up-from-under scowl. Would he redeem himself? Would the humiliation of the 100 meters final be canceled out in one last magnificent surge? Can't recall what happened, or even if Team America won. My daughter returned to her room to nurse her sleeplessness. We live in a society of spectacle. It's hard to hold our attention.

Primo Levi was born in Turin, Italy, in 1919. He was arrested during the Second World War as a member of the anti-Fascist resistance and deported to Auschwitz in 1944. He was interred in one of the camp's subsidiaries, Buna-Monowitz, where he worked in a chemical facility till 1945, year of Russian liberation. His experiences in the camp and subsequent travels through Eastern Europe and Russia were the subjects of his memoirs, *Surviving Auschwitz* and *The Drowned and the Saved*, and several works of fiction and poetry. Forty years after his imprisonment, in the spring of 1982, Levi returned to the camp —"in the role," as he says, "of a tourist." The experience was recorded and broadcast in 1983 by Radiotelevisione Italiana. Levi died in Turin in April 1987. What would he have made of all this? In Krakow, in a hotel perhaps not so dissimilar to ours, he mentions two drunks he met in an elevator. He was impressed by their speech. It reminded him of his first visit to Poland, the guards. They spoke in harsh consonantal curses, a language of "nothing," a "truly hellish" speech. The memory of the event, not the event itself, is what overwhelms and shocks.

August 29th. The road to the town of Oswiecim was a single-lane highway. After the motorway-tangled outskirts and chain-smoking foundries, we were suddenly speeding through lines of mature poplars, swelling hills, and generous pasture. There were ponds with men and boys fishing, a monastery on a hill. "Look, monster, *ja!*" our driver, neck tensing under its soft pink folds, gestured manically.

"Monster? Where?" I yipped.

"Monastery, dad."

"Monastery, ah, yes, good!" craning to look back at some slate roofs among the trees, displaying my touristic interest and gratitude for our driver's visual gifts. We passed through toy-town villages (gray brick church, single-tank petrol station, white-washed post-office) and acre after acre of yellow flowers. "Look! Shops, *ja!*"

"Shops?"—my swiveling head—"Wow!" Sometimes imposture becomes grotesque. I felt my daughter looking at me.

Near Oswiecim, we passed a train moving along an embankment. I began to ask the driver whether that was the actual line that... He didn't understand what I was saying. He was accustomed to using German with his customers, not English. Maybe it didn't matter what language was spoken, anyway. I imagined him thinking: Better to anticipate what the silly man says and just bellow infantile rubbish at him. His enthusiasms careered down the slope of this decision.

"*Ja, choof-choof, ja!* Yes! Okay! Two minutes to museum, no problem! Then we are go Birkenhau! All is good! No problem! That is football stadium." The town opened out with the awful dreary sameness of a suburb anywhere. We came to an electrified fence (scrubbed new looking; three meters tall; walking-stick-shaped concrete poles, handles facing outwards), then a car park, sleek double-decker coaches, people consulting guidebooks. "I wait two hours, three hours, no problem! Then Birkenhau, yes? All is good! No problem!" The crass simplifications ("Don't worry, be happy," "There is a God," "Of course"), the shocking nudity of words stripped of decoration or reticence.

I said we'd be back in a couple of hours.

"Two hours, *ja,* yes, okay! No problem! I am here, *ja,* yes, okay? All is good!" Our driver looked as if he wanted to smite me on the back and emit a lusty roar, so great was his sense of universal good.

"Thank you. Yes. No problem. Good."

Levi recalled the dislocation he'd felt when the guards had spoken only Polish or Yiddish and he and his companions had understood neither. After travelling for seven days in a boxcar, water-less, licking frozen breath on the steel latches for sustenance, he'd heard these strange new words, commands, questions. What to do? What to say? Say anything. It was, he said, as if he'd lost his reason, or the ability to reason altogether.

The museum looked almost benign in the summer sunshine. With its sturdy gabled buildings arranged in phalanxes, its full-grown leafy trees, its cobbled concourses, its tour groups bent over their camcorders or cigarette lighters—witness, witness—it had the pleasing architectural simplicity and low-key festive air of an art gallery, a modishly ugly one, the sort of structure that might do for a redeveloped city-centre, Wolverhampton, say, or Brussels. The spot-lit black-and-white photo-shoots, the sexy industrial chic, the blown-up charcoal drawings, the artificial wall-section (a pocked gray plastic imitation of the wall they used to shoot "politicals" against) with its pile of off-centered wreaths, the wooden gibbets, even the dank hot cellars with their eye-level arrows, explanatory notices, and stifling shoulder-jostling passages. These could have been the exhibits, the wire-suspended installations, the interactive sets of a South Bank art gallery, laid out for us to cruise and coo in. In Block 4, Room 5, a white-haired couple, cool in black sweaters and skin-tight black jeans, were scrutinizing with finger-cocked chins the Zyklon B canisters exhibit. In the same room there was a glass panel running the length of the wall. I had to wait an age while another tourist fiddled over his light-settings and angles, before I too could close in on the mounds of human hair.

The restored crematorium was a less sensational place. Too dark, too badly lit. Clammy cement walls. Lumpy machinery and razor-sharp cogs. Two ovens. The doors were open. Staring, we kept tripping on pipes and track. It was not silent in there. A guide, towing his own human cargo, was bawling cavernously in French.

In the car park, we saw our driver leap up, gesticulating. His high-pitched happiness made me think of the sort of jolly rosy-cheeked Mittel-European who figures in '50s travel posters, clutching bratwurst in one hand, a tankard of frothing beer in the other, and laughing out loud through healthy, gappy teeth. "Come! Enjoy! No problem!" Still beaming, he drove us a mile or so down the main road, took a right, then cruised along a dirt road beside another high fence, so that—he gave us to understand—we might appreciate the sheer enormousness of Birkenhau (at its height it contained 10,000 prisoners), the length and breadth of its 175 hectares, the simple unadorned woodenness of its huts, the algebraic elegance of its sewage system.

In one hut I mistook recent graffiti (covering a wall with the intricate density of 50 years of vandalism and courtship) for the last-minute fumbled execrations of Levi's drowned. Crematoria II and III, which were dynamited by the fleeing Germans, had been left as the Russians found them, burst apart, lying in tarry slabs, with gloomy disheveled underneaths, now housing thuggish cats and discarded Marlboro Lite packs. A few people—a handholding group in Shetland jumpers, and me—bent and stretched, digital cameras glinting in our fists. The railway line, a double row of track, one for coming, one for going (to avoid time-consuming waits), moved towards us, broadening from a single point of origin. Near a watchtower at the middle, a tour group attended to its guide, swaying slightly with the disciplined syncopation of a choir. Across a stretch of grass, dragonflies played now you see me, now you don't. Following them, we finished up at a pretty little pool, green with algae and fat lilies.

Watching glossy green frogs plop, we chatted about nothing. I chewed on a blade of grass. Later, I found that the pool, according to the guidebook, was "the pond into which ashes were tipped."

Aura is repeatedly conjured and as repeatedly magicked away by books and blockbuster movies, by what is promulgated in schools, places of worship, and other institutions—by all that is drilled into us over and over again. Aura needs distance; it won't survive being turned over in the fingers like a coin. Aura is memory without the frills, therefore no memory at all. What is left is a blank space, a wall, say, onto which we scrawl our own terrors and avowals, personal, fitful, largely trivial. In 1983, Primo Levi found it "comical," acceptably comical, that the museum should have a restaurant (a resort should have a restaurant, shouldn't it?). The thing that really troubled him was that the Polish government had appropriated Auschwitz as a monument to Polish martyrs. He didn't mean that the museum should not memorialize Polish internees; he meant that the camp was, or should have been, before that, and after that, the site of a larger, less parochial site of witness—one where language, faltering before the irreproducible, engages with its responsibility. In *The Drowned and the Saved*, he remembers a crippled three-year-old boy called Hurbinek who could not speak yet whose eyes were fierce with demand and assertion, and who, one day, uttered a barely intelligible word that was neither message nor revelation, that was probably meaningless, but which, for Levi, articulated with absolute clarity the effort he had to make.

Benjamin says that if the auratic object is detached from tradition, if the unique existence dissolves into its copies, at the same time, reproduction can "reactivate the object" by "meeting the beholder in his own particular situation." *In his own particular situation.* This is a hard thing to grasp because it seems to equalize evil and goodness even as it devalues privilege, because it seems to ameliorate shame even as it rescues aura for private speculation. Alone with our thoughts, are we not able to go where others, sharing theirs, have neither time nor leisure nor hope of going? Yet there is room still for community, or cruelty. Where Levi spoke of a football match between the SS and Sonderkommandos as the true horror (normalcy performing itself next door to slowly accumulating slaughter), others could be aroused by the plump bottom of a nurse in the camp infirmary only a few hundred yards away from the columns of shivering heat.

What is left for us now of Hurbinek's attempt at speech, or Levi's words? Dumb open mouth that through referential promiscuity and repetition, the slick transformational grammar of postmodernity, turns into something out of a tongue-in-cheek slasher flick. After recycling, after reimaging, the look of horror returns as ohmigod, the dropped jaw of automatic dismay. We shed gelatin tears. ("Auschwitz," the Atrium's concierge told me later, pushing across the guidebook and speaking with the disturbing flatness of tone only a second language speaker can ever achieve, "is the saddest place on earth.") This is what remains of aura.

Theodore Adorno said that there could be no more poetry after Auschwitz. The camp introduced the unspeakable, the unimaginable, the inhuman into language and history. Adorno's shock fed into the idea of "holocaust," which Levi, for one, distrusted. (Holocaust, which alludes to sacrifice by fire, or to burnt offering, struck him as "wrong," "rhetorical.") Giorgio Agamben finds in Adorno's impossibility (or his shock) an ethic of possibility: the inhuman begets the human, the unspeakable requires the speakable, Hrubinek's babble drives Levi's eloquence. We do write poetry, but it has become cautious, perhaps spellbound by those negative prefixes, perhaps conscious of the respect due those who were silenced, perhaps ashamed of its own prolixity and too easily acquired decency.

> I should not be so proud
> of my latecomeliness of virtue
> My tongue moves latterly

and disproportionately
over the atrocious.

Others choose Adorno's route into silence. Jean Améry, also confined in Buna-Monowitz, conceived of language as a vast hibernation from which he could only emerge (in the '60s) as proponent of a specific identity and self-slaughter.

Agamben sees in the concentration camp the biopolitical paradigm of the modern world and its power structures; the camp, the Lager, is where power confronts human life in the raw, without mediation. Here, there is no such entity as a citizen, there are only bodies, stripped, exposed, rendered down, ready to be remade, numbered, categorized, used, reused, or not. Agamben doesn't wonder how the crimes of Auschwitz could have been committed. Rather he wonders how the crimes could have become so normalized, so commonplace and natural, as to lose all taint of criminality, of wrong. By what singular and remarkable socio-juridical process, he asks, do human beings reduce other human beings to things? The curious, the unseemly fact is that the same wonder must apply to our own reductions now. By what process, as singular and remarkable no doubt, has this scene of horror become, for us, an object of pleasure? Levi writes:

> Many people—many nations—find themselves holding, more or less wittingly, that "every stranger is an enemy." For the most part this conviction lies deep down like some latent infection... and does not lie at the base of a system of reason. But when this does come about, when the unspoken dogma becomes the major premise in a syllogism, then, at the end of the chain, there is the Lager.

Substitute "a thing" for "an enemy," though it hardly makes any difference.

In Auschwitz, bodies were differentiated one by one. They were tattooed and labeled, each label (a red, yellow, pink, violet, black, or green triangle) conferring identity on them—identity, that is, in our special modern sense of national or cultural, religious or racial, sexual, social or physical differences—as in: the (Polish or Russian) political body (red), the Jewish body (yellow), the Gypsy body (black), the homosexual body (pink), the Jehovah's Witness body (violet), the criminal body (green). Auschwitz survivors mention other kinds of bodies, bodies that spoke and bodies that did not (Mussulmeinen, or Muslims, as they were known, after their posture of seeming prayer— heads bowed, hands clasped to breast), bodies that rebelled and bodies that did not (the Sonderkommandos), bodies that were shot, bodies that were sterilized, bodies that were starved, bodies that were cut up, bodies that were injected with dye, bodies that had toxic substances rubbed into their surfaces. Therein, perhaps, we find a way of reading our own situation. If the careful labeling and categorization of bodies (by race, religion, nationality, sexuality, gender) is the modern practice of power, then our silence or complicity, our resentment or enjoyment, marks an end to another syllogistic chain.

Agamben observes:

Behind the powerlessness of God peeps the powerlessness of men, who continue to cry, "May that never happen again!" when it is clear that "that" is, by now, everywhere.

Everywhere, my friend.

BOBBI LURIE

My Son Works in the Museum of Intolerance

From October/November 2012

MY SON WORKS in The Museum of Intolerance. His job is to get people to sign a sheet of paper when they walk through the door. The sign-in sheet makes them "official" and helps justify the museum's existence.

Once they sign in, my son offers to show them around the exhibits of human atrocities, made up mostly of photos. My son has become an expert on human cruelty. "Why are people such creeps?" he often asks.

"Why don't you ever come and visit the museum?" he asks today.

"Because I can't bear to learn anything more about The Holocaust," I tell him. He knows our family history. He knows about my life in Israel.

"It's more than The Holocaust, Ma," he says. "It isn't just about Hitler, Ma. They killed people faster in Rwanda." My son is on the autism spectrum. What this means, to me, not "them," is that my son cannot comprehend human cruelty. It makes no sense to him.

"Why was I ever born, Ma?" he asks me, as he always does. "Don't you think the world would be better off if there were no people?"

"Yes." He knows my answer.

"Why did you have me anyway?"

"Because you taught me what love is," I say, as I always do.

"But isn't that selfish?"

"Yes," I say. I always say yes.

A long pause as usual and then, as expected, I pose the question, "Will you eat tonight?"

We are fighting anorexia. "We," meaning any doctor who has ever met my 96-pound son. "We," meaning me, not him.

"The anesthesia makes eating hard. I need to stop eating," says my son, one up on me. He has an excuse these past few days. The surgery in Miami. The surgeon from China, the genius who gave him back his one good eye after Stevens Johnson TEN and an injection of prednisone, inserted into the wrong part of the eyeball, blinded him in his left eye. The doctors said he would soon go completely blind in his right eye as well. His eyelids, after Stevens Johnson TEN attacked his entire body, turned to a texture like sandpaper, scratching his corneas every time he blinked. The surface of the cornea grew thinner and thinner; he could not bear the light; his head was always down; blood vessels were growing into the cornea, and if they reached deep enough into his remaining eye, he would be blinded forever.

The destruction wrought by Stevens Johnson TEN keeps progressing. He can no longer make tears. The type of severe dry eye he has causes blindness.

I decide not to push him to eat. *He's alive. He can see.* We found a doctor who surgically altered the eyelids in his right eye, smoothing them out with the skin from inside his mouth, allowing him to look into the light for the first time in two years, allowing the blood vessels in his right eye to retreat for the time being.

"Did you take your drops?" I pray he did. An infection would destroy everything.

He hems and haws. My eyes must have been shut. I did not see him go. I hear the front door close. He is gone. We live in the middle of nowhere. I pray he can see well enough. It is dusk.

After surgery he tore the bandages off his eyes. The day before the surgery, he said, "I don't care if I go blind." Instincts took over after surgery. I thought I could see his heart pounding through his chest. I begged the anesthesiologist to give him something to calm him down. I've heard anorexics die of heart attacks.

Where did he go? Where is he now? It's getting dark. Can he see?

I take a Xanax. I have lost count of how many I have taken so far today. I've been taking them for years. I don't think they work anymore, but doctors have warned me that going off them can create a nightmarish situation. The backlash of medications is familiar to me. My son's disease was caused by a severe reaction to pharmaceuticals.

An hour later he walks back inside.

"Where were you?" I know he won't answer. I decide not to ask about food. I decide not to ask if he will take the drops.

"Do you want to watch a comedy?" I pull out *Curb Your Enthusiasm.*

"I gave that to you, you know."

"Yes, I know." I pull him close to me.

"Why did you have me?" I say nothing. I pull him closer still.

Because without you, I would not know what love is.

DOROTHEE LANG

Berlin, Alexanderplatz

From October/November 2008

October 1980

"I'VE NEVER BEEN there, in Berlin," I say, my finger pointed towards the TV screen, as if Berlin was right there, behind the glass. Chrissie shrugs. Her grandparents live there, but the place is no big deal to her. Nothing is. I am not sure what to say next, so I shrug, too, and take another spoonful of ice cream.

"It's a grand city," Lola explains.

Lola is Chrissie's mother. It was her idea to watch TV, to enjoy vanilla ice cream, there, on her French bed, together with the Siamese cats.

The scenes on the screen are dark, the persons are all adults. The story is one of violence. While the vanilla ice melts on my tongue, I watch a blond woman enter a restaurant. There is a man waiting for her at one of the tables. At the counter, there are soldiers. Suddenly there are swearwords shouted in a language I don't understand. Then a fight starts. I try to figure out what's going on but am interrupted by

Lola, who turns to me and Chrissie. "Get out," she orders angrily. "These obscenities are not for your ears."

Chrissie shrugs, picks up her ice, and leaves the room. I take another look at the screen and follow her. The Siamese cats are allowed to stay on the French bed, though, to keep Lola company.

July 1986

She ignores us. I am sitting at a restaurant table in Berlin, together with six classmates. We are ready to order, but the waitress pretends we aren't there. Like the others, I am unsure how to deal with the situation. It's as if we had stumbled into the wrong classroom without a teacher present. So we decide to leave, the money we need to spend still in our pockets: 15 Ostmark each, the amount you have to exchange at the socialistic rate of 1 to 1 at the Berlin-Berlin border, even when you only visit the other side for a mere two and a half hours.

We walk back to the Alexanderplatz, to the meeting point. At a book shop, we stop, trying once more to spend our money. Yet the books look as tedious as the ones we have to read for the literature class in school: plain-colored covers outside, too many words on too thin paper inside, and the authors, a far step from the current bestseller lists.

There is still an hour of time left when we arrive back at the Alexanderplatz, but most of the others are there already, too. We are sitting on the steps of a fountain guarded by stone snakes, waiting for the bus to arrive, to take us back to our hotel in the Westside. Overhyped and dazed, we pull the unused bills of Ostmark from our pockets and turn them into planes, into boats that drown in the snake fountain.

April 1998

And now what. I'm standing at the sidewalk, in front of an office building made of glass, metal, and concrete. The project meeting ended earlier than planned due to a phone call of a team member who forwarded the news of yet another major problem that has to be taken care of not only as soon as possible, but immediately. Thus, after frantic preparations, important TOPs, endless To-Dos, and a rushed goodbye, I suddenly find myself with time on my hands. One hour of unscheduled emptiness. When the taxi arrives, I tell the driver to take me to the city centre instead of the airport.

"Kurfürstendamm," the taxi driver says.

"*Ja,*" I answer.

Twenty minutes later, the taxi stops. I am there. It's late afternoon. I walk down the street, together with 5,000 other persons. I pass MediaStore, McDonalds, KarstadtSport, NikeTown. I pass a stone church. The tower of the church is broken, has been for 55 years. It stands there, a clock on it, timeless.

At the Bahnhof Zoo, I turn around once more to see the broken tower, then board the bus that will take me straight to the airport. It's in that moment that I am really there, in Berlin, for a second.

May 2008

There is no way. There are rows and rows of concrete blocks, rising from tumbling ground, reaching to my hips, to my shoulders, over my head. I turn, then turn again. There is Fay somewhere, and Erin, and there are others, couples, tour groups, school classes. We get lost, each of us in our own time and direction, in this monument. There are no words written on the blocks, no explanations given. There is not even an entry.

Yet, to my surprise, there is an exit in the midst of the stones. I walk toward the steps leading downstairs, maybe to a tunnel passage.

When I see the sign attached to the door, I stop. So do the school girls who followed me.

"Is this not the exit?" one of them asks.

"No, it's just for emergencies," I explain.

One of them shakes her head in frustration. "And, how do we get out now?" she asks.

They are about the age I was when I visited Berlin, years and years ago. Back then, this Holocaust Memorial hadn't even been a plan. It had been as unimaginable as the reunion of Germany, as the Y2K-hysteria, as the terror attack of September 11th. This space, here, had been part of the death corridor, part of the wall area. Now it is part of the centre again.

I turn and keep walking until the maze of concrete blocks shrinks again, until the ground rises, until I can see the green of the trees, the pink of Fay's shirt, the yellow of Erin's top.

"I am here," I say.

May 2008, a day later

It's our last day together. We all will leave tomorrow, Erin via Tegel, Fay and me via Schönefeld. Our goodbye comes in green, and is named Berliner Weisse: a beer that looks like a cocktail and is served with a straw. We clink glasses there, in this café next to a concrete fountain, next to the church with the broken tower. We take some more pictures. We are surrounded by streets, by people. It's five, the blue hour, the time of work ending, of the weekend starting.

When I look at the broken church tower, I see a sky of darkness moving in like a float. The waiters start to close the parasols.

"Let's leave," I say to Fay.

"You don't have to leave," the waiter assures us when we ask to pay.

"It looks like there is a storm coming," I say.

"Yes," he answers, his expression unchanged.

On the way to the s-train station, we walk past a monk riding a turtle. Both the monk and the turtle are frozen in motion, in metal. In front of the turtle, there's a plate.

Alles verzehrt am Ende die eine Macht: die Macht der Zeit, it states.

Everything is swallowed in the end by the one power: the power of time.

The church tower rises above us, its clock ticking silently, just like the clouds. Underground, we take the wrong direction first but realize the mistake after the next stop. When the train reaches the surface of the city, there's hard rain falling, and it's another city, barren and gray.

"So now we get a glimpse of Berlin in November," Erin says.

July 2008

They are not there. I search through the box of 1980 photos again, but it doesn't contain the Berlin photos. There's no transit bus, no Checkpoint Charlie, no group hug, no paper boats drowning in the snake fountain. Nothing.

I should be collecting my keys, should be gone already. Instead I try the 1979 box, then the 1981 box. Again, nothing.

Irritated, I start with 1980 again.

Finally I leave, the library card in my pocket, my mind still in Berlin while I drive along the B10, while I search for a parking spot, while I invent an excuse.

In the library, I walk straight to the D-shelf. D like Dürrenmatt's *Physicians*, D like Dostojewski's *Demons*, D like Döblin's *Berlin-Alexanderplatz*, a book no one made us read at school.

Back home in the garden, in Berlin, I open its pages. I sit and read. I taste the ice again. I keep searching for those lines I wasn't supposed to hear, that I couldn't understand in 1980.

STUART GELZER

The Watermelon Hunters

From October/November 2013

1

IN THE DAYS after we settle into our apartment on Araqishvili Street, Alan, sleeping on a sheet draped over a red velvet sofa in his makeshift bedroom, finds himself waking every morning to the faint sound of jazz piano. If you're near a window, it seems to come from outside, but from the middle of the windowless dining room, it's clear the piano is right overhead. Alan sings along with Oscar Peterson's version of "Summertime" as he makes breakfast. Even though my interest in jazz is nil, I can tell the guy upstairs is good. The swing comes through the ceiling along with the thump of the pedal.

The invisible pianist slaps the keys in a few places to clear the air, then starts a new piece. Alan looks up from the stove and smiles. "Dave Brubeck, 'Blue Rondo á la Turque.' Tasty. And you know what else? His piano is in tune! Our upstairs neighbor has the only in-tune piano in all of Georgia!" It's true. To a musical ear, one painful consequence of the post-Soviet collapse of the Georgian economy is that pianos everywhere have slid, then fallen, then plunged out of tune. No one can afford to pay a tuner, so the tuners now do other, more necessary work, like selling cigarettes on street corners. It seems to be universal; even the piano the Rustavi Ensemble uses in its rehearsal room sounds like a honky-tonk after the shootout. But the piano upstairs is right on.

A week or so later, I come back from an early evening photographic stroll around Tbilisi, trying to catch the Old Town's ornate wooden balconies at sunset, and find a short note on the dining room table:

Gone upstairs to visit the piano player. Come join me. —A.

Carl returns from his own wanderings at about the same time, and together we go upstairs and knock. The door is opened by a slim, well-dressed, red-haired man in his 40s, quite drunk. "Aha!" he shouts in strongly accented English, "the friends of Alan!" We find Alan curled up in an easy chair in the living room, able to smile broadly but not do much more.

Alan has been here a couple of hours already. When he first showed up at the door, he and our host, Tengiz, established their bona fides by running through some jazz duets together. After the roaring success of "Summertime" and the revelation that Alan lives in Toronto, home of "my teacher, Oskar Petersoni," Tengiz brought out a bottle of *chacha*, homemade brandy from the village, double- or triple-distilled from grape skins.

At the mention of the word "chacha" in Alan's slurred report on the evening so far, I glance with alarm at the table and am relieved to see I got here just in time. The bottle has only one round left in it. That's good for me but bad for Alan. Half the bottle is already inside him. Worse yet, Tengiz's wife and five-year-old daughter are away visiting relatives in western Georgia, so there is nothing to eat in the house. For the last two hours, Tengiz and Alan have been eating walnuts and cheese puffs. The coffee table is heaped with broken shells, and the only thing left from a large bag of cheese puffs is the bright, powdery orange residue on their fingers.

One glance at Alan is enough to make clear that if the three of us are going to do what we do best (and what a Georgian drinking party requires), we'd better sing a song fast while Alan can still help. As we sing—a simple *mravalzhamier,* whose entire text means "Long life, long life, good health to you"—Tengiz's eyes widen farther and farther. These are not just three Americans who know a common Georgian song, these are The American Singers from TV! Fortunately, he doesn't spoil the fun by turning respectful. Instead he starts laughing and can't stop: the idea that three media babies have been living downstairs from him all these weeks and are now sitting around his coffee table singing, and one of them is about to pass out!

Tengiz is a physicist. Academic life in Georgia having been turned upside down along with everything else in the last few years, he now teaches physics at four different technical institutes, scrambling for any work he can find. Serious research is impossible. There is no money for equipment, no money for travel to conferences, no money even for journal subscriptions. So Tengiz has gone back to his first love, jazz piano. He tells us he learned English listening to Willis Conover, the host of a jazz program on Voice of America.

At this point Alan wakes up, turns green, and mutters between clenched teeth, "Take me home." As Carl and I maneuver Alan down the stairs, Tengiz, standing at his doorway looking even pinker and more exuberant than when we arrived, cries out after us, "You are all my friends! But Alan is my highest friend, because he heard music and knocked on my door!"

2

In early September, soon after Tengiz has moved out and the new owners have begun the noisy demolition of his apartment, he telephones us and invites us to go on a trip to Kakheti, the easternmost region of Georgia. Great, we say: steep gas prices, unreliable gas supply in rural areas, and terrible roads everywhere have prevented us from seeing as much as we would like of the country outside Tbilisi. And it's the right place at the right time: Kakheti is wine country, and the grape harvest is going on now. Tengiz says we would be joining his friend Vazha and a few of Vazha's friends. Fine, we say; we've met Vazha, another physics teacher, and he's good company in the same way Tengiz is: easy-going, dry sense of humor, interested in the world. Sounds great. One thing though: can we extend the invitation to our friend and translator Maia? Tengiz hesitates and then signs off abruptly.

The answer comes from Maia herself, speaking over the phone with some urgency: "Stuart, listen to me, this man Vazha called me, I don't know him, by the way, and he told me you're not going for the grape harvest, you're going hunting!"

Hunting? Hunting what?

"I don't know! How should I know what people hunt? Wild animals! Also, he told me it will be very hard. You will sleep on the ground and maybe stand up to your necks in the river." Translation: no girls.

Alan, Carl, and I debate the proposal in this new light. Carl thinks it sounds like a macho joyride, and he wants out. Alan thinks most of what Vazha told Maia was just made up to scare her off (it worked). Alan and I both think Tengiz and Vazha wouldn't be involved in something completely Neanderthal. They're too sophisticated and too self-aware, and neither of them could be mistaken for an outdoorsman. I say, "It's just a weekend hunting trip. How bad can it be?"

Both Alan and Carl stare at me. "But, Stuart, you're a vegetarian!"

It's true, I am. It seems like that ought to present an ethical problem, but after self-examination I find I can't locate the problem. After all, I don't prevent other people at table with me from eating meat. "Oh well," I answer cheerfully, "on the extreme off-chance I find myself actually pointing a gun at a live animal, I can just miss!"

In the end, Alan and I opt to go, and Carl opts to stay behind—but not to let Tengiz know in advance, to avoid having his arm twisted. So Friday noon Tengiz pulls up in the street outside our windows and honks, and Alan and I go out, and Tengiz says, "Where is Carl?" and we say, rubbing our stomachs, "He doesn't feel well."

On hearing this, not only does Tengiz turn pale, but Vazha gets out of the car and turns pale with him. "Very bad, very bad. Only two, you cannot sing." I'm wondering if their task was to produce the American singers, and two out of three doesn't count, but Tengiz explains tragically, "If you don't sing, no choice: they will make us to hunt." Tengiz and Vazha sink back into the car with very long faces, and Alan and I in the back seat have plenty of time to digest our fate as we drive east out of Tbilisi.

In broad terms, Georgia occupies the groove between two roughly parallel mountain ranges: the Northern Caucasus, along which runs the border with Russia, and the lower and less linear Southern Caucasus, separating Georgia from Turkey and Armenia. It's a narrow space. From some points near the southern border, on a clear day you can see the snow-capped peaks along the northern border. The long east-west lowland is broken into almost equal halves by a north-south range of hills. To the west the rivers run to the Black Sea; to the east they run into Azerbaijan and finally, below sea level, into the Caspian Sea. Moist air off the Black Sea makes western Georgia humid, fertile, even in places swampy, but the central north-south range of hills casts a rain shadow across the east. Eastern Georgia is dry, and drier the further east you go.

At first we drive through grape country—acres of gnarled vines stretching away from the road and up the slopes of isolated, irregular hills. The leaves and even the thick clusters of grapes are all the color of dust. Lines of tall poplars divide the fields, and the dry, rocky creek beds and gullies are marked by majestic walnut trees. We pass horse carts carrying firewood and ox carts loaded with cut vines. When I ask out of curiosity where we are going, Tengiz answers sadly, "I don't know, Vazha don't know." Then, because he can't fight his sense of the absurdity of our predicament, he adds, "Too late to ask where we go. Now we only go. And we hunt." He throws up his hands: "*Ara ushavs!*"—an expression lying at the intersection of "no problem," "never mind," "could be worse," and "heigh ho!"

It turns out our physicist friends have directions only to a rendezvous point, a featureless crossroads in the fields. Waiting for us there on the shoulder is a Soviet military jeep with blotchy green camouflage paint. Inside it sit four men. Three of them are wearing camouflage fatigues that allow them to blend perfectly into the jeep. All three have terse little Sandhurst moustaches and, though they all appear to be in their early 30s, distinguished streaks of silver in their hair. Alan immediately names them "the Grecian Formula gang." Zurab, his brother Gia, and The Driver (a man never named in my hearing) are members of the border patrol police, and they seem to have borrowed quite a list of office supplies for their weekend trip, starting with the jeep and several Kalashnikovs. The fourth and only un-camouflaged man, Tamaz, a tall, lean fellow in a black tank top, with his tonsure of silver hair, his deep-set, searching eyes, and his deliberate calm, looks like a model for an Orthodox icon. He is in fact a painter. The muscles in his shoulders suggest he could wrestle any number of Abstract Expressionists to the studio floor.

These men are not Vazha's friends but rather friends of his friends, not known to him. After greetings all around, we set off again with them in the lead. The jeep has no windows or roof, just a canvas top stretched over rods, so from our car we have a good view of Tamaz and one of the Grecian Formula brothers in the back seat. Long silence in our car as we contemplate our weekend companions. Finally, after carefully recasting the verb agreement in my head, I say in

Georgian, "They are already real hunters." Tengiz almost goes off the road laughing. Then we all take turns singing out recklessly, "*Ara ushavs!* No problem!"

3

We drive another hour east and southeast, through land ever drier. Vineyards have given way to nondescript yellow scrub. Only a few trees hang on here, and even the bushes by the road seem discouraged. Finally we come to the sleepy town of Dedoplis Tsqaro: Queen's Spring (known of course as Red Spring during the Soviet era). As in many country towns in Georgia, the life we see as we drive up the main street consists mostly of tiny, dusty pigs. The humans are hidden in courtyards behind high iron walls painted pastel blue, green, or pink, and from the street we can see the tops of grape arbors, fig trees, and pomegranate trees peeking over the walls. We pull up outside one house, and the jeep honks until someone comes out to swing open the gate so we can pull in and park under the grape arbor. Here we meet the last carload of our party.

A smooth, chubby little man in a nice knit shirt bustles forward to greet us with a gravelly voice: "My daahlings, what an extra, ordinary pleasure!" He seems to have the remarkable ability to boom through his nose with a voice and an intonation that make Alan and me stop and stare: is he for real? He is. His name is Mikha, he is the English teacher in Dedoplis Tsqaro, and he is trembling with nervous energy because we are the first native English speakers he has ever met. Even after two days together, when we are entirely used to him and he himself has calmed down, it's still hard for us to believe this is not a put-on—that Mikha really teaches English to small-town grade-schoolers in remote eastern Georgia in a hyperactive, campy, smooth-as-honey self-mocking style suggesting Jim Belushi doing Robin Williams doing Marlene Dietrich doing Touchstone the Fool on Broadway.

The other men from Dedoplis Tsqaro—one old and two young—certainly don't seem surprised by Mikha's behavior; if anything, they demand it. He is the licensed town clown, brought along by the serious hunters for his entertainment value (rather like those singing Americans). The older villager is a grizzled little man with a mock-fierce manner whose form of conversation with foreigners is to grip them firmly by the hand for minutes at a time without a word. The two young men, whom Alan and I dub "the Gung-ho Hunters," seem as shy of the big-city people as they are of the foreigners, and they mostly keep quiet.

The last of our party is a man Alan and I have met before at a *supra* at Vazha's house. He is the only person Vazha himself knows here. Tall, thin, serious, dressed in a shabby button-down shirt, Vakhtang looks and acts much more like my idea of a village schoolteacher than the clown Mikha does. In fact, Vakhtang is a lawyer and a politician and, best of all, the author of the new Georgian Constitution. What he is not, however, is a citified academic indoorsman like Tengiz and Vazha. Vakhtang and his beautiful ten-year-old son, who is also along, spend all their free time on the trip carefully cleaning and polishing their shotguns. (From the easy friendship Vakhtang has with the other men from Dedoplis Tsqaro, I assume he's the Member of Parliament for this region. Only several months later, after the national elections, do I discover he was actually the representative for my own district, Vaké, an elite neighborhood of Tbilisi. I say "was" because by the time I find out, at yet another *supra* with Tengiz and Vazha, Vakhtang has lost his seat. Vazha was his campaign manager, and the *supra* is a defeat post-mortem—but not a solemn one: Tengiz announces to everyone that it was my fault, since I failed to vote in my neighborhood.)

The hunting party has gathered at the home of one of the shy young men. His family spreads out an astonishing feast as an afternoon snack, and I face the delicate moment of explaining to a dozen hunters that I don't eat meat. As the young man's grandmother bears down on me with a platter of kabobs, I murmur to Tengiz, "You remember that I'm a vegetarian?" He nods and says matter-of-factly in Georgian to the table at large, "This one eats no meat"—a sentence I am perfectly capable of myself; it's nerve I lack. The men around the table stop talking and look at me for a second, then, in unison, scan the dishes nearby for vegetables to send my way. Since the Georgian custom is to serve each food in many small dishes scattered around the table, I soon have three dishes of fried eggplant, four dishes of roast tomato, and a pile of cucumbers in front of me. (As a rule, it is infinitely harder for Carl to get away with refusing wine than for me to decline meat; there are few things more important to Georgian culture than food, but wine is one of them.)

When the meal is over, under a golden late-afternoon sun, a jeep and two cars head southeast carrying 13 men, a boy, two dogs, more than enough shotguns and submachine guns, an assortment of guitars and a three-stringed Georgian lute called the *panduri*, about a quart of water, and a 30-gallon keg of wine.

We cross an uncluttered landscape: no trees, no bushes, nothing but brown grass and sunflowers in all directions. At dusk we pass through the last habitation we will see: a line of crumbling cement huts, home to the ethnic Azeris who used to work on the collective sunflower farm and at this hour haul water from the village well in buckets, herd geese with a stick, and watch us drive by. We are headed for the easternmost place in the country, Shavi Mta, Black Mountain, "the last mountain in Georgia."

The road, always bad, turns into a track, a pair of wheel ruts dug by farm machinery, climbing up and down through the sunflower fields. A couple of times we all have to back up 100 yards or so to a fork after we find the track we were on ends in the middle of a field. As darkness comes on, the car from Dedoplis Tsqaro blows a tire. That would not normally be an insurmountable problem, but in this case the flat tire is already the spare: we stopped once earlier to change that tire.

All three cars now stop at the crest of a small rise. There is just enough light left in the sky to see we are surrounded, all the way to the hills on the horizon, by the stubble of harvested sunflowers. The wheel comes off the crippled car easily enough, but the tire resists being pried from the hub—which it must be to get at the inner tube. Lots of advice, arguing, and hammering in the gathering dark. Finally the wheel is placed flat on the ground, and The Driver, with plenty of hand-waving and hollering help, maneuvers one front wheel of the jeep onto the flat tire, off center: the plan is to use the weight of the jeep to pop the tire off its hub. As if this activity by itself weren't odd enough, Mikha, the schoolteacher from Dedoplis Tsqaro, dances around singing in his Gypsy Kings-, Jacques Brel-, smoker's rasp, "What's the buzz? Tell me what's a-happenin'! What's the buzz? Tell me what's a-happenin'!"

The brute-force method of tire repair not only fails to work but further cracks the low-grade rubber of the flat tire and probably warps the hub, too. Now, with the whole party clearly stuck here for the night, the division between real hunters and hangers-on is formalized. The hunters pile into the jeep to go hunt for dinner; the rest of us wait at camp. Gia, one of the border guards, is delegated to stay, armed with a Kalashnikov to protect us from the brigands known to lurk in remote sunflower fields. The hunters run a wire from the jeep's battery to a big hand-held spotlight, roll back the canvas roof so they can stand up and aim the light in all directions to spot game, and drive off bristling with guns.

4

The roar of the jeep engine fades slowly to a murmur and then to nothing. For a while we can still see the searchlight bobbing up and down as the track alternately climbs and descends through the sunflower fields. Then even that disappears, and we are alone. On a blanket spread over trampled sunflower straw, we set out the condiments to go with the eventual dinner: unleavened bread, hard salty cheese, tomatoes, tiny onions, coarse-grained salt, and wine (that 30-gallon keg). A full moon rises from Azerbaijan. Mikha, tuning his guitar, stops and looks up at the shining sky. He calls out, "Gentlemen, daahlings, listen!

> We are as clouds that veil the midnight moon;
> How restlessly they speed, and gleam, and quiver,
> Streaking the darkness radiantly!—yet soon
> Night closes round, and they are lost for ever.

"Percy Bysshe Shelley, 'Mutability.'" Mikha looks away and strums a quiet chord on his guitar.

Alan and I are momentarily silenced—I couldn't have dredged up a single line of Shelley, to say nothing of a whole stanza, much less something apposite—but while Gia the border patrol guy asks Mikha to explain what he said in Georgian, Alan whispers to me, "You know, he kinda creeped me out at first, but this Mikha is turning out to be good value."

Around ten o'clock we give up waiting for the hunters and sit down to eat what there is. We have no fire: early in the evening, experiment showed that a lit pile of dry sunflower stalks generates no more than a wan glow and turns to ash within a minute. But the food is wonderful, and so is the wine, though we have to share the few wooden cups. Before we drink, however, we must have a *tamada*, a toastmaster. At a Georgian table, wine may be drunk only in response to a toast. (Our blanket spread on the ground counts as a table, since the Georgian synecdoche for banquet, *supra*, actually means "tablecloth.") But not anyone who pleases may propose a toast. Instead, the *tamada* makes the toasts, and the rest of the company speaks only in response to what the *tamada* has said. Many traditions, including an elaborate order of toasting subjects, surround this most characteristic of Georgian rituals, and a foreigner at his first Georgian *supra* may feel as if he has stumbled into an unfamiliar church service and doesn't know when to stand, when to kneel, and when to say "Amen."

At home, the host of a *supra* will either take on the role of *tamada* himself or choose an honored or especially eloquent guest to replace him. Out here in the fields, nobody can claim to be host. Before we drink the first cup, Tengiz tells the other Georgians the story of Alan following the mysterious music upstairs to his door, ending with the *chacha* and the walnuts. Amid some gentle laughter at Alan's expense, Tengiz nominates Alan to be *tamada*.

During our several visits to Georgia, we have listened to countless *tamadas* at numberless banquets—often with Maia leaning over and quietly translating the proceedings for us while adding her own sarcastic commentary to the high-flown sentiments wafting over the table once the *tamada* has had a few—so Alan knows what to do. He makes the necessary toasts in pretty much the required order: to our meeting, to friendship, to music—the music that brought about his friendship with Tengiz and indeed our very presence in Georgia—to the bonds between Georgia and America, to love. He speaks in English, and Mikha translates. As Alan pushes farther down the list of mandated subjects, his toasts get shorter and Mikha's translations get longer. He is using Alan's words as a mere sketch, a hint of what really ought to be said. Eventually he begins to interject remarks in English while Alan is speaking: witty examples, nice turns of phrase, telling analogies to help Alan give the toast some weight before Mikha himself embroiders it in Georgian.

Some time later, the hunters return empty-handed. They decline offers of food and wine and go straight to bed. It's nearly midnight, and they want to be fresh for an early morning expedition, but I think pride is also a factor. These weekend hunters want to live off what they kill, so if they don't kill, they won't eat. Instead, almost without a word, they roll themselves up in blankets on the stubbly ground around us. The Parliamentarian's ten-year-old son beds down with his shotgun cradled in his arms. But the moon is high now, flooding the land with soft light, and the wine is good, so for the rest of us the party goes on.

Gia is certainly a real hunter, and his job guarding us is done now that the rest are back, but he's been inspired and doesn't want the night to end. He is determined to speak to the Americans. He could use Mikha to translate, but he wants no middlemen, so he finds something he can say using the little Georgian we know. He points west: "Georgia." He points north: "Azerbaijan." He points east: "Azerbaijan." He points south: "Azerbaijan." We are in the easternmost finger of Georgia. He should know—he's a border guard. He spreads his arms to indicate the space around us. "Here, there is no water. This is the Shiraki Plain."

Alan and I sit up at once. "The Shiraki Plain?" Mikha jumps in to amplify in English. The Shiraki Plain is a flat area at the eastern tip of Georgia, surrounded by low hills and therefore not watered by the rivers (the Alazani and the Iori) that flank it to north and south. But Alan and I are not interested in geography right now—we know this name from a poem we have half-learned. *"Shirakis velze mivdivar,"* I say haltingly: "I am traveling in the Shiraki Plain."

Gia chuckles and picks up his *panduri*, and then—softly at first, for the sake of the sleeping hunters, but gradually louder because it's irresistible—he sings:

> *shirakis velze mivdivar,*
> *ukan mabrunebs kario.*
> *tsin shemeqara pepela,*
> *tsitlad uchanda mkhario*
> *saqvarlis kabas vamsgavse.*
> *ghmerto, damtsere jvario.*

I am traveling in the Shiraki Plain.
The wind tells me to turn back.
I encounter a butterfly,
The red of whose wings
Resembles my beloved's dress.
God, You marked me with the sign of the Cross.

"Marked with the sign of the Cross" in this case means marked for death. It's a great melody, fast and light like that butterfly, and Mikha quickly tunes his guitar like a *panduri* (turning a six-stringed instrument into a three-stringed one) and joins Gia for the next verse and the verse after that. Alan and I don't know the rest of the words, but there's a good *oo-ing* bass part. Tengiz leans over to me and says, "You want to learn Georgian songs. This is where real Georgian songs are, not in Tbilisi. You should have your tape recorder here."

"I do," I say and point to my head. I am indeed taking it all in to remember: Gia's high, sweet tenor and the way he sings to his left hand so he can watch the fingerings; Mikha's husky, honking rasp—sounding, after several hours of drinking, less like Marlene Dietrich and more like Louis Armstrong—and the way he strums his guitar high up the neck to reduce its resonance and make it sound more like a backwoods *panduri*; Alan swaying slightly, eyes closed, as he tries to sing and catch a little nap at the same time; one of the hunters stretched out nearby giving up on sleep and sitting up groggily to join the party; and over us all, the moon.

When it's time for the next toast, Alan is discovered to be fast asleep. Tengiz and Vazha wake him so he can do his job as *tamada*. He mumbles something about travelers everywhere and then drifts off again while the rest of us drink to travelers everywhere—"May they all find what they seek," to travelers caught outside by nightfall while their loved ones await them, to travelers marked with the Cross. Mikha is inspired to recount for us all, in English and in Georgian, a long and thrilling Jack London story about a traveler in distress. What story exactly, I don't remember. I am drifting off intermittently myself by now. At 4:00 AM, with the story over and Alan unwakeable, the party suddenly ends. Most of the men just lean back and fall asleep where they have been sitting, but I, not eager to lie on sunflower stubble, follow Tengiz to his car. He drags the back seat out onto the ground for himself, and I get in and use the reclined front passenger seat as my bed.

5

Any night so close to Heaven must be followed by a morning near Hell. I wake at eight, still drunk, in time to see the hunters—including some who got up in the night to party until four—gather for an expedition on foot. Vakhtang the Parliamentarian mischievously wakes Vazha to ask if he wants to go, and together they wake Tengiz for the pleasure of hearing his cries for mercy as he curls into a ball on his car seat. Then the hunters, armed with shotguns and dogs, set off walking across the sunflower fields, and the rest of us fall back to sleep.

It seems that in the heat of independence from the Soviet Union, in 1991, some politician (not, of course, the Constitution Writer), insisted that for Georgia to stay in the same time zone as Moscow was a form of Russian hegemony. This remarkable individual actually went on a hunger strike until the rest of Parliament agreed to move Georgia, chronologically speaking, not one but two hours to the east. The result is a kind of permanent double daylight savings time: the sky is light until 11:00 in midsummer (though Tbilisi is at the same latitude as Rome), and, at 8:00 AM in the middle of September, when the hunters rise and head off into the sunflower fields, the sky is only just beginning to think about getting pink.

By nine, however, the sun is well up and as huge and close as the moon was all night, but a thousand times brighter. I stagger out of the car, no longer drunk but hungover, desperate for water and shade.

There is no water—the quart we brought is long gone—but there is still plenty of wine. As for shade, a couple of other early risers have discovered a nearby line of low, sparse bramble bushes separating two sunflower fields. Together we crouch under this mostly imaginary cover, picking thorns out of our necks and trying to get our tongues to move in our parched mouths.

Gia and The Driver get ready to drive the jeep back to the Azeri village with the crippled wheel of the other car. Before they leave, however, Gia decides it's time to wake the remaining sleepers: Alan, Tengiz, Vazha, and Mikha, stretched out in the blazing sun, their heads wrapped in towels or coats. Gia hands me his Kalashnikov, first carefully setting it to single fire. I admire the ingenious hinged butt that folds away to make the gun handier in tight corners. Then I aim into the air (but not straight up!) and pull the trigger: *BLAM!* The sleepers sit bolt upright, blinking and cursing.

The jeep drives away, and all of us now take cover under the brambles, whose shadow-casting power, anemic to start with, diminishes noticeably as the sun climbs higher. The near-silence that follows for the next couple of hours is the product of no water, no food, no shade, no sleep, and pounding headaches. There is, of course, food—more of the same condiments we ate last night—but the unspoken understanding seems to be that for the non-hunters to eat again while the hunters are away would be bad form. So we huddle under the brambles, shifting every few minutes to adjust for the sun's movement, croaking feebly when we settle on new thorns. Once or twice we hear the hunters' guns faintly in the distance, and everybody grunts approval. Then we lapse back into our own thoughts. I will never drink again... I will never leave the cool shade of my home again... What kind of sick culture produces grown men who drive off for a weekend in the wilderness with a single quart of water and 30 gallons of wine?... I will never drink again...

The hunters finally return, bearing three partridges and two quail. I won't learn the English equivalents of the Georgian names until I get back to my big dictionary in Tbilisi. All I can be sure of now is that these five small, limp birds will have their work cut out for them to feed a dozen men, most of whom ate nothing the night before. While the rest of the party retreats to the shade of the brambles, one of the young Gung-ho Hunters from Dedoplis Tsqaro plucks the birds— reducing their bulk even further, so that the largest now fits neatly in the palm of his hand.

Then he borrows the Parliamentarian's cigarette lighter and sets fire to the matted sunflower straw. By repeated applications of the lighter, he gets scattered patches to smolder long enough to singe the last feathers off the birds. The old man meanwhile gathers dry sticks from the bramble bushes with his bare hands—a job which the rest of us watch with respect and no great urge to jump up and help him— and prepares a real fire of the only thing around here resembling wood. The young man guts and spits the birds and gives them to the old man for grilling. The young man's hands are covered in blood when he's done, and there is no water, so he kneels while someone else carefully tips the 30-gallon keg and pours out a thin trickle of wine, in which he washes his hands.

As the smell of cooking bird spreads in the hot, still air, Mikha finally wakes up enough to get back into first gear. "Fee, fie, foe, fum," he rasps, "I smell the blood of an Englishman." The jeep returns with the repaired wheel for the crippled car, and when the wheel is in place, it's time to eat. Someone has the bright idea that, since Alan was *tamada* yesterday, I should be *tamada* today—all day. Mikha may have reached first gear, but he's clearly not turning over fast enough to connect the dots for me in translation, so as we gather around the jeep's khaki tarpaulin, spread on the ground as a tablecloth, I make a mental checklist of what needs to be said in a low-key setting like this. Holding with no great eagerness the day's first cup of wine (first cup

of anything), I scan the food to see what I can eat. The same as last
night, naturally—beautiful quartered tomato, tiny raw onions, day-
old puri flat bread. I drink a toast to the hunters for all their work. As
I speak, I feel as if my salivary glands are producing pickle brine.

It takes only a couple of minutes for a dozen men to eat those five
tiny birds, so we are on our way as soon as the wine keg can be loaded
onto the jeep. Our course appears to proceed less and less along even
the doubtful tracks we have followed up to now, and more and more
straight across country. The jeep tears along happily, but those of us in
the two cars following it feel the sunflower stubble scraping along the
undercarriage and hear the engine gasping as we climb straight up yet
another hillock. Nosing our way gingerly down one steep slope into a
gully, we can see the equally steep ascent ahead of us. Hoping to get
some momentum, Tengiz floors it, and we roar downhill past the
village car and the jeep. We make it less than halfway up the other side,
however, before Tengiz's proud little Moskvich grows tired. Vazha,
Alan, and I get out and push, and the jeep and the other car climb past
us, jeering. After a few repetitions we become resigned: barrel
downhill, whine uphill, get out and push, walk to the top where
Tengiz waits for us once the lightened car has gained escape velocity.
Throughout this performance, Tengiz—liable at any time while
driving to slap the dashboard and cry out, "Moskvich! Best car!"—
maintains a distant and dignified little smile, like an explorer in a
palanquin borne by clumsy natives.

Speeding downhill past the jeep, Tengiz suddenly leans out the
window and shouts "Ivan Susanin!" and gets blank stares in return. He
turns halfway to the back seat and asks Alan and me, "You know Ivan
Susanin? Enemies of Russia, Polish maybe,"—here Vazha interrupts
to suggest it was the Mongols.—"No, Polish."—"Mongols." We get
out to push again, and the jeep and the other car pass us again. When
we are all back in the car, Tengiz picks up the story. "Enemies of
Russia, nobody know who, ask Ivan Susanin to lead their army to Tsar.

If he refuse, they kill him. So Ivan Susanin lead enemies far into forest, deep, deep, deep into forest, with many turns. 'Where is Tsar?' they ask him. 'Soon, soon, over this hill.' But in fact they are lost, he lose them, they never find Tsar, they all die in forest, and Russia is saved from Polish—and Mongols."

"And what about Ivan?" I ask. "Weren't the Polish and the Mongols a little upset with him when they found out?"

"Ivan Susanin die, but Russia saved." Tengiz gets a quaver in his voice as he does his best to pretend to care about the fate of Russia. Then he points ahead at the jeep. "Up, down, up, down. They are Ivan Susanin, leading us in circle."

When we get back in after pushing the car up the next hill, Alan, who knows his opera synopses, says, "Isn't that the plot of Glinka's opera, *A Life for the Tsar*?"

Tengiz does a little dance in the driver's seat. "Oho, bravo Alan! Bravo Glinka!" This time as we pass the jeep he leans out and shouts in English, "You, you are all Ivan Susanin! But we will not be fooled! We have education, and we know Glinka!"

The loyal little Moskvich does its best to save us, absolutely refusing to go up the steepest, longest ascent of all—which turns out to be Shavi Mta itself—and overheating to make its point. We sit for an hour, drowsing in the afternoon heat, listening to a soccer game from Tbilisi on the radio, while we wait for the jeep to lead the other car up and come back down to tow the Moskvich the last practically vertical mile, to the top of Shavi Mta.

6

At the exact top—where the land drops away smoothly on all sides and, if not for the dusty haze, you could see for miles in every direction, because Shavi Mta is the highest thing around—at the top sits one building, a decrepit hunting lodge. The layout inside is simple: two rooms full of beds, one room full of firewood, and a chicken-wired porch with a cement hearth and a big table, around which all waking activity takes place.

The fenced yard holds a few turkeys, a few chickens, half a dozen cows, and the Hound of the Baskervilles—a mongrel dog with the size and build of a St. Bernard and the teeth and temper of a wolverine— whose job is to guard the cows when they go outside the yard to graze, and at other times to attack anything that moves. Strangely, the dog wears a six-inch-wide, hand-beaten metal collar, as if to protect him from the jaws of predators. If there are any bears left in Georgia, they are surely hiding in the remotest folds of the high Caucasus, not on this treeless knob surrounded by sunflower fields, so maybe it's just vestigial armor.

A couple of young men occupy the lodge: the caretaker and a long-term visiting hunter in army fatigues. Neither one seems to have bathed this year, and the hunter's thick hair, packed with grease and dust, stands several inches high, Eraserhead-style: like Eduard Shevardnadze in his luxurious compound high above Tbilisi, these men live at the top of a hill without water. I refer to one of them as the caretaker, because he behaves like someone temporarily responsible and not rooted here, but he might well be the owner. The about-face from a communist economy, in which the state owned all property and occupants paid a nominal rent, to an economy of private ownership, was accomplished with bold simplicity: whatever you occupy at this magic moment, you own. It's as if the whole country went co-op overnight but the apartments were free. If you were living in a beautiful prewar penthouse in the heart of Tbilisi, it's now yours, and you can sell it to a foreign embassy and move to France on the proceeds if you want. On the other hand, if at the magic moment you had the bad luck to be occupying a crumbling cement hovel without power or water on a windswept hilltop at the extremest tip of Georgia, it's yours, too, and if you can't find a sucker to sell it to, you might spend the rest of your life there.

While some in our party set about boiling beef for dinner over a wood fire on the hearth, and The Driver and Zurab, the elder of the Grecian Formula border patrol brothers, take the jeep down to a stream to refill the lodge's water containers, others settle down at the long table for a loud game of dominoes. Tamaz, the quiet painter who looks like an icon, sits surrounded by the slamming down of dominoes and the shouts of triumph and protest, completely absorbed in a dog-eared paperback. Tilting my head, I slowly decipher the stylized Georgian script on the cover: *Rojer Akroidi's Murder,* by Agata Kristi.

As I am stepping off the porch to go take a leak, the caretaker stops me and puts into my hands a seven-foot-long wooden pole that stands by the door. "Bad dog," he says in Georgian while he makes the motion of swinging the stick in a vigorous arc around him. Fortunately just the sight of the stick is enough to discourage the dog, and he stays at a safe distance, barking savagely, as I pick my way past the cow pats and the waist-high thistles growing out of the cow pats, to a suitably distant corner of the yard—only to find that this spot, hidden behind a solid bank of thistles, is already crowded with nervous, shuffling turkeys.

When we all sit down for a five o'clock meal, I realize the water fetched by the jeep was intended for washing and cooking; as long as there is wine, no one plans to drink water—and there is still plenty of wine, now partly decanted into a teakettle for ease of pouring. But, as I am reminded as soon as we sit down, I am still *tamada*. Rank has its privileges, and I thereupon order a large chipped enamel cup to be filled with water. I don't care what lives in this water or what defecated upstream of its collection point—it's water and will never turn to wine. I drain the cup, feeling the water flow to all parts of me in an instant like adrenaline, and then I order up another round in the same cup (the only one not already full of wine) for Alan.

There is not a fork or spoon to be seen, and the only knives are the men's personal hunting knives. Chunks of boiled beef are pushed onto flowery china dessert plates with the same stick that was used to stir the pot, and then we all eat with our hands. The food options for me, however, remain the same as ever: tomato chunks, little onions, and old puri—unless I want to try a piece of the large round loaf of bread that sits inscrutably in the middle of the table throughout our stay, its crust almost invisible under a furry carpet of mold. Soon enough, however, my hunger for anything not a tomato is smothered by the familiar buzz of wine, especially after the caretaker insists on drinking a *vakhtanguri* with me. He is our host, and as *tamada* I am right now our party's representative, so I can hardly refuse this ritual of friendship. We stand up, entwine our drinking arms, and each drain a full cup of wine, shaking the last drops onto the table to prove it done. The caretaker then solemnly kisses me on the lips.

It's another short meal. The hunters are eager to be off, and they push back the benches and pile into the jeep. But I didn't come all this way and drink all that wine just to sit around the lodge listening to the dog bark. I walk out to the jeep. "I want to go hunting," I say in Georgian to nobody in particular. "Is it possible?"

The jeep, which is only a hair bigger than its American equivalent, holds at this moment eight men, one boy, two dogs, and a lot of guns. Everybody turns to look at me, even the dogs. Tengiz and Vazha, who have settled down with a backgammon board across their knees, and Alan, who is on his way to the back rooms for a nap, all stop and stare at me as if I have lost my mind. The hunters, however, recover in a moment from their surprise, squeeze in tighter, and offer me six inches of unoccupied seat. I climb on board. Somebody looks around and realizes there is no English speaker along to translate for me. They all turn and shout, "Mikha!"

Mikha, still seated at the table, happily tuning his guitar, looks up with such an expression of horror that I say, "*Ara ushavs, ara ushavs!*"—no problem! And off we go.

7

We barrel down the mountain on a different track from the one we came up. I have been placed toward the middle of the rear seat (there are five of us sharing it, including the boy) so that the hunters along the outside can have an unobstructed shot. Next to me is Aliko, the stiff-haired hunter from the lodge, who I now learn used to be in the Soviet Army, stationed in East Germany. That he is also a crack shot I soon discover. A flash of color arcs over the jeep and disappears in a field of knee-high sunflower stubble. Before The Driver can hit the brakes, Aliko leans out and fires his shotgun into the field. A pheasant breaks into the air, flapping, then drops. Aliko jumps out, followed by the black retriever from Dedoplis Tsqaro. (Since the dog has to bound out from under the feet of half a dozen men with cocked firearms, it's remarkable no one shoots himself.) Aliko brings back the pheasant, which is unharmed aside from a broken wing, and gives it to the boy, Irakli, to hold on his lap.

The road winds always downhill, and soon we leave behind the open sunflower fields and descend into a region of steep, eroded gullies and scrubby forest. The pheasant's iridescent feathers are astonishingly beautiful, and Irakli strokes them gently. The bird sits motionless except for the rapid pounding of its chest. The road gets worse and worse, and The Driver switches to four-wheel drive and downshifts to first gear to negotiate the ridges of dry mud where the road crosses and recrosses washed-out creek bottoms. After half an hour Irakli relaxes his grip for an instant, and the pheasant breaks for freedom. From one moment to the next, before Irakli can even cry out in surprise, the jeep is suddenly filled with flapping bird—in our faces, at our feet, against the windshield, over the back seat, into our laps again. Both dogs lunge for it, but it is Zurab, laughing, who grabs the pheasant by the wing, hugs it tight to his chest, and wraps it in twine, still alive. He stashes it under our feet.

The gully opens out onto a broad, treeless expanse overlooking the Alazani River. "Overlooking" is the problem: we are on a bluff a hundred feet above the water, and nobody seems to remember the best way down. So we drive parallel to the river for a few miles, nosing the jeep experimentally down every break in the plateau, but each attempt ends eventually at a sheer drop, laughter, and exasperated I-told-you-so's.

Where the plateau is wide and flat enough, it has been turned into watermelon fields. A debate on whether to stop and pick some is ended by the sight of a truck piled high with watermelons, parked unattended in the shade of a tree. A couple of hunters jump out of the jeep, climb the sides of the truck, and start heaving down watermelons. They stop when we have about ten rolling around at our feet along with the dogs and the pheasant. A few hundred yards farther, The Driver sees a track down to the river he thinks he can negotiate, but there's enough of a chance he'll flip the jeep on the way down that he makes the rest of us dismount and walk. Then he creeps down the track in first gear, watermelons rumbling forward as the slope increases.

At water's edge Zurab takes out his fancy foot-long hunting knife, opens a watermelon, and hands out slices. Vakhtang the Constitution Writer, meanwhile, strips down to his underwear and goes in for a swim. Tamaz the artist unrolls a net and wades in to go fishing. I myself am content to touch this river. A famous Georgian folk song, Gaprindi Shavo Mertskhalo, mentions the Alazani, so it's a name I have known since long before I spoke a word of Georgian:

> Fly away, black swallow,
> Follow the banks of the Alazani.
> Bring me news of my brother
> Who has gone to war.
> I went along the Alazani,
> I saw red grass.

Fly away, black swallow,
Down the banks of the Alazani.

So here I am on the banks of the Alazani. I can easily picture the
sparse, dry, foot-high grass around me stained red with blood, but I see
no swallows, though it seems like a perfect place for them. The
opposite side of the river, which is about the width of a six-lane
highway, is a sheer 100-foot-high cliff of crumbly sandstone, with
countless eroded hollows suitable for nesting. Gia thinks so, too, and
he begins firing his Kalashnikov at the cliff to bring out whatever
birds are hiding there. We're standing at the apex of a tight bend in
the river, and the cliff throws the gun report back at us from three
sides. No reaction from any birds, but Tamaz, standing knee-deep in
the river and casting his net like some Disciple in Galilee, shouts at
Gia to cut it out before he scares the fish away.

After all the weaving around we did to get here, it's a little hard to
pinpoint exactly where we are, but according to the map in my head,
as well as the map I consult when I get home, this stretch of the
Alazani forms the border between Georgia and Azerbaijan. That
doesn't keep Zurab, one of the three border patrol officers present,
from proposing to everyone (and explaining to me with gestures and
well-placed Georgian words) a walk upstream to a fording point.
Apparently the piles of fallen rock at the foot of the cliff on the other
side are a likely place to find foxes. I'm not familiar with *mela*, the
word for "fox," but Zurab's pantomime—big ears, high tail, and
wicked eye—is so much fun to watch that I'm briefly tempted to
pretend I still haven't guessed it so he won't stop.

No one else thinks much of the plan, but I follow Zurab and Aliko,
the high-haired hunter who bagged the pheasant, upstream away from
the group. If anybody is going to do some serious hunting, it's these
two guys. It's about 8:00 PM, but that's Georgian time, so the sun
itself has only just set behind the bluffs southwest of us, and the sky is
still bright blue. Ten minutes of scrambling over pebbled banks takes

us around another bend in the river, where the Alazani narrows to the width of a city street. This is the crossing point. Zurab walks out fully dressed into the river, holding his shotgun over his head as he wades toward Azerbaijan. (I assume that, as a border patrol officer, he knows what he's doing; maybe the fact that the base of the cliff is inaccessible from the Azeri side makes it okay.)

Before Zurab gets halfway across, the water is up to his waist. He pauses, bracing himself against the current, which is naturally much stronger here at the narrows than where the river spreads out again below. He notices that the cartridge belt across his chest is in danger of a soaking, so he tries to gather it up and sling it around his neck. In the process, his very best hunting knife slips out of its sheath on his cartridge belt and vanishes into the river. Groans of sympathy from Aliko and me on shore. Zurab gives us a wry smile, shrugs his shoulders, and wades back out of the river on the Georgian side. The foxes are safe.

8

The three of us walk uphill, away from the river, through a swath of thorn bushes. At first Zurab and Aliko move quietly, alert for game, but as dusk approaches and the chances recede of spotting an animal in the darkening underbrush, Zurab—still soaking wet up to his armpits—drops back to chat with me in my brand of simple declarative Georgian.

He and his brother live in the city of Telavi (not near a border, so I assume they serve rotating field duty). His wife is an English teacher, but he speaks no English. He would like to learn English, and he would like to live in America someday. Where do I live? I live in New York. Manhattan? No, Brooklyn. Ah, yes, Brooklyn. Zurab nods knowingly. (Because of the huge Russian-speaking émigré community in Brighton Beach, Brooklyn is known to millions of people who have never heard of the Dodgers.) And what work do I do? From my very first Georgian lesson, Ivdit has prepared me with the vocabulary to answer this common question. I work as a film editor. But the next question is one I am not prepared for. Zurab stops at the edge of another thorny patch and asks, "How much money in one day?"

My first impulse is to lie, but Zurab seems so open, so hungry for communication, that I find I can't do it. What's the use of sharing an experience like this trip with someone if you can't be honest with him? Since I can't lie to him, but I'm not ready to tell the truth yet, I stall. "Me?"

"Yeah. Your job. How much money in one day?"

I wave my hands to illustrate the cost of living. "Apartments are very high."

He nods, not distracted. "How much does your job pay?"

"Food is very high. One loaf of bread—"

Laughing, he holds up a hand to stop me. "I know. Your job, how much in one day?"

I'm going to have to tell him the truth, and I don't have the vocabulary to qualify it with ideas like "freelance" or "months in a row without work" or "self-employment tax." I take a deep breath and tell him the truth, an amount measured in hundreds of dollars per day.

Zurab flushes deep red. He's angry that I would try to mock his credulity—or maybe he's embarrassed for me for having told such a flagrant whopper. I'm embarrassed, too, because I know that, though as a member of a military force, Zurab probably makes more than the common government salary of three dollars a month, he certainly makes much less in a year than I do in a day.

After a few seconds Zurab can see I'm not joking. His eyes narrow, and he stares into the distance, trying to picture that much money and my consequent life of decadence. He repeats the figure I just gave him. I nod. He turns on his heel and leads the way uphill without another word. I should have lied.

When we finally reach the plateau at the top of the bluff, we find ourselves in the same watermelon field we crossed in the jeep. Aliko is already hard at work, circling back and forth in the gathering gloom, tapping watermelons. The three of us fan out, crouching to tap, shuffling to the next, crouching to tap again. Aliko finds a ripe one and, without taking the time to cut it off the vine, opens it with the only knife we have left. The bright red flesh is warm from the sun, but anything with the word "water" in it presents a still badly needed chance to rehydrate, and I eat until I'm bloated. Aliko walks a few feet farther and opens another one, and then another, and we eat only the sweet centers, leaving a wake of disemboweled fruit.

A dilapidated farm vehicle with one uncertain headlight bounces slowly toward us. It's the owner, I think, wiping my mouth. Now there'll be trouble. It is indeed the watermelon farmer, but no trouble follows. He gets out wearily, greets us, and accepts a slice of watermelon from Aliko, and we all stand around in the dark, eating. Collective farming was as hated in Georgia as elsewhere in the Soviet Union, but the new concept of private ownership is not yet strong enough to overcome the old understanding—ingrained by decades of habit—that everything worth anything belongs to the government, which is to say to nobody, and therefore nobody will miss it. Even the farmer helping us eat his own watermelon thinks he's getting away with something.

The jeep, still ballasted with its own haul of watermelons, climbs up from the river to meet us. On the ride home the day-at-the-beach atmosphere disappears, and the hunters get serious again. Like last night, the canvas roof is rolled away and tied so that two men can stand up in the back seat. Zurab holds the searchlight and scans the ground on either side as we go, and beside him Aliko follows the beam with his shotgun barrel. Except for the boy Irakli, fast asleep against his father, everyone is alert, leaning out into the dark, ready to loose both barrels at anything that moves. We see nothing at all until we climb out of the wooded hollows onto the high, open sunflower fields. There a few night birds, owls probably, flit across the spotlight beam, and everybody tenses for an instant before looking away.

Then, only minutes from home, as we are about to head up the slope of Shavi Mta, there is suddenly motion at the pale extremity of the light beam: a hare, at least a hundred yards away across the fields, already spooked and bounding away from us, no more than a bouncing dot of pale fur against the night sky. Hopeless, I think. Aliko fires. Another bound; the next will take the hare over the crest of a gentle rise and out of sight. Aliko fires the other barrel, and at the same moment Gia, in the front passenger seat, fires one round out the window from his Kalashnikov. The hare flips over in mid-air and falls.

The Driver turns the wheel and aims the jeep straight across the bumpy sunflower field. If it was Gia who hit it, there will be nothing but raw stew out there. But the hare proves to be intact and still twitching when the spotlight finds it. We pull up beside it, and Irakli, wide awake now, is dispatched to get it. He stands over the hare and watches until the last tremor has passed, then brings it back to the jeep, holding it at arm's length by the ears with two hands.

The roving spotlight and the general alert routine resume as we drive on up Shavi Mta, but the pressure is off: we have dinner. Back at the lodge, while the meat is cooking, the caretaker turns on the television, which requires starting up an outdoor generator that seems to have no other purpose. For one hour of Tbilisi television, one liter of gasoline.

When we sit down to eat, I discover that Tamaz, who knows I won't eat pheasant or hare, has put his entire catch—half a dozen finger-sized fish—on my plate. Nobody will accept my offers to share, so I eat all the fish (seriously bony and tasting remarkably of hare) myself—with my fingers, of course. But it's after midnight of an incomprehensibly long day, and though by strictly enforced house rules I am still *tamada,* I can barely keep my eyes open. Fortunately,

Mikha is well rested and happy to spin my aimless mumblings into recognizable toasts in Georgian. Tengiz, fresh from hours of backgammon, says, "You see? This is what happen when you go hunting. Are you hunter? No. You are singer of Georgian folk music."

Alan, who has not forgotten that he is indeed a singer of Georgian folk music, has spent his evening profitably quizzing Mikha for the words to additional verses of the Shiraki Plain song. They perform it together, Mikha with his guitar, Gia with his *panduri*, and Alan with his notebook of lyrics. Whenever Alan stumbles over the fast-moving, unfamiliar words (nonsense to him), he raises his hand to claim the error like a well-trained choral performer at rehearsal, a superfluous nicety here—since he's the only one who doesn't know the words by heart—that earns him a roar of approving laughter.

At the moment when I can't keep my head up anymore and am about to commit the kind of breach—the *tamada* quitting the table for bed—that only a foreigner could get away with, the serious hunters rise from the table as a group and make their excuses in a good-night toast. I'm not the only one who's tired, I think, but no. Leaving the table, they pile into the jeep and drive off, at 1:00 AM, to hunt some more. As for me, I ponder the likelihood of lice for about three seconds before collapsing fully dressed onto one of the half-dozen trough-shaped beds in the back room.

9

The noise that wakes me at eight the next morning is the sound of those same hunters climbing into the jeep to go out again. That they really did go hunting last night is confirmed when I wander outside and almost step on the guts and severed heads of two more hares. Breakfast is watermelon, and the old man and I, armed with the anti-dog stick, walk to the eastern edge of the yard to blow seeds and admire the sun rising over the snowy ridge of the Caucasus, 25 miles away: a 10,000-foot-high wall stretching unbroken across our entire field of vision, crowned with a jagged frosting of pink-edged white. Between us and the mountains, under morning mist, lies the valley of the Alazani River. The old man doesn't have Zurab's patience in constructing a Georgian conversation that I can share. He breaks our companionable silence only twice. The first time he points down into the valley with a watermelon rind and announces "Azerbaijan." I nod. A few minutes later he points over the snow mountains. "Chechnya."

"Very good," I answer.

Having bonded, he and I walk back to the lodge and join a game of dominoes. The rules are a lot more complicated than I remember from my childhood. We play in teams of partners across the table, like bridge, and whenever the dots on the tiles at the playable ends total a multiple of five, there is a lot of shouting and Vakhtang the Constitution Writer racks up the score on the abacus. There are other rules, too, but I don't worry about them because the old man and I are playing as one person. He has the easy job: deciding what tile to lay down where. My part is much more challenging: I have to hold all our tiles in my hand the approved way, stacked edge to edge between fingers and thumb at just the right pressure. Too little, and they collapse into a pile in my palm. Too much, and they fly across the porch and the chickens rush over to peck at them.

The skinned bodies of the two hares, hanging to drip blood into a pan, attract a party of bees. Mikha, who has been watching the dominoes game, suddenly flaps his hand and shouts, "Aaaah! Sting, stung, stung!" Still extracting the bee from his finger, he explains. "In Georgian a bee bites you, like a dog." He points at Irakli's cocker spaniel, which did not go hunting this morning: "Bite, bit, bitten!" Back at the bees hovering over the pan of blood: "Sting, stung, stung!" Back to the mystified dog: "Bite, bit, bitten!... Sting, stung, stung!"

The hunters return with three more pheasants, which are left intact for taking home. Tamaz, who has spent the whole morning with his nose in his Agatha Christie, jumps up and gets The Driver to take him on a short mystery expedition that turns out to be a special fishing trip for me. Meanwhile the rest of us gather in the yard for a shooting contest. The target is a ceramic insulator on top of an electric pole across the yard. Thanks to Lenin and Peace, Land, and Rural Electrification (a slogan that always struck me as too perfect an illustration of bathos to be real), power once reached to the top of Shavi Mta—or at least the poles got this far. There are no wires to be seen between any of the poles marching down the mountain toward Tbilisi; maybe the wires were part of a different, less fully achieved Five Year Plan. The men lining up to take turns with Gia's Kalashnikov—men who grew up surrounded by Soviet shabbiness and are now living through the collapse of even that rotten infrastructure—obviously don't believe that in their lifetimes this pole will ever serve as anything better than target practice. Several bullets, including mine, land loudly in the pole itself, but nobody hits the insulator until Mikha, showing unexpected concentration, takes the white ceramic knob cleanly off the pole with one shot. He dances around the yard, flapping his arms and crowing, "I am the Greatest!" in a tone designed to tell the rueful hunters he could beat them any day at their silly hunting games if only it were worth the bother.

They get their revenge at lunch. The old man is *tamada* today, and halfway through the meal he stands up and begins a toast to Mikha. The toast goes on and on, and since Mikha is being addressed, he can't turn aside to translate. After tuning out for a while (as one must occasionally do in these cases or go mad), I am brought back by a long, slow wave of laughter and by the old man, with an absolute poker face, declaiming something that sounds remarkably like "Sting, stung, stung!" pronounced in a singsong like an American child's parody of Chinese. The Georgians at the table, including Mikha, are weeping with laughter, and I have to shake Tengiz to get a translation.

"This old man say Mikha never speak to Americans before. He... congratulate him for speaking with you. He say he love to see Mikha talk to you and Alan these last days, talking-talking-talking and you understand everything he say, and he understand everything you say, even you talk fast. He say it's a great, happy thing for Dedoplis Tsqaro to have such a good teacher of English."

Tengiz has said all this in a tone that suggests the other shoe is about to drop. I prompt him. "Yeah? But?"

"Then he say nobody in Dedoplis Tsqaro speak English as good as Mikha. All his life nobody understand him. He has nobody to practice English. So he go to the... the place where pigs are kept. He speak to pigs in English. He teach them English. He say, 'Sting, stung, stung!' And pigs answer him, 'Sting, stung, stung!' Together they have English conversation. Pigs are his friends."

The old man, having come to an end without once cracking a smile, kisses Mikha on both cheeks and drinks with him. The meal is almost over, and the *tamada* turns his attention to Alan and me. Fortunately, he goes easier on his foreign guests than on an old friend, thanking us for our singing and our cheerful company and drinking to the next time we all meet and go hunting.

When several people are the subject of a collective toast, it's normal for one of them to respond for all. Alan quickly elects me, and I get to my feet. What to say? Toasting is inescapably a branch of the higher blather, and nobody is on oath about matters of mere fact when the point is to let the heart speak, but when I can I still try not to tell bald lies. A future repetition of this magic time seems like a vanishingly remote possibility—and not even a self-evidently good idea. But what to say? From the other end of the table Mikha watches me closely, ready to translate and if necessary invent. I take a deep breath and begin, with no idea where I am going.

"Gentlemen, who knows if we will ever be together again? Alan and I live far from Georgia, and many of you live far from Tbilisi." While Mikha translates that much, I finally see where I am headed. "But there is a way we can always be together: in a photograph. I can send you a copy from America and you can stick it right here,"—I slap the sooty wall behind me—"and you can see that we are together each time you come up here. I want everybody outside for a group picture: every man, every dog, every shotgun, every Kalashnikov, every guitar, every *panduri*, everything!"

With a roar of approval, my wish is carried out to the last detail—except the part about every dog: the caretaker's monstrous watchdog is wisely not invited, and in fact is kept at bay with the pole.

We take a different road back to Dedoplis Tsqaro. Only once do we meet a hill so steep that we have to get out and push, and only once does the other car get a flat tire. After we all part ways, one of the morning's pheasants winds up in our car, rolling limply from side to side in the back as Tengiz maneuvers around potholes on the road back to Tbilisi. The final event of the weekend, when we pull into the courtyard of our apartment building, is the struggle over the pheasant. Tengiz quietly tries to add it to the luggage Alan and I are unloading. "For Carl," he says when I stop him.

"But we don't know how to cook it."

"Your housekeeper knows."

"But it's Sunday, which is our housekeeper's day off, and this bird must be cooked today."

I have him, but he still wriggles. "I also don't know how to cook it."

"But your wife knows." He's beaten, and the pheasant goes back in the car: a tiny win for the visitors in the never-ending Georgian hospitality wars.

10

In my lesson the next day, Ivdit makes me tell her the whole story of my trip. At first she insists I tell it in Georgian, which handcuffs me considerably, but after a while she stops objecting to my lapses into English and just listens. At the end she says, "My husband often goes hunting, but he never told me about it." She shakes her head in amazement. "So this is what men do!" Then, remembering her job, she gives me as homework the task of writing out my story in Georgian.

With my dictionary in front of me, I am able to eke out a bald three-page account, but it takes me all my homework time for a week to do it. The title of my essay is "The Watermelon Hunters." On the day it's finished, I leave it open on my desk when I go out, to remind myself to recopy it neatly before tomorrow. When I come back and sit down to my manuscript in the evening, I discover that every verb conjugation—the one thing my dictionary can't help me with, since it gives only infinitives—has been neatly corrected in faint pencil. Lia, our housekeeper, came in to dust my room while I was out, saw my work, sat down to read it (or more likely stood, since she would feel like a trespasser sitting down), and couldn't resist fixing my errors.

I incorporate Lia's corrections in the clean copy, but the next morning, when Ivdit gets to the first difficult verb and exclaims at my excellent grammar, I tell her what happened, assuming she will find it as sweetly funny as I did. Instead Ivdit flies into a righteous temper and intercepts Lia as soon as she walks in the door: "How dare you? Who is teaching these boys Georgian grammar—you or I?" Lia apologizes meekly, but later, when I slip into the kitchen to get some lunch during Carl's lesson, she does a fine imitation at the stove of Ivdit carrying on and wagging her finger while in danger of bursting out of her tight clothes with outraged dignity.

11

A month passes. Late one evening a few days before Alan leaves to go back to Toronto, Tengiz drops in unannounced. He's already pretty drunk, and he's carrying cans of German beer he must have bought at a sidewalk kiosk on his way here. He sits down at our table, invites us to join him, and opens one beer, which he pours carefully into glasses for all of us.

He lifts his glass and then purses his lips, struggling to find the right words in English. Finally he says, "My good friend Alan is leaving. Soon all of you will be gone away. We had good friendship. What will happen then?" Alan promises to write, but Tengiz waves that away. "What is a letter? It is not your friend. A friend is here." He grabs hold of each of us in turn. Alan responds that we will come back, but again Tengiz waves that away. "You say you come back, but who knows? Many things happen. Your life is there; my life is here."

Carl answers, "But our life is here, too."

Tengiz murmurs something in Georgian, snapping his fingers with frustration at his inability to translate it. Then he says, "Bring me your Georgian writing notebook." I fetch mine, and right after the homework I have just finished, Tengiz scrawls two lines in pencil. "Ask your teacher what says this. She can say it in English. I cannot." He reads the lines to himself, murmuring the words in Georgian and looking sadder every moment. Then suddenly he looks up and cries, "But why so sentimental? *Ara ushavs!*" He clinks each of our glasses vigorously, knocks back his own, and is up and through the door and gone before we have time to rise and see him out.

At my next lesson, Ivdit carefully examines the words pencilled after my homework and declares them to be illegible. "Was your friend drunk?"

KEVIN O'CUINN

Coffee and Eyelashes, a Story of Budapest

From July/August 2005

THE SULLEN SMILE with my name pencilled on a piece of paper said, "*Horshue Sempeela.*"

"Nice to meet you, too," I answered.

"No, not nice to meet you, *hor-shue sempeeela*—you have very long eyelashes."

Any doubts I'd had about grad school in Budapest evaporated on the spot. It was a below freezing January evening, but somewhere inside a fire started. She said her name was Marta and added, "Give me your questions, when you have them." Cool, I thought, my own personal Oracle.

Legends recall that in the fifth century AD, Attila the Hun—the then scourge of everything and body (God supposedly included), arrived in what was to become known as Budapest. He cast an eye over the city and decided to name it in honor of his baby brother, whose name just happened to be "Buda." I jest not, and no relation to The Enlightened One.

The Romans vacated the settlement shortly before Attila's arrival, his reputation preceding him. He left fine architecture and lots of baths. Attila's pace slowed after Budapest. He took to the place, as I did, too.

Fifteen centuries later...

There was something in the air. Airborne, a softness nobody escaped. People had stopped complaining about the small planes humming over the city, once it had been established they were spraying a dopamine-based compound that kept the blues at bay. That was the answer I preferred to the oft-asked, "What's with all those planes?" Others insisted it was a new tourist scam, others still that it was a new breed of property surveyor. After a while nobody cared or noticed, hence my logic for siding with the dopamine fraction. The mix had a side-effect of making you want to stay. Like I said to Diana Ross on the flight back to Germany the following July, "I don't want to leave," but more about that later.

Once upon a lifetime ago. Six short months. Different scene, different being, different seeing.

Andrea, on one of her barnstorming visits, said that it was how she imagined France after the war, THE war, minus the camembert. Despite her having the status of "love of my life," we'd become undisputed world champions in domestic squabbling. But now with her in Germany, me in Hungary, and good old Austria as a buffer between us, things could only get better, no? Either way, I was resolute that in Hungary there would be no exchanging of bodily fluids with others. I was here to learn, and *Affairs of the Heart* was not on the syllabus.

Hungarians not only lead the world in hammer throwing and child-birthing techniques, they are also second to none when it comes to pedagogy. Thus the reason for my journey East, to master the intricacies of English Language Teaching. My days were full of Krashen and Chomsky—the other Chomsky, Chomsky the rebel linguist. Truth be told, I wasn't confident of making the grade when it came to sitting the exam. On good days I thought of myself as an okay teacher but one lousy student. How I'd gotten this far, I do not know. I was forever waiting for the eternal tap on the shoulder and a voice to say. "*Oi!* You! Call yourself a teacher? Don't make me laugh! You're an impostor, not a teacher! Go on, out!" Not the best attitude to embark with, I admit. In the weeks that followed, I did my best to avoid questions and the glare of my peers. I even faked a coughing fit to get out of an "assisted" (observed) teaching assignment.

The school rented me a one-room flat, my home for the next 24 weeks, on the Buda side of the Danube. From the window I had an eyeful of the Hungarian Parliament buildings on the Pest side of the river. An exact replica of the House of Parliament in Westminster, England—Marta assured me it was too complicated to explain why. Main thing was, the place was cheap, central, and halfway clean. Oh, and it was warm, very warm. Blistering hot in fact. Or if you liked, you could turn the heating off. One or the other. I opted for the former and got used to it. It felt like Christmas should, toasty, until April, whereupon the radiators turned to ice.

I recommended rope-skipping to regain a semblance of my not very hot (but somewhat slimmer) former self. The old lady downstairs paid me a visit four minutes later and complained in very colorful language, not a word of which I understood. Her message however was crystal clear, so I reverted to the age-old strategy of leaving a bottle of Bailey's Irish Cream outside her door. Works every time, though I doubt she enjoyed me practicing my saxophone, either.

Within a week I'd made myself known to a few of the locals in the vicinity. In the following six months we went a long way to creating a new Pidgin, incorporating English, school French, bar-German, and ample servings of an as yet undocumented sign language.

Linguistically, I hold anyone in awe (Hungarian included) who learns to speak Hungarian. I had my trials and tribulations, my half successes and disappointments, and after learning the absolute essentials, gave up after two days.

After "*Horsue sempeela*," the top of my list was how to order a cup of coffee. "Easy," Marta said, "Just say, *edge KAR-vet, car-wreck say pan.* But say it really quick, like you're in a hurry." With practice, it actually worked, like a caffeine dream. Thereafter I relied on pointing, smiling, and pot luck. One evening my neighbor's tantric imploring of *mage, mage, mage!* led me to chance ordering *MAGE edge kar-vet?* in hopes of receiving a second coffee. Voila!

I once dreamed I could learn languages via osmosis, that just by listening I could become hip and articulate in tongues going back to Babel. So I tuned in to a local FM station each morning before going off to class, hoping to pick up a phrase or two. From the signature music at 7:30, I figured someone at Danube FM had decided to serialize *Star Trek*. I might have been wrong. However, after a couple of weeks, I could differentiate between the main protagonists. Speaking Hungarian with a Scottish accent cannot be easy. Kirk seemed his smug self, McCoy sounded stressed, Spock was Spock. My linguistic output however, stayed firmly in the "eyelashes & coffee" department.

Like other East-European metropoles, Budapest has a long history of revolution, culture, and lousy rock bands. The crumbling decay of old-world architecture is, however, more dangerous than charming. I'd come from Frankfurt, in parts of which people walk in the street to avoid the junkies shooting up on the sidewalks. In Budapest I walked in the street to avoid falling balconies. A city coming down around you is disorienting for a newcomer. Just when you think you know your way around, somebody pulls down your landmark. It's annoying. Major restorations were underway. People stood misty-eyed in front of construction sites. The city was reinventing itself to much talk of "former glory." After more than 40 years behind the Iron Curtain, Rumpelstiltskin was having a makeover. "The Pearl of the Danube" was very much reopened for business. Forty years of irritation had only enhanced its shine.

Like the other countries of the former Soviet block, the Hungarians had, since the fall of the "Evil Empire," pulled down all the old statues celebrating the icons of Communism. Cheerio, Joe; *arrividerci,* Vlad. But unlike their neighbors, they didn't smash them to dust to the delight of CNN camera teams. Oh no, they did something far more suave. The Hungarians carefully hauled their statues of the icons of Communism to the outskirts of Budapest AND OPENED A THEME PARK! You really have to admire them for that. There's always a line, but it's worth a visit at $8 entry.

The Turks, marauding, conquering people they once were, visited Budapest on more than one occasion, the last time if I remember correctly for 120 years. They did the usual raping, pillaging, and plundering, renovated the baths, but all importantly, brought coffee.

My guidebook was so overwhelming in historical points of interest that I became nauseated and discarded it. All I kept was its list of recommended coffee houses. In those early days I obediently did the rounds and paid extravagant prices—by local standards. The list promised "old ladies in fur hats... writers... intelligentsia..." Oh, dear. They were all there, plus busloads of tourists; pot-bellied, greasy-haired men in dark suits; and my personal favorite, high-class hookers. A real *Muppet Show.* And everyone high on copious quantities of *kavet.*

I tried not to take it personally when waiters sighed at me returning to their establishment. They were used to once-off tourist custom and weren't interested in familiarity. I took it as a compliment; I'd shaken off my tourist mantle.

I found a place outside the guide in Buda. It was on my way to school, and I loved to stand at the bar and watch the trams come and go. Soon, like the locals, I looked up when the tram drivers rang their bells to signal end of shift. Shortly after, in they'd come, cursing the cold (I think) and stomping snow from their boots. They served coffee in shot glasses because they had to. Porcelain was expensive and in short supply. And the sawdust on the floor was not just decorative. People drank till they were sick and, I learned, vomit on sawdust is conducive to brushing.

There was a small transistor radio behind the bar, which could occasionally be heard above the rush of the numbers 4 & 6 trams on the avenue. More often than not the radio sounded like a leg of lamb crackling in an oven between Hungarian folk songs. And though I'm sure nobody understood a word, there was much tapping of feet when Sheryl Crowe stormed the airwaves, even of the Hungarian folk station, with "all I wanna do is have some fun, I get the feeling..." During the six months in Budapest, I added a new word to my (English) vocabulary and used it often: "Incongruous." Before then, I'd only read about it.

They called it "The worst Winter in a generation." No holds barred, textbook—or rather, picture-book—stuff. A meter and half of snow fell in a day. The omnipotent snowploughs worked with messianic endeavor. Having diverted the snow east and west, crews of men and women, yes, men *and* women, shoveled the snow into trucks with a gusto reminiscent of me with a spoon left alone with a Baked Alaska dessert. I liked to think they ferried the snow off to children in more temperate climates where it was scarce. Or maybe they were building a monster snowman out at the statue park. "On your left Vladimir Iliych, known as Lenin, on your right, for a short time only, Frosty the Snowman."

The snow carried gentleness. For the first time it made sense that the first flower of Spring should be the snowdrop. The lingering memory of the Real McCoy. Marta, my personal oracle, informed me that every snowflake is unique. Apparently if melted and then refrozen, it will revert exactly to its original crystal form.

Quayside cafés, galleries, and antique shops were just the ticket for my hunger and curiosity. I had, after all, spent the previous 12 months (according to *The Rough Guide*) "in the dullest, grayest, most boring city in the western hemisphere," Frankfurt. It's changed, Frankfurt, in the intervening years, a little.

One snowy afternoon I wandered around the Alliance Francaise, the bastion of Frenchness abroad. A photo exhibition lauded the musicality of the nomadic Romany people of Central and Eastern Europe. Their proud faces couldn't hide the confusion that someone with a camera should be interested in their antique violins and beat-up saxophones. Their soundtrack was the history of their travels, yet all I could hear was snow, snow, snow.

In the toasty heat of the cafeteria, I indulged my lust for poppy-seed pastry and looked out over the city. By and by a guy asked if he could join me. He introduced himself as the Ukrainian attaché to Hungary. He even offered his card. He seemed like a nice young man. Out of politeness I wouldn't have refused, but anyway scanned the tables around me for open space. I hadn't noticed the place filling up, and nodded my ascent. Andre didn't seem familiar with small talk. "Are you lonely? I like your accent," and yes, "Do you come here often?" I wondered how well his approach reflected the state of flirtation in the former Soviet Union. He baited me with a ticket to the recital that was about to begin in the auditorium. He wasn't really my type (being male), and despite not normally being such an easy touch, I acquiesced. So what? Okay, I was lonely, and flattered.

I wasn't questioning my sexuality, at least not at that point. No, I didn't get worried until 40 minutes into the recital when a balding, middle-aged cello player, from 200 yards away, gave me an erection. Yes, I know, I gave myself the erection, but the cello played its part. I became aware of the people around me. I think I sighed. The lady on my right fidgeted. Andre came closer. My vision narrowed. I felt his arm against mine. Turning my head 90 degrees, I looked at him and saw three blackheads on his cheekbone. He patted my hand, which was clenching my knee. Hurriedly, and not eloquently, I clambered across the row of people into the aisle and out through the exit. I heard the audience break into applause and told myself repeatedly they did so because the concert was ending. I didn't look back till I was home. Dvorak would never be the same.

Of course my actions reflected an innate lack of maturity in dealing with anything outside my regular scope of reference, and as ever when an incident came along I felt uneasy with, I did the Quinn Thing... tucked it neatly away in the recesses of my cerebrum, and went back to the mediocrity of daily routine.

This wasn't difficult as I was at school most of the day. I enjoyed Language Acquisition class and how babies mistake birds for dogs and clouds for grandmas, but otherwise I wasn't learning a whole lot. Plus all my peers and tutors insisted on using textbook grammar. So I wasn't having a particularly good time. And most of the food in the vicinity was deep-fat fried. In high school I played my role of empty vessel stoically—just fill me up with all the garbage necessary to pass the test, leave me alone, and I'll go learn it. Here, however, tutors feigning interest in my opinions took a certain amount of readjustment.

Looking back, it would have been a richer learning environment if they'd just cut the adult democracy bullshit and said, "This is the way it is, accept it, learn it, and you might pass the exam." People generally decide I'm flaky when they realize my opinions change with each passing cloud. My Budapest tutors saw this as craziness, provocation, learning difficulties, or as an amalgamation of all three. I was there to play their game, but they weren't very forthcoming with the rules of engagement.

We were 12 in the class, all of us drop-outs or fall-outs from other disciplines. Tinker, tailor, journalist, sex slave, fisherman, lawyer, architect, thief. Normally this might be considered a good recipe for cocktail conversation, but we were all too self-important and constipated to exchange anything more than pleasantries and feedback on course-related material. Yawn.

A wolf escaped from the zoo around this time, and everyone had a theory as to where the fugitive might be hiding out. As the bars of his cage were bent inwards, it was thought he may have had an accomplice. I remember the incident so well because it was one of the few times we discussed anything as a group. The wolf turned up in the statue park, scared out of his wits.

Of the group of 12, I got on best with Sebastian. We were the only partnerless two, so we made an effort to take in some sights together. We walked, talked football, and swallowed lots of *kavet*. Then, quite suddenly one day, we were comfortable sitting in silence with one another. He had one of those English public school accents that could only have been acquired at the best grammar school. He was, in his own way, borderless. Daddy had represented the British Council abroad at least all of Sebastian's life. Ex-empire-trotting for Queen and wanderlust. We covered a lot of ground. Budapest is a shoe-friendly kind of place. We even found a bar called "Champions," which of course, as the name suggests, was full of losers.

The snow moved on, the rains came. Seb and I watched. There were days the world was but a rainy windshield. Colors ran into each other until everything around was one great gray mass, and the Danube licking its sides our liturgy. Recipes brewed inside me of the most nutritiously delicious ingredients: two cups of lust, a smattering of love, a waitress's furtive glance, a pinch of tease. Simmer till you're in a frenzy, then let it set. Rain does that to me. There were hours in those rains I longed to hold Andrea and, together under an umbrella, hurry across a busy Avenue in Spring's growing light. And laugh until forever came.

Seb and I finally found "Sixtus Kapolna," the Sistine Chapel, the place that was to become my emotional El Dorado for the duration of my stay. It wasn't easy to find, and they didn't advertise. And anyone we met who'd heard about the place had never actually been there. It was beginning to acquire mythical proportions. At one point we'd decided it was in fact a rumor. Who would have the tenacity to find the place? Certainly not drunks. Eventually Marta the Oracle drew me a map and told me to trust it when I met "nameless streets." And as ever, she knew best.

Sixtus had a short but colorful history. It was smack in the middle of the Jewish quarter. In the name of decorum, the proprietors, Oran and Hans, had been asked by the local rabbi to remove the name sign hanging out front. And so it would remain, nameless and inconspicuous. Oran and Hans were a testimony to Irish-Dutch friendship, if ever there were such a thing. They both spoke flawless English but nevertheless chose to speak Hungarian to each other. It was but a mild peculiarity about the place. It was like they didn't understand what a weird and difficult language Hungarian was. They opened their mouths, and out it poured:

"*Yo nappot kivanok, hogy vagy?*" Which means, "Hey, what's up?" See?

Sixtus Kapolna is where I met Judit. She didn't so much as catch my eye as disembowel me with a glance from across the bar. I was distracted, in trouble right from the start. She had those eyes, dark like night, and a warm embrace. Though I didn't know about the embrace then. But still I was determined: there'd be no involvement, no distraction. *Affairs of the Heart* was not on the syllabus.

Next time I saw Marta, she confided, for no apparent reason, that Hungarian women are perhaps even more beautiful than Slovenian women, but automatically gain 300 lbs on their 30th birthday, and I had better be warned.

"What, what?" I asked her.

"I see it in your eyes, my friend."

A month or more after the embarrassing cello incident with the Ukranian attaché, I sat in Boris's kitchen, waiting as he printed me a counterfeit train ticket to Bratislava. I'd wanted to go there from the moment I'd heard the name. A regular ticket was within my budget, but cloak and dagger normally wasn't.

Boris spoke all the time and smelled like the underside of a bridge. The question "sweat or pee?" was continually on my mind. I still wonder what language it was he spoke. He offered me a slug of a yellow liquor, but I refrained. He seemed to be just about finishing, the ticket and the bottle, when the cello-thing started over. How embarrassing. I hadn't given it any thought since the evening with Andre. It's a Quinn Thing.

Boris smiled coyly, seeming to sense what was going through my mind, or rather groin. He revelled in my shortness of breath, which I hoped was my asthma. He winked at me, then nodded at a photograph on the wall of a woman I supposed to be Mrs. Boris. He swayed and hummed, and only then did I realize that the music was not coming from some threatened area of my skull. It was a couple of floors up in the courtyard. Relief! I smiled and heaved a joyous sigh. Boris laughed. I wasn't the pervert I'd feared myself to be. Cello music turned me on, that was all, perfectly normal, nothing to worry about. Perfectly normal.

I moved closer to the kitchen window overlooking the courtyard. I opened it and caught a breeze full of Debussy's "The Girl With The Flaxen Hair."

God, I laughed. I pointed a couple of floors up and did a Marcel Marceau with cello. None too impressed, Boris tutted, wagged a hairy finger across my face, and proceeded to do a much more credible impression. He turned his head high and left, clenched his eyes shut, squatted low, and with pearls of sweat across his face, he pulled an imaginary bow left, right, and left again. Then, regaining his usual slovenly posture, he took a step back, bowed until his forehead touched the ground, and fell over.

I applauded enthusiastically, but he actually got quite a bad carpet burn down one side of his face. He seemed a little offended when I interrupted the build-up to his next impression, which may have been a plumber. I'd loved to have stayed and played charades, but, well, I don't play charades with guys named Boris in the early afternoon, at least not when sober. He was good, though.

As I left, Boris looked wistfully into the courtyard and sighed a long, lustful "Juuudiiiit." I understood two words from his next half dozen sentences. "Sixtus Kapolna." One and the same. Stunned, happily stunned, but stunned nonetheless, I gesticulated skyward, repeated "Judit" and "Sixtus Kapolna" in as good a questioning tone as I could muster in Hungarian. Boris nodded affirmation, slapped me on the back a couple of times and pointed an ink-stained finger into my face. Suddenly I felt much better about my cello fixation. I didn't exactly leave Boris with a spring in my step as freak snowstorms had again hit the city the day before. Treacherous ground. Yesterday's snow, tomorrow's black ice. When I did invariably lose my footing, I fell head over heels. But that was much later.

I never made it to Bratislava, by the way. The counterfeit ticket expired six months later, in so far as counterfeit tickets ever expire, but I couldn't bring myself to throw it away. Memorabilia of time well spent.

No question of involvement, no distraction. I was in Budapest to learn, or at least to pass an examination. No affairs, no *Affairs of the*

Heart. An innocent inquiry later and I knew that Judit was very much recently single, but not on the lookout for the type of male companionship that might lead to the exchange of bodily fluids. This I could deal with. I was okay with it, really. I would not become involved. Nor would she. But God.

So I sat at the bar for months and tried not to watch her. I looked at her, that was all. As discretely as my eyes would let me. She became an aftersight, background to my musings. The bar was made of black marble and generally I could restrict my gaze to her reflection there. Each day we had the same exchange: "Hi" "Kavet?" "Thanks." "There you go." "Thanks." "No problem." And later, *Mage edge?*" "Thanks." "Here you go. "Thanks." "Welcome."

The break from Andrea was doing us both good. We wrote and called regularly, had stopped reprimanding each other, and actually discussed things as we once used to: art, history, literature, biology, technology, archaeology, politics, combustion, astro-travel, psychiatry, economics, dentistry, and American foreign policy in the former Yugoslavia. We often disagreed, but we were remembering to respect each others' opinions. Once, taking shelter under a shop's canopy, I mistook tears in my ears for raindrops. There in the shop-front display was a bottle of the perfume Andrea used. It brought her flooding into me. I missed her then; I miss her still.

Seb became fed up of over-frequenting Sixtus and absconded to the arms of Fran. Women loved to ponder what might be the cause of the faraway look in his eyes. I knew it was his long-suffering soccer team, Queen's Park Rangers, though of course I told no one. Fran had a wonderful laugh, wore Doc Martens, and had a shadow-friendly face. She was quite a catch, though probably he was, too. I was happy for them to have found each other in the midst of the multi-million conurbation.

So I was left alone to make the trip from hilly Buda where I spent my days to my evenings in the flatlands of Pest.

While keeping Oran company in Sixtus one afternoon, Judit arrived through the door. "Kevin," she said, "please help me." She held out an earring and pointed an ear at me. I took the earring and brushed her hair over her ear with the outsides of my fingers, running it along the rim of her ear till I finally held her earlobe between my index finger and thumb. I inserted it and returned the hair to where it had previously fallen. The shadow of the earring swung to and fro on her neck. She tilted her head slightly and looked far inside me. A moment before, Oran and I had been discussing the importance of mythology to everyday life, I think. Now his silence was an intolerable din. I remember I squinted and bit my lower lip. She said, "Thank you," as if I'd just saved her from a burning car wreck, turned, and left.

Oran never said a word. He pulled up a stool, rolled a cigarette, and handed me his tobacco. We sat and smoked. Words were futile. Now we were three. Three minutes earlier I'd been alone.

When I was 16, I fell in love with Nastassja Kinski. I'd just seen her in Polanski's "Vampire" thing and developed an ever-so-acute dose of infatuation. She would have been 22 at the time. Now she's 40 and has three kids. Of course I'm happy for her, I just wonder what might have been if ever we'd had a chance. Having a crush back then was difficult. Today it's eeeeasy. Thank the Internet. Everyone's got half a million websites. Back then we didn't even have foreign newspapers. And there was no "Breaking News" on CNN. In fact, there was no CNN. Yes, I know it's a difficult thing to imagine. It all took place in your head. And dreams.

All I'm saying is, I recognized the symptoms.

In the weeks that followed, Oran shared our secret with respectful silence. If more than four people gathered into the bar including myself and Judit, he would distract himself, so long as there was quiet. Polish a glass, write a letter, and occasionally to the consternation of thirsty guests, go for a walk.

The silence grew, and only three of us knew what it was. It became contagious, and far from complaining, people seemed to enjoy it. People spoke about it elsewhere, the silence that had fallen on Sixtus

Kapolna. Orders were whispered, sometimes pointed, conversations became muted. Nobody asked why. And it was good for business. A quiet bar.

It didn't take long before two other bars had opened in the vicinity with this "theme" in mind. The first was called "sssshhh," the second I don't recall. They had strippers and tequila nights, neither of which was particularly conducive to... well, you get the picture.

By the time my exams came around, I was actually beginning to believe I might pass. I didn't, of course, but I thought I had a chance at the time. Could be my diet played a part. Apart from coffee, the only solids I remember ingesting in my last two months in Budapest were chocolate-coated cottage cheese bars (*toros*), which I highly recommend, and *kavet* cookies.

I also made friends with a spider, a small one I shared my bath with.

It was my final evening in Budapest. My Austrian friend Phillip called from Vienna to say he was coming down for a cup of coffee. People don't normally cross international frontiers to have a coffee, but that's Phil. We hadn't seen each other since I'd kicked his ass at table-tennis two years previously.

I went to Kiraly station to meet all two meters of him from the train. As Hungary had once been part of the Austrian empire, he said he was having a "moment" after he got off the train. He lowered his head and muttered something only audible to himself. Then we hugged, and he said, "So Kevy, how have you been?" like he always does. As it was his first time in Budapest, we thought a little sightseeing might be in order. It was late though, so we didn't. His disappointment lifted when I suggested we take in a couple of Irish pubs and a pizzeria on the way to Sixtus.

It was busy when we arrived, shortly before closing. Oran had my coffee on before the door closed behind me. I introduced Phil around, and we found a seat out back away from the bustle of the bar. It was probably the Guinness in his veins that made Phil feel edgy about the attention people showed him. For a big guy, he enjoys a low profile.

I'd hardly mentioned to people that I was leaving on the next morning's 7:00 AM flight to Frankfurt, and when I did, they reacted strangely, starting sentences that didn't end. I hadn't talked about leaving. I'd been too concerned with being there. I realized that people would miss me, and I them, and I felt selfish at not having given them more forewarning. I had told Oran, and I could feel his recognition in his playing of all my favorite tunes by Sly & The Family Stone.

Shortly before 2:00 AM, to a chorus of disgruntled groans, he stopped serving, squeezed in beside where I was sitting, and offered me his tobacco. We sat and smoked a while as people started to drift away. Phil was engrossed in conversation with two very beautiful Hungarian-speaking Romanian girls. They were captivated. One interrupted every couple of minutes to translate for her friend, who shook her head and opened her mouth as if to accept a ladle of soup, or threw back same head and laughed silently while holding one hand to her stomach. Phil was on a roll.

Judit didn't stop washing glasses when I approached where she stood behind the counter.

"I heard you were leaving."

"Yes. I just wanted to say goodbye."

"Goodbye, Kevin."

"Goodbye, Judit."

I turned to the door, wanting to leave, with haste. I was happy. There had been no famous final scene, no tears, no broken hearts. I wanted to board the plane right then. I caught Phil's eye, and he came straight over. Oran was behind him. It wasn't the first time I'd been last in the house.

"Time to go, I'll call from Frankfurt, thank you, thank you..." Phil pushed me out the door, calling behind to Oran that we'd see him in half an hour in "Piaf's," sounding like he'd been there a thousand times before.

Piaf, the little sparrow. The illustrious French chanteuse whose name hangs over a small club half a mile south. The club where Hungary's film and rock stars drank until prohibited by law.

Phil had decided he liked Budapest. In fact, he thought he might stick around a few days and check out the coffee culture. Vienna, after all, a 90-minute train ride away, would wait. "Vienna will wait." He repeated "Vienna will wait" 20 or 30 times, each time sounding different; each time there was something else to hear. I left that morning, but Phil is still in Budapest, six years later.

Piaf's was full of faces from Sixtus. One or two waved to us, and we made our way over to a table. Phil's fan club made space for us and introductions were made. I bought a round. The music was far away now. People wished me well. They told me to come back soon. They told me I was a fool to go.

I noticed Oran bouncing around the dance floor but not Judit arriving until she sat down beside me and everyone else left en masse. It was then I had the first inkling of a sentiment that all and asunder had been privy to the liaison I had believed to be taking place, to a large extent, in the privacy of my head. Their mass departure coincided with the drum-thumping of Iggy Pop's "Lust for Life."

"Hey," I said.

"What time is your flight?"

"Seven."

"Who's taking you to the airport?"

"Huh? Nobody."

"But that's sad, to leave alone. You seemed so happy here."

"I have been."

"Want me to go to the airport with you?"

Inside I almost nodded my head off in affirmation. Go, Iggy, go.

"No, Judit. But thanks for offering."

"Come on, it's already four, you don't want to miss your flight. "

With that she stood and walked to the exit. I was embraced in a monster group hug, lifted, and deposited outside. Nobody said goodbye. They waved for a moment and then were gone back inside to the life I did not want to leave.

Judit took my hand, and we began to walk. We crossed the Danube just as the enormous neon signs on its banks extinguished, as if in the reflection in the water below us. On Margit Island a couple were arguing in German. Not a good omen, I thought. For the first time in ages, I really wanted a beer. A fresh cold beer—or six, enough to take away my fear.

I opened the door to my flat, and in we went. I turned on the lights and started to busy myself. It was too late for foolishness. My heart was still intact, four chambers and all aorta. I was almost smug, not quite, but not far off.

Judit sat on the one chair in the place and pointed at my saxophone-case.

"What's in the box?"

"Oh, it's my saxophone."

"I didn't know you play sax."

"A little, and not very well," I told her, overplaying the modesty.

"Well, better a little than none at all. I play cello."

"Oh really? Wow, that's great! I had no idea."

The mention of the word "cello" made me want to chew my knuckles. I excused myself and retreated to the bathroom, where a quick change of shirt and a spray of deodorant awaited me. Composure regathered, I went back to where Judit was looking out across the city from the window.

"It's really beautiful at this time. We better hurry. I'll take your saxophone."

I closed the door behind us and put the keys through the letter box, and then noticed she'd been crying. I wasn't sure what to say, so I said nothing. I handed her a tissue, she blew her nose and put it back into the pocket of my jacket. I didn't mention it.

We took the metro from Bethyany to Elisabeth Square. I had loved to stand on the platform and feel the gale-force gusts being pushed ahead of the trains long before I could even hear them coming. I remember them arriving at acute almost-right angles to the rails, in a hurry. The next one was two and a half minutes behind, like anytime else, day or night. We didn't speak. We wouldn't have been able to hear each other anyway, but we didn't try.

At Elisabeth Square we had enough time for a final *kavet* before the airport bus left. A digital clock, moonlighting as a thermometer, told me it was 26 degrees warm and 5:30 AM dark. I was not so familiar with this time of day. My hearing was off, and words felt slower. It was going to be another beautiful day in Budapest.

The driver started the engine, and we boarded. Judit sat beside the window, and despite the narrow seat I didn't so much as brush against her when I sat beside her. Nobody's heart had been so much as bruised, though that was how the sky now seemed, bruised dark blue and purple. A rampant celestial bruise, a sky that spoke of hurt.

Outside the city, as if on cue, the sun began its ascent. Judit was relaying to me Oscar Wilde's "The Student and The Rose," I think. I wasn't really paying attention. Wilde boredom, and that from a countryman. No, I was enthralled by the choreography of sun and shadow taking place in the speeding bus across her neck, face, and chest. Light and dark dashed and bounced around her. The sun had finally found a worthy stage. I smiled occasionally or raised an eyebrow when she nodded to me. Once, she touched my arm. I know because I saw her do it, but I couldn't feel a thing. It was then I noticed the long black hair lying across her chest. Taking its chances to go it alone. I'll take it, I thought. And let my greedy fingers find their hungry way inside that shirt, to a throbbing breast and embrace it for all I'm worth, consume... but I didn't, it was too late for foolishness.

As the bus slowed and pulled into Ferihegy International, the great shadow ballet slowed before my eyes and collapsed into darkness and then light.

Departures, second floor.

There were a lot of private security personnel eyeballing those arriving and talking into blazer lapels. Funny how those not wanting to be noticed do so in such a conspicuous manner.

Judit went off in search of a restroom, and I checked in. Boarding pass in hand, I wandered around the check-in area without any goal, before seeing her, Judit, watching me from far across the terminal.

"*Szia*," she said after approaching. It always sounded to me like "see ya," but is Hungarian for "hello" and "goodbye." How screwed is that? Hello doesn't generally hurt so much.

"You checked in okay?"

"No problem."

"So, I better give this back. Don't forget to practice."

"Yeah, you, too. Thanks for carrying it. I'm glad you came along."

"It's not good to leave alone."

The planes above came lower, closer, closer. The air filled with mist. Then somehow my world stopped. It stopped, just stopped. The newspapers would report that the crop dusters released instant-freeze on an unsuspecting airport. Pigeons, trapped in the terminal, stopped in mid-flight. Announcements went unfinished. Drawn breaths were not exhaled. I turned all around. A passer-by smiled at Judit and me, perpetually. Judit blinked, and realization struck me with all the force of life's cruel games.

"Kevin?"

"Judit... no." I put my face in my hands and shook my head in wonder.

"What is it?"

"Judit, I'm really going to miss you."

For a moment her hair turned white and her dark eyes combusted into deep green flames. She smiled fire and nodded softly, and as the color came back to her face, she looked at me and said, "Same here Kevin, same here."

I heard my name on the public address system. The world had returned.

"*Szia*, Kevin."

"*Szia*, Judit."

We embraced. She turned. She was lost in the crowd.

I boarded flight LH3453 in disarray. My heart was full of confusion and my face full of tears. It quickly became apparent why there had been such a heavy security presence outside. In the first seat of the first row sat Diana Ross. I'd seen posters advertising a concert, but I wasn't a fan. At least, that is, not since the Supremes. But she caught my eye, took my hand and in a heartbeat closed my fingers around a tissue. "What's wrong, dear?" What's wrong?"

What... is... wrong... in a teary, snot-filled sentence I blurted, "It's okay. It's just an eyelash. I just have a lash in my eye, really."

But again, "What's wrong, dear. You gonna be okay?"

And this time, "I don't want to leave!"

She said something else, something I don't recall.

"The Scourge of God," aka Attila the Hun, died in 453 AD of a nasal hemorrhage following nocturnal passions with his new bride. I wonder would he have preferred the battlefield. Legends recall that he was laid to rest in a triple-layered coffin of gold-silver-lead, which was left to fall to the depths of the river Tisza. Though no doubt his remains will one day be found, the Huns, having killed the pallbearers, never returned there.

FERNANDO MORRO EMERSON

Diamond Subdivision

From January/February 2009

MY MOTHER SPOKE English with a Spanish accent. She styled her hair like Jacquelyn Kennedy's and wore fashionable clothes. I remember walking with her in a town square in Puerto Rico where shoppers milled, when a paddy wagon veered and policemen jumped to the curb. They swung batons at a group of shoeshine boys who dropped their shine boxes and scattered. I heard batons smack naked backs. My mother pulled at my hand, but I resisted—those boys were my age but they were different, darker-skinned and wearing ragged clothes. Running in fear. In the security of my mother's hand, I realized my state of grace in the world. A status I found out later could change without warning.

I remember my father with his widow's peak hair shined back, wearing aviator sunglasses and playing the bongos. After heating the drum skins over the stove, he thumped them to exquisite pops, then sat and pounded them with cool ferocity. Me, the toddler with charcoal smudge eyebrows, spellbound by his elegant mastery of brute percussion. I still wonder how a pale Anglo of English/German extraction could possess such rhythmic intensity. Yet, I realize now that his voice was his true instrument. He had a radio drawl that instilled calm, yet he could project command voice like a drill sergeant. Command voice moved soldiers through unholy conditions. His voice brought him far from a broken home in the broken American South. Moved him at the speed of sound.

With duffle slung over his shoulder, he reported to the flight line. Not long after takeoff he found himself strapped by the open door of an overloaded C-54 as the cargo plane strained to gain altitude over looming mountains. The plane skimmed slopes, evaded pinnacles, crossed voids. Word crackled through the headsets: they had to jettison cargo or they weren't going to make it. In the bitter cold windblasts, he and another crewmember heaved crates to the yawning gape, watched them burst on the rocks, saw plumes of snow fly.

In Germany some local nuns came to the Air Base to teach Catechism. Their faces were deeply lined. They stood in front of my fifth-grade class and told of eating shoe leather to survive as the bombs rained. They held ritual roll call. When the nuns called my name, I raised my arms to the light streaming in from the window and said, "Here I am o' lord," and felt embarrassed, but I obeyed as I had been taught.

On family drives in our black Pontiac, we saw token remnants of World War II: buildings shattered by bombs, legislated to remain rubble, to remind Germans of the price paid for aggression. My father parked at the edge of an overlook where we marveled at the Mosel valley, the gray curve of the river, the hillsides lush with Riesling grapes. Even in youth I knew to view it with a sense of history. Renewal in a land where men like my father had once rained bombs.

"If there is a heaven, it will look like this," my father said in an aside to my mother.

"Will we all be together in heaven?" I asked, standing between them.

He smiled and said, "You and your mother will be at the top of the hill." He used his hand to show a high horizon and then lowered his hand like a plane coming in for a landing. "I will probably be down here."

"But will you still be in heaven?" I asked.

In the Hunsruck Mountains, military convoys hauled missiles past farm tractors. The countryside smelled of hay and manure. In farm towns, bell-ringing criers shouted the news. Beyond the forested horizon another threat loomed. The nuns told us that someday we would be tempted to lie and steal and possibly in conflict, find ourselves swept into the madness of the most mortal of sins.

The Air Base waged Cold War against the Soviets. Each night, I lay my head on my pillow and listened as the bugler played "Taps" over the Giant Voice system. Soon after, a roar came from the flight line. When the F-104s fired their afterburners in the darkness and passed overhead on their way toward the frontier, I knew the nuns had it right.

I wrote a paper in Catechism entitled "The Valley of Friends and Enemies," about a timeless place where hostilities have ceased but peace does not quite reign, because there are things worth having passion for, even worth fighting for, but it is better if they are worked out.

Reginald would be in my valley. A barrel-chested, African-American Captain, he lived next door to us in the Philippines. He watched over me when it was my father's turn to go to Vietnam. Reginald took a baseball bat and killed a rat that ran loose in our house. Reginald tutored me in the strikes and blocks of Karate, so a 16-year-old boy could stand against the Filipino gangs of Balibago Angeles City. I never had a chance to thank him, for when it was his turn to go to Vietnam, he didn't return.

In Balibago Angeles City, days rose bright and hot, and nights fell to a black velvet canvas daubed in painted lights. Jeepneys and motorbikes rolled along an artery of broken mirror nightclubs. Capillaries terminated in guarded compounds. Diamond Subdivision was our compound.

One night, I attended a house party with Jeffcoat. We left the party and walked down a tree-lined street as Jimi Hendrix feedbacks faded behind us. Zinc roofs shone under the streetlamps. Bats dove into the cones of light and flew off. We were high on Darvons and Scotch.

We passed a bus bench where a big Samoan wearing a jean vest was hanging out with two girls. I recognized the Samoan from school. A gang of Filipinos that had been hiding in the shadows leapt into the street and surrounded us. I recognized them as Los Teenersbugs and the young man who led them as Reny. I had heard that Reny's father beat him with chains and that he sometimes went shirtless to show his scars. His hawk face and lean tension recalled a coiled cobra as he jutted a finger toward us and challenged us to fight.

"It wouldn't be fair," I said, "all of you against just us two." I could see there was no way out. I was glad Jeffcoat was there, gangly and tall as an adult. "Let me find more guys," I pleaded, "to even things out." A few guys had left the party but steered wide of us. "Hey, help us out over here," I pleaded, but they only moved away faster.

Reny kicked me in the chest, hard. I was shoved back, but fear snapped into anger. I lunged wildly at him and swung but missed. I was attacked from both flanks, and I vigorously blocked the punches with a degree of control. A punch I never saw burst my lip. I saw white light for an instant, then swung with a roundhouse that connected by luck. As they swarmed into me, I saw Jeffcoat break into a run. The son-of-a-bitch deserted.

I knew if I went down I would be stomped. I knew I had to stay standing no matter what came. I felt as if a wave were crashing over me. I heard someone yelling and saw the big Samoan approaching.

"I know this guy," he was telling them, "He's alright." The Samoan broke through the group, put a big arm around my neck and said,

"He's my friend." I felt dwarfed, dominated. He let go, and I recoiled slightly and wiped blood from my lip.

Reny's narrow eyes glittered. "You're all right," he virtually hissed. "You're all right with us."

I walked home alone that night, angry, bruised, and cursing Jeffcoat, wishing my father was back from Vietnam.

A few months passed. One Friday night a group of us hid in the jungle brush by the edge of the base where the Caraboa Bus Line (Caraboa Butt Licker to us) made a stop. It was a part of the base where thieves cut through the fence, so some nights the Military Police fired parachute flares over the area. We watched the flares drift in the darkness and rock the shadows of the brush. The police weren't interested in dependents inside the fence, though we hunkered in ambush. Our ammunition: egg, both hardboiled and raw.

Bayoni and Honesto were with us. (Honesto, whose father would one day be assassinated, and who as an adult would triumphantly step into his place in Filipino politics.)

The bus approached, a gray and red school bus with particleboard windows that slid up to offer protection from rain or slid down into a slot when it was hot. The windows were down, and along the length of the bus, elbows hung out. The GIs were dressed in their Friday-night best as they headed toward Angeles City with its Wild West nightclubs and bordellos.

I don't remember our signal, but the eggs hit rapid-fire with sickening crunches. Shouts and curses tore the balmy repose. The bus jolted to a halt. In the momentum, doors swung open. GIs swarmed out like shaken hornets, and we boys were suddenly running through the bush toward the NCO housing area.

I heard grunts, pants, and branches snapping behind me. In the surreal light, I saw a GI break out across a backyard toward me, when out of the corner of my eyes I saw something miraculous. The GI was at a full run when he was suddenly jerked horizontal. His feet flew straight out, and for an instant he floated suspended above the ground like a magic carpet. Then he dropped flat onto his back into the dirt, gagging and clutching his throat. It took me a second before I realized the poor bastard had been clothes-lined.

I broke out around the building into a quadrangle of town homes, and then I spotted Honesto, all legs and bounding up a short stairway of a home that wasn't his. The GIs burst into the quadrangle hollering for vengeance. I had just disappeared around a corner.

It wasn't until later that I found out Honesto had simply opened some stranger's front door, turned as if leaving, pulled a comb from his pocket, and started slicking the Tancho pomade in his jet-black hair like he was out for an evening lark.

"Did you see some guys run by here?" the panting GIs asked. Honesto was cool except for one thing. He pointed out the direction the rest of us had run!

Behind the houses, I led single file with Jeffcoat running behind me. I sensed at least three GIs gaining on us. I could hear screams and shouts, and I knew Bayoni was caught somewhere. I rounded a corner just in time to duck into the shadow of an elevated back porch. Jeffcoat burst around and two GIs grabbed him. I held my breath and made ready to lunge when something held me fixed. My conscience wrestled with duty, fear, and remembrance as I watched from the shadows as the two GIs punched Turncoat. I had gotten my revenge at a shameful cost.

It was rare that I would spend time indoors, but in our tropical home in Diamond Subdivision, I stretched out on a rattan chaise lounge and read my father's survival manual. I glanced up and through the window and saw our Philippine Constabulary guard by the wall at the end of the driveway, sitting in his chair under a tree and cradling an M-16. His face was bronze, his cheekbones high, his eyes furtively watching from the shadows. Another guard joined him, and the two lunched on dog meat.

I also read the log of Captain Bligh of the Bounty who was cast adrift by mutineers, and who survived in an open boat packed with crewmembers for 47 days. Dangerously dehydrated, some of his men drank seawater that proved to be fatal. What a mad hope for nature to dangle, afloat in a world where life-giving water is in reality undrinkable brine.

One night, I lay in bed, the ceiling fan rattling with the window slats open to the night air. I heard a sound outside. I don't know how I differentiated that rustle from the rattle of the fan, but I did. I knelt up in bed and pressed my face to the screen. All I could see in the backyard was a papaya tree and the high wall embedded with glass. I lay back down and stared at the window until a shadow moved across the slats and a face loomed in the window. Washed in moonlight, the face appeared ghostly. I froze and feigned sleep but watched through narrowed eyes. The face looked around. When it backed away from the window, I slid to the floor and crawled to my parent's bedroom. My father woke with a start, but in whispers gleaned the situation, and in one motion swung his long legs onto the floor and removed a .45 Colt from a night table. Wearing only dark pajama trousers, he headed for the door, but before he got to the driveway we heard gunfire several houses away, which turned out to be warning shots and a return volley.

A man operating a canister of anesthetic gas was apprehended and arrested. That man was our guard. A ring of guards was implicated. Wearing gasmasks, they had incapacitated an entire family in order to rob at leisure. A child with spinal bifida was on life support.

I understood appearances could be deceiving. "Look to actions for truth," father said, "not words." But I wondered how anyone could have seen the treachery of our guards. I suppose even Captain Bligh could have made the argument for eternal vigilance.

After my father had been back in the Philippines for several months, he came home one night, walked grimly up to my mother and spoke to her in whispers. My mother gasped. My father looked expectantly at me and then walked out the door. My mother approached me and said a friend who served with my father had left weeks ago to Thailand where he had been unable to connect with his Air America helicopter at Ubon. The man was one of eight men to load drums of diesel fuel into an SOS Pony Express helicopter and fly to a remote site in Laos, where they had come under enemy fire. The helicopter crashed. Three men jumped from the craft and escaped into the jungle, injured but alive. The other five men were burned beyond recognition. Who had escaped alive and who had burned was still a mystery. The news had splintered their family, and so my mother asked if it were okay if the son bunked with me until they made the identifications. She said the boy was in my class at school, that he needed a friend. I said, "Sure." Moments later my father walked in with Jeffcoat.

I had not spoken to Jeffcoat since the night of the bus ambush. There in the living room came the turnabout—security was a facade, and I found myself just as suddenly as Jeffcoat plunged into the valley of friends and enemies. My father didn't speak a word, which was itself a miracle. In my room, I indicated to Jeffcoat that he could take the bottom bunk and I would take the top bunk. I climbed up the ladder. Jeffcoat hung his shirt on a hanger, folded his trousers over the desk chair, aligned the creases with deliberate precision, lined his shoes up under the chair, and then crawled into his bunk.

We talked in the darkness about a cologne that was popular among the guys at school, Hai Karate, with its martial arts name and superfluous sharp, spicy scents. We talked about girls we liked and then about Liz, a 12-year old girl who was having sex with groups of boys in the woods behind the school. Not that we weren't as sexually curious as everyone else, but not so much so that we would take advantage of someone of such tender age, and we wondered how it came to be that she was so scandalously promiscuous, and what her father would do if he returned from Vietnam. We didn't talk about our own scandalous behavior. We talked about how it could be that Jeffcoat's father was shot down in Laos when the war was supposed to be in Vietnam. In the darkness, we strolled in the bright sunshine along the gray curve of the river in the valley of friends and enemies until at last we fell asleep. Days and nights continued to pass in Diamond Subdivision. A week later, the identification that we all awaited finally arrived: Jeffcoat's father was among the dead.

A few nights before my father left for Vietnam, he had a dream. He was in a coffin, buried alive. He began hitting his head against the side, determined to kill himself rather than suffer slow suffocation. He described this dream to us the next morning while standing on the shining clay tiles in the living room. When he finished speaking, there was only the shush, shush, shush of the maid buffing the waxed floor, her skirt hiked and held at the thigh, her bare brown leg and foot atop a coconut shell-half abrading the floor in a circular motion, shush, shush, shush.

My mother looked only at her husband of 17 years. They had been married almost as many years as he'd been in the military. He had been a loving father, a good provider who answered to a personal and professional code. I silently concurred with the look in her eyes. A few days later he shipped out.

My mother worked as a Nurse's aide at the Base hospital, assisting the wounded who had been flown directly from Vietnam to the advanced surgical wards at Clark Air Base.

Passing a door, she heard a voice call to her. She went in and saw a young man bandaged and propped up on the bed. He had neither arms nor legs.

"Ma'am, could you help me smoke a cigarette?" he said in a Southern drawl.

"Of course." She forced a cheerful smile as she plucked a Lucky Strike from a packet on the bedside. After putting a cigarette in her mouth, she lit it and took a puff. She then placed the cigarette to his mouth and held it as he puffed, removed it until he appeared ready.

"This is my life," he said. "This is it from now on. Forever. I have a car back home, up on blocks. I had hoped to restore it." He tried to hold back his tears. She struggled, having practiced being a rock of cheer, a fighting-back-bitter-tears rock of cheer. He finished the cigarette, and she laid it in the ashtray.

"Thank you," he said.

"You're quite welcome. You heal up now. There's a lot of people waiting to see you back home." She left to the emergency stairwell and behind closed doors, sobbed.

That night when we sat around the dinner table, she told us what had happened at the hospital. My father listened and served from a casserole dish into our plates.

"This war is wrong," she said. It had just slipped out. All activity at the table stopped.

"But mom," I said, "The teacher said we are supporting the South Vietnamese against—"

"Your mother has spoken, Son," my father said in his quiet drawl that this time rippled through me like command voice.

He looked at his wife, my mother. She pushed a strand of hair off her forehead. I could see admiration in his eyes. My mother had kept our home together the best she could during his tours of duty. She had kept herself productive at the hospital, kept herself fit at the base bowling alley. Whenever he returned, they danced in the living room and she taught him every Latin step the former bongo king lived for.

My father scooped from the casserole dish into her plate. "Anyway honey," he said, putting down the casserole dish. "I have to leave again at the end of the month."

"I know," she said, putting her napkin in her lap.

LYN FUCHS

Dying with Dignity, Mexican Style

From October/November 2007

For Whom the Bowl Flushes

MY LIFE IN Mexico began with the cockroach incident. First morning in my new home, a toilet wouldn't flush, and a rising desert sun promised to bake the unsavory contents. I stepped into the shower.

Shampoo had just covered my closed eyes when I felt the tile floor move. One eye cocked open. An antennae-waving mega-roach scurried frantically around my feet. I yelled. I danced. We were trapped together like Aztec prisoners in a stone ball court. As he darted up my leg, I jerked, flinging him into the nearby fecal stew.

Several deep breaths stopped my trembling. La cucaracha paddled desperately through putrid seas while I stood above in godlike indifference to his plight. His fate was not so special. For many, life is crappy and then you die. I came to Queretaro for such existential reflection, but first, I needed a plunger.

Took a taxi across town. Decals of the grim reaper and a laughing skull adorned my side of the windshield. Conversation pieces perhaps? Or maybe, while other cabs post assurances of the driver's safety record, Mexican taxis prefer to remind us that death comes to us all in our own time, thus the beer-scented chauffeur furiously street racing his amigos has nothing to do with it.

Ah, the philosopher/cabby. Stickers of Catholic saints nearly blocking out his field of vision offered further proof of his enlightened (if impeded) view. Now, that's faith! Plus, the white-knuckled passenger received a potent evangelistic pitch to make peace with his maker.

I disembarked at Jardin Zenea. Children strolled with ice cream cones, and couples kissed with uninhibited passion. Church bells clanged. The sound emanated from a stonework dome towering over the ochre-plastered Templo de San Francisco, which was founded in the 1500s as a convent. I descended into the dark interior. A gory, life-sized crucifix forced me left, where flickering candlelight revealed a chapel and an imposing glass crypt dominated the scene. Inside, an orange-haired, green-faced Jesus bled profusely onto his white-cotton death shroud, looking much like a reject from a bad CSI set. Revulsion outweighed inspiration.

Mexicans have an obsession with death that tends to mystify and mortify gringos. Yet, could it be our culture's ritual denial that is truly bizarre? I was determined to wallow in the macabre to find out. A policeman posted just outside the cathedral with pistol, automatic rifle, and ammunition strap reiterated that death is a fact of life the locals make no effort to conceal.

A Cock and Bull Story

Friday was National Independence Day. My death pilgrimage led me to the *corrida de toros* or charging of the bulls. Hemingway loved such bullfights for the romance. I was here because the sun also sets, and in Mexico it often sets blood red.

The crowd was mildly inebriated. We sat on brick risers between a dusty arena and a misty waterfall. Flamenco guitar filled the air. A black bull hurled itself into the walls as sleek men in gilded, pastel costumes tormented it from all sides. Snack vendors combed the aisles.

A blindfolded and padded horse served as victim for the bull's furious goring to facilitate its rider grinding a spear into the bull's neck. (This wound forces the animal to charge head downward and horns forward.) A thick magenta mantle oozed over taurine torso and coagulated on a yellow prize ribbon. Mothers chatted with babysitters via cell phone. The beast took on a glazed stare as bloody slather dripped from its lifeless, leathery tongue. Matador Fernando Ochoa stepped out to roaring applause.

El toro and *el matador* (the latter means killer) danced a swirling ballet. With each turn, horns and bulk passed within inches of the *machismo artiste,* who skillfully hypnotized a mountain of taurine testosterone into a delirious death cadence. The romance was highly questionable, but the finesse was indisputable.

The famous red cape conceals a silver sword. Fernando brandished it like a crosshair between raging eyes and snorting nostrils a yard away. (The fatal stab must be timed when hooves are together thus splaying shoulder blades.) Silence—the lunge, the strike, the collapse. This creature, born to hulking domination, crumbled finally into breathless submission. *El toro* had left the building. A pathetic bag of bones was dragged away with little dignity or notice.

Torrential rain swept in. The drag marks became a long, purple puddle, and the arena floor became a terra cotta swamp. A yellow bull stormed out with a raspy roar. Attacking his tormentors, he lost footing, crashed into a barrier, and broke off half a horn. His sound and fury signifying nothing, he now appeared an inelegant adversary and was soon replaced by a 600 kilogram, reddish, bellowing streak of anger who nearly hurdled the wall on entrance.

Matador Rafael Ortega took off his shoes for mud traction. Time after time, slip after slide, his lance missed the mark, turning all efforts to end the misery into meatball surgery. Japanese executives in cowboy hats clapped as if this was a new twist on Teppan-Yaki. The bullring became a lake. Rafael and apprentices retreated to high ground, where they discussed the logistical nightmare; elite patrons retreated to shelter, where they bemoaned the damp inconvenience. Across still-rising waters, a solitary clump of flesh occasionally twitched.

Were this Transylvania, the night's bloodlust would likely have been satisfied. However, this was Mexico. Our movable fiesta migrated to the crumbling stone bowels of an old Franciscan mission for the *torneo de gallos* or cockfight. (Perhaps, the Spaniards weren't such an obvious choice to "civilize" the indigenous peoples.) How do I characterize this cultural event? Picture 700 men with 500 cigars, 300 tequila bottles, and 100 women of the sort who become sexually aroused by homicidal chickens.

Amidst the smoky, drunken chaos, bets were placed two ways. Officials threw around a slotted tennis ball into which you crammed your wager, or spectators shoved money in your face which you were expected to match. Disputes were resolved quickly or violently.

The well-bred cocks were a lustrous green or red. Claws were accentuated with razor-sharp steel blades. Tournaments were a momentary flurry of screeches and feathers. Losers were often dead. When a bird survived, the owner orally sucked the blood from its throat to protect his investment. When both competitors were unresponsive, they were laid together and the winner (using the term loosely) was he whose beak hit the floor last.

Finding no thrill in animal cruelty, I was just about to leave when I noticed the curvaceous aficionado next to me licking her lips. "Well," I sillygized, "if animals are going to suffer, mankind should receive some benefit." Not all the cocks that parried and thrust that night had feathers, and that's no worn-out, wet and dirty bull.

Bootylicious and Decomposing Bodies

The following weekend, I discovered Mexicans not only enjoy watching death, they like flirting with it as well. Drove to San Miguel de Allende. This picturesque pseudo-authentic town keeps its rustic charms with a combination of modern zoning laws, tourist cash flow, and quaint shops run by bohemian foreigners. The authentic Mexicans, of course, are mostly busy in non-authentic places, hustling jobs to spare their children from quaint, rustic poverty. In short, San Miguel is theater, a place where white folks find burros and sombreros while brown folks elsewhere seek carros and cappuccinos.

Today was slightly different. The main drag was packed with rich boys in white shirts and red bandannas (*chico rico rancheros*) putting on a good buzz and awaiting the release of the bulls. (I'm not saying that youth is wasted on the young; I'm simply noting that some youth were wasted on the street.)

When the terrified little cows finally came scampering down the cobblestone, it was about as glamorous as watching tipsy Mardi Gras revelers dodging parade floats. The bulls tried their best to avoid the staggering morons and were generally successful. "Bowling for drunks" pretty well sums it up.

My flirting-with-death reference had nothing to do with these bovine/hooligan antics. The real danger was in the crowd. Each tiny side street held a standing-by ambulance and about 1,000 liquored-up *fresas* pressing against the barricade. (*Fresa* is Spanish for strawberry, or for a girl who thinks shopping is the purpose of life.)

The strawberries and I were quickly becoming compote. As I was compressed from the front ambulance bumper to the door to the gas tank to the rear wheel, my will to live and my will to be smushed to death by beautiful women struck up an internal dialog. However, in the crucial moments my duty to you the reader kept me alive.

Every few minutes, some unconscious person was passed back through the crowd. Without warning, an unsuccessful ambulance-climber sat on my head. She apologized, but this only confused me since it was pretty much the highlight of my day. I think I saw a bull running, but with my face plastered against the filthy window of an open rear ambulance door, it's difficult to say for sure. Next time, I'll play it safe and run with the bulls.

With near death and animal death behind me, I felt prepared for something truly hard-core. Time for another road trip. My destination city of Guanajuato wasn't so much constructed as sculpted out of solid rock. From the subterranean labyrinth of stone tunnels to the stone palaces of historic mining barons, to the stone streets, lampposts, walls and bridges, this town was hewn to last.

Even mortal flesh lingers here. Guanajuato's ground minerals not only sustain the living, they preserve the dead. A bizarre sampling of pickled Homo sapiens has been warehoused to enlighten and disgust at the Mummy Museum. Thanks to many locals who can no longer afford grave rental for barely decomposing relatives, this establishment serves up a daily visual feast of peasant under glass.

I bought my ticket and swallowed hard. First came a black and white photo gallery where parents held deceased children. The poses were reserved, but the eyes burned with grief. Mothers looked stunned and distant; fathers seemed bursting with rage or crumbling with despair. A miner in a dirty suit cradled his sleeping princess in a white frilly dress. A circle of gaunt children tenderly supported their lost sibling's slumping head. This was life, the movie, not coming soon to a theater near you.

Perhaps using dead children for spiritual education props and pay-per-view entertainment is inappropriate. If so, someone forgot to tell the Mexicans. One proprietor acknowledged the tackiness, then pointed to hordes of foreign tourists, quipping, "Which is worse: to sin for pay or to pay for sin?" Savvy museum official 1, sanctimonious journalist 0.

The threshold of the Mummy Museum proper passed beneath signage reading, "As you see me, so you shall be." A faint smell of musty rot offered further forewarning of things to come. Inside, the walls were stacked with glass vaults containing leathery remains that once walked and talked.

A sincere but incompetent friend strove to translate the tour narration. Our guide would speak for several minutes, then my pal would say, "This is another mummy; he's dead," or "More mummies; they're dead, too." I abandoned the tour de farce for the company of those who say nothing but communicate much.

Some corpses were organized in bone rows by human hands seeking meaning and order, but most had succumbed under nature's hand into varying degrees of chaos—clumps of hair, sagging flesh, loose fingernails, deflated lips, shriveled penises, dried-up eyeballs, broken-off toes, and peeling-off faces.

A skeleton in pleated shirt and silk waistcoat grimaced the word "Nooooo!" with enough terror to make Edward Munch's "The Scream" look like a Monet garden. One resident in cowboy boots held a note: "Simon Lozano, miner, died 1900, exhumed 1907." How ironic to spend your life in underground darkness and your death under floodlights.

I stood in absolute horror before a woman with dusty, petrified labia, still-visible clitoris, tightly-clutched breasts, and head jerked back in an agonized scream suggesting that death and orgasm are nearly indistinguishable and the former may be more familiar to us than we wish to believe.

The mummies continued ad nauseum. A fetus showed an umbilical cord dried across a tiny chest. A baby in diaper and blue sweater with chubby rotting cheeks gripped a doll with its few remaining fingers. A blackened, crispy elder retained beard, mustache, and pubic hairs. A pregnant woman bore heaps of collapsed belly skin and breasts like dehydrated figs.

The sickening parade ended, and I finally emerged into sunlight. A street vendor extended arms loaded with toy mummies. I laughed in disbelief. "More mummies? More mummies? Do I want more mummies? Are you kidding?" I found a place to sit down and think about anything but mummies.

Christmas Greetings from the Inferno

The gringo/Latino death-perspective-gap can also be found traveling southeast from the Bajio. I arrived in Bernal one weekend along with swarms of tourists. The village had few services, dirt lot pay parking, and rental toilets with extra charge for paper. So, why was everyone there? Only one reason: Bernal has a rock. Granted, it's a big, beautiful rock with a stunning view from the top, but it's still a rock. Hippies and retirees flock to the rock and its reputed life-sustaining aura, whatever that means. Mexican locals are quite content to turn their backs on the monolith to welcome tourists with their life-sustaining aura of cash.

Nearly all of these visitors come to the rock through the junction town of San Juan Del Rio. Very few stop at the straightforwardly-named "Museum of Death," though admission and parking are free. My tour group included only young Mexican couples on what some would consider an odd first date. Here you walk across many elegantly carved rocks with mystical symbols. However, these are burial headstones. Rather than offering a panoramic vista, they provide only a glimpse into the abyss. Our guide expounded passionately on displayed artwork portraying all manner of persons awaiting their appointment with death. While most gringos are vaguely conscious of this inevitability, when it comes to metaphysics, we prefer less talk, more rock.

I returned to Queretaro on Sunday night to learn that even Christmas can't escape the kiss of death in Mexico. Though still early in the season, the main plaza had transformed into an elaborate, twinkling Navidad display, divided into four quadrants. The first illustrated the star trek of wise men from the East, the second offered shepherds prostrate before the angelic messengers, the third glorified the baby in a barn lying in a manger.

With this totally unsecularized presentation, readers may wonder if the city fathers provided anything relevant to those of other faiths or none. Why, yes, they did. The fourth quadrant portrayed a flaming hell with the damned in eternal death surrounded by 12-foot-tall nightmarish demons.

Now, if you're a little shaky on the connection between tidings of great joy and tidings of your ass is grass, I'm with you. However, one needed only scan the beaming faces packing the square to see that most locals were quite comfortable with a yuletide admonition of "Joy to the world, or else." Don't tell Bing Crosby, but not everyone is dreaming of a white man's Christmas.

Come Wednesday, death made another appearance on an even less expected occasion. Have you ever been to a children's birthday party where you felt like killing a couple of kids? Who hasn't? Yet, only in Mexico have I seen the deed actually done.

Preparations began six hours before celebration time. Two woolly, bleating kids were tethered to a tree. Suddenly, one was seized, its legs bound with coarse, biting rope. A knife was inserted by a neck jab you could feel; then came a shocked convulsive squirm, a dramatic sigh with a simultaneous expulsion of poop pellets, a mixture of drowning and breathing from the neck gash, a bucket filling with goopy cherry-red blood, a woozy docile resistance followed by unconscious reflexive resistance followed by stillness.

The sibling stood by waiting his turn as obliviously as most of us do. The bloody knife lay on the cream tile looking like a movie poster.

When a stick was thrust up the lifeless hind leg, long-closed eyes horribly snapped open. Using this entryway, the carcass was blown up like a raft to separate the meat for butchery. The dead animal was then hung from a hook with the head dragging clunkily across the stones and a gaping white aorta dripping like PCP pipe.

The inflators spit the bad taste from their mouths while I wondered if I should do the same. Our sibling sensed something negative and preferred to face the other way. Don't we all? Behind patio-door glass, a three-year-old brown face was sobbing. I assumed she was weeping for the kid; turned out she was crying because she had wanted to see. Perhaps aversion to death is learned, not inborn.

The distilled blood was cooked with chilies, onions, herbs, and green tomatoes to make taco filling. The flesh and bones were grilled over a pot of garbanzos, potatoes, carrots, and onions, resting on white hot coals in a stone pit. This was covered with maguey leaves, plywood, and finally a mound of dirt. Four hours later, the pile was shoveled off to reveal succulent meat and zesty consommé.

A long fiesta table was spread over the spot where the killing took place. Small burgundy stains under the chairs went unnoticed. The greasy broth, served with chopped onions and cilantro, was strong as goat gravy mixed with sheep bathwater. The solidified-blood tacos had virtually no flavor, for which I was truly grateful. Our sacrificial lambs even attained an afterlife in the many photos of guests gnawing bones. A fly-covered bucket of hooves and organs, abandoned off to one side, comprised the final frame in my memory—a birthday, a deathday, a normal Mexican day.

Gettin' Drunk with Dead Relatives

Why are Mexicans so unusually comfortable with death? One possible reason is that they are less likely to die alone or forgotten than their northern counterparts. Death, like everything else here, is a family affair.

On November 2nd, the Day of the Dead, I went with a friend's family to a little town called Pueblito, which means "little town." The cemetery was packed with crowds of people and rows of porta-potties. Carnival-like vendors sold fresh bouquets and chocolate skulls. We negotiated the maze of above-ground cement rectangles, some of which were being lovingly painted and others of which were serving as picnic tables, to their grandather's plot. After arranging flowers and reciting rosaries, we sat on grandpa's grave to play guitar and drink *pulque* cactus beer. (The man resting beneath us had died trying to cross a desert on foot into the US. How dare he scorn the immigration laws made by esteemed men like Richard Nixon and Bill Clinton in order to feed his offspring? I guess he got what he deserved.)

In theory, Day of the Dead is to remind people that life must be lived with gusto and forebears should be remembered with gratitude. In practice, it's more like a tailgate party on a tomb. However, compared to Halloween, where we introduce children to the occult while jumpstarting their diabetes, this is good clean fun.

I for one would be happy to have my bone box used for dining furniture or an accordion concert, if it helped the next generation view life more as spiritual quest than shopping spree. (I would also be thrilled to have this writing constitute a legal will, if it reduces the global lawyer population by one. I would thus herein claim to be of sound mind and body, but those who've read my work or seen me naked could easily testify otherwise.)

Liked the Holocaust? You'll love the Aztecs!

Another likely contributor to the Mesoamerican death fetish is the longstanding local tradition of brutality and slaughter. Regional history somewhat resembles the Mel Gibson flick. Plus, don't tell Mel, but the Mayans were sissies compared to the Aztecs.

One lazy afternoon, I stood inside the Pyramid of the Feathered Serpent Quetzalcoatl at Mexico City's Museum of Anthropology.

Below me were skeletons of sacrificial victims wearing human jawbone necklaces—Mexico's answer to the Hawaiian lei. Spend a day in this world-renowned art collection, and you'll see clearly that the death cult has long been inseparable from Mesoamerican civilization.

Olmecs near Veracruz portrayed the death god well before 1,000 BC. Half skull / half face shamanic masks, along with evidence of ritual roasting, boiling, and defleshing cannibalism likewise survive from these early times. First millennium citizens of Teotihuacán dubbed their main drag "The Avenue of the Dead," then mass produced gleaming obsidian blades and needle-sharp skewers for daily executions. Early second millennium Toltec gave their reclining deity Chac Mool a belly bowl for stockpiling human hearts. (So much for those "wild fraternity ritual" stories.)

Just before closing time, I gawked at the famous Aztec Sun Stone, which celebrates the source of all life and currently adorns the ten-peso coin. Gringos like to pretend it's a calendar. Mexicans know it's a sacrificial altar. The center sun face has a knife tongue and holds two beating hearts. (Not so surprising from folks who roofed their buildings with skulls, covered every other flat surface with grinning death god motifs, and decapitated someone for each ball court foul. Even ratings-starved NBA owners haven't tried this.) The sheer number of Aztec altars that have survived time ravaging and Spanish purging boggles the mind, without even noticing the built-in drain holes and trenches engineered to dispense with an ocean of blood. Need I go on? Suffice it to say: death themes are as common to Mexican heritage as corn.

Mesoamerican history loudly argues for the brevity and tragedy of existence rather than happily-ever-after Hollywood endings. So, to some extent, omnipresent mortality is a permanent fixture in Mexican psychology. There abides a Sun Tzu-like conviction that death is coeval with life and to prevail without resistance is best. Still, my experience suggests a deeper and more current explanation for why these people stare death squarely between the eyes.

With Mexican Chocolate, Who Needs Peyote?

While leaving Mexico, I had one more sobering brush with death—death by chocolate. The day was scorching hot. My vehicle had no air-conditioning. The more delirious I became, the more determined I was to reach Zacatecas. Stopped for food and drink. The gas station had neither, except for the Mexican chocolate bars made entirely of cocoa, cinnamon, and sugar. I munched happily with no awareness of the dehydrating effects or of a fireball sunset magnifying through the rear window onto the back of my head.

Stuffed into a narrow canyon between craggy, arid mountains, Zacatecas often shimmers like a mirage. On that day, though, in my waterless, sunstroked state, it positively wobbled back and forth and zoomed in and out. Near passing out, I negotiated a one-lane cobblestone alley with cars parked on both sidewalks toward a hotel shown on my map. Dead end.

Backing out was impossible, and blacking out seemed inevitable. Could things get any worse? Suddenly, a street person, wearing an arm sling clearly concealing something other than an injury, stepped from the shadows and began urgently whistling for his accomplices. Putting a hand on my open window, he hissed that he'd help me if I'd just hand him the keys. I froze for an eternal second, wavering between fight and flight, until a police car lit up behind me. Ten minutes later, I stumbled into a Howard Johnson suite, threw up, and fell into bed.

The next morning as I loaded my suitcase, a passerby offered me $3,000 US to ride in my trunk across two days of desert and over the border. Imagine. He was willing to pay dearly for a deadly ordeal that made mine of the day before look easy. Why? Because most Mexicans are all too aware of what we have in North America: economic wealth.

However, little human cargo goes the other way, since most North Americans have no idea what treasures lie South of the Rio Grande.

Frankl-ly Speaking, Kevorkian Don't Know Jack

Friedrich Nietzsche said he who has a why to live can bear with almost any how. In concentration camps, Viktor Frankl confirmed this with his observation that those who saw purpose and meaning in life were able to face even a death of ultimate degradation and injustice. I've met Mexicans living in many degrees of pain and squalor, but I've known very few who face life or death without a belief that God is there and cares. In fact, if you confess to a typical Mexican that you doubt whether God exists or gives a damn, he will likely flash you the poor-pathetic-gringo-look and offer to buy you a beer.

Perhaps he has a point. While most Mexicans have little faith in the workings of democracy or the benefits of exercise, they pity the desperate fool who finds himself in a spiritual void. It may be that in our flight from moralism to unlimited freedom, we North Americans have sold our souls to the—well, of course, we don't believe in *him*, either.

In *Man's Search for Meaning*, Dr. Frankl contends the depression, aggression, and addiction of Western society cannot be comprehended without recognizing the existential vacuum underlying them. He furthermore suggests that the Statue of Liberty should be supplemented by a Statue of Moral Responsibility, lest freedom degenerate into a meaningless existence.

Ironically, while Latinos do a majority of the physical suffering in the Americas, gringos do almost all of the clamoring for the right to assisted suicide. In Auschwitz, Frankl conducted doctor-assisted non-suicides, dissuading comrades from offing themselves by helping them find meaning in all life, even suffering. If Kevorkian were right, then Frankl was denying people dignity rather than restoring it. When would-be suiciders argued they had nothing more to expect from life,

Frankl boldly suggested "life was still expecting something from them."

I came to Mexico with the gringo values of effective-time-management and cleanliness-next-to-godliness; I came away with a deep conviction that life and death can be faced with purpose and courage. John Steinbeck once combined a Mexican folktale and a parable of Jesus to caution that the pearl of divine and family love should never be traded for the pearl of worldly wealth and leisure. Mexican Don Juan DeMarco (Johnny Dep) similarly enlightened his gringo psychologist (Marlon Brando) that all the questions in life worth asking have the same answer: love. For some reason, most of my brown friends don't have to be told this. They know people need reasons for living, not just resources.

Heading North on the highway from Zacatecas, I watched red ponies grazing in yellow daisies and ashen burros slumbering among brown corn-stalk pyramids. Slowly, the cactus took over—blue agave, grayish maguey, pale green organo, and red-fruited garambullo.

To the physical eye, the desert is a lifeless place. When seen under the midday sun, it appears still as a corpse and dry as a crypt. Yet, locals know the truth. As darkness closes in, the coyote and the tarantula come to life.

Like the biblical Samaritan woman, ancient Aztecs found living water in a parched land. Beneath a forbidding surface, the cactus gushes with moisture. For those who endure prickly discomfort, it provides the vegetable *nopal*, the *tuna* fruit, and the beverage tequila. As people draw near to death, they often sense more life in this equally forlorn prickly place than meets the eye.

When my mother lay dying from cancer and diabetes, a doctor proffered her a quicker exit to avoid the approaching days of pain. Instead, she hung on and suffered as humans often do, until her children and grandchildren arrived by car and plane. Though I'm not suggesting Kevorkian's clients were taking the "coward's way out," neither can I endorse the politically correct notion that those who pass in agony fail to "die with dignity."

In a world where many suffer guilt from unresolved relations, my mother gave a precious gift in the midst of her pain. One day, dialysis became impossible, which meant that afternoon's 15 minutes of consciousness would be her last. I was choking and drowning on the knowledge that we were having our final conversation, but Mom simply squeezed my hand and spoke a concluding sentence: "I'll see you soon." I take her at her word.

Everything I know about facing death, I learned from my mother or those crazy Mexicans. *Gracias mis amigos, hasta luego mi mama.*

KATHLEEN McCALL

Sand Memories

From April/May 2002

My 11-year old daughter tells me, "They're making the airplanes fly lower now, since the eleventh."

"You think? What makes you say that?"

"Because I never used to hear them before, and now I hear them all the time."

Saudi Arabia, 1974

WHEN I WAS 17, I could do anything. Nothing frightened me. When I was 17, a world where they cut a man's hand off in the square below my parents' hotel was a play world, not real. I didn't see it, even though they told me it happened all the time. "Stealing is a great crime here," they said. "You can feel safe, you know."

I didn't feel safe in my long sleeves and my long skirt and my bandanna—all of it red to match the skirt, the long red print skirt I had made because they'd written to me, "Bring long skirts. It's all you can wear in public." I found fabric already gathered at the top and just stitched up the sides. Done. I would not be an Ugly American. I would not. I wore the skirt, I covered my head, and I did not know the red would scream my profanity there.

I didn't feel safe because they looked at me, looked at me right in my face, my profane face, the face I showed in their marketplace; I was alone, I was undressed, to them, naked. They stared and they talked to each other, guttural, as though my name was spit. *Hawadji*, they said. Infidel? White person? Woman who dares wear red and go about our market in her bare face?

But I was 17, and Allah was no God to me, and these were men who cut off hands, and I was *not* safe, and I knew myself a stranger in a large desert and very far away from laws I'd thought were written in stone. I had not seen they were written in English, until then.

I had a letter to mail in the *souk*, and I had some money, although it was play money—all reds and blues and oversized bills. We had gotten them yesterday from the moneychanger in the *souk*. He kept the bills on clips on a big board behind him. Thousands of dollars. "No one steals here." But I did not know the right ones, and I did not know which way to go, and to stand was to be stared at. The taxis did not stop for the white women, the bare ones, even though King Faisal had said they must.

A crowd of dark young men approached me. *Hawadji*. I heard them say it. Young men, dark-browed, white *thobes*, the white headdresses and coiled ropes we called napkins and fanbelts behind their backs. I had nothing. No words, no defenses. They closed around me, as we do not, here. They took my letter from my hand. And then they took my money.

They did not touch me.

They closed around me, and we went, swept without touching, moving me quickly in their deep, throat-clearing language, talking not to me since I was bare and uncomprehending, but to each other, every other word Allah, or maybe not.

They took me to the post office, and when the clerk told them how much for the airmail flimsy to home, they said no no no no—*la la la la*—and gave him less, and gave me back the rest.

And they smiled at me and were gone.

Can I put this flag poster up in my window?
Sure you can, if you like.
Why don't you put one up, too?
Because I am too sad right now.
Is that why you have just the candles then?

Zaid was Ethiopian. Or Eritrean. Or Amheric. I never quite got any of that straight; the politics were so intense and so compressed, like Maine hates Rhode Island. We were told she couldn't go home, because of politics. Her sister wrote her there was work in Jeddah, working for American families. It paid well. So she came to live with my parents. Her son was still at home, though. I didn't know why. She didn't speak of it.

She spoke a little English, and I spoke a little Arabic, but we didn't talk. I just said, "Good morning," and a lot of embarrassed thank yous. I didn't like her washing and ironing my underwear. I didn't like it that when I came to visit my parents, she had to move in down the street with her sister and just come in daytimes, while I slept in her bed under her Coptic cross. I was a young, rawboned liberal; noblesse made me blush.

Zaid wore white dresses embroidered at the bottom and no shoes. Never any shoes. She did the wash in the bathtub, holding her skirts high and kneading with her pink-soled feet in the Tide-foamy water. My parents had a washer, but it never worked. It was always in pieces on the stone tile floor, waiting for parts (yes, yes, tomorrow, Inshallah, tomorrow) that never seemed to come. I don't think she would have used it, anyway.

Zaid ironed everything. She was one ironing woman. When the power went out—it always did—she kept ironing, squeezing out that last little bit of heat, making it last. Sheets, shirts, underwear. Washed, hung on the back balcony to bleach dry in the Saudi sun, ironed, put away.

Her salary was nothing really, a tiny dipperful out of my father's salary. His salary was an even tinier dipper from the vast ocean of oil money that was washing out the old sand culture in those years, creating an urban desert, airlifting technology and dropping it right into the dunes. And those vast oil fortunes would only be a tiny dipperful compared to the loss of a son, I think. Odd commerce.

Zaid seemed to like us. Someone said Captain liked lime Jell-o; and lime Jell-o we had—she called it "jelly"—every day for a month. My father, no more comfortable than I with noblesse, ate it quietly.

She made us *ziggini* sometimes: cubes of some meat she bought in the market, simmered in a spice blend she had brought with her in a jar when she left Ethiopia. *Berbere*, she called the spice blend. She couldn't get any more, but sometimes, for us, she would open her precious jar from home.

Mommy, what does "civilian" mean?
Civilians are the sons and mothers and fathers and daughters of soldiers.

I have a tape somewhere, an old 90-minute cassette with only the scratchy first few minutes recorded. I recorded it more than 25 years ago, on a borrowed cassette recorder, from a friend's apartment balcony, at about four o'clock in the morning. I recorded it and kept it because it is haunting. It is music of the soul, just as is a Gregorian chant or a Southern spiritual. It is the calling of the Muslim faithful to dawn prayers.

In the cities now, and even then, I know they use recorded calls. But in the outlying mosques in those years, the *muezzin* sat in the tower, traditionally with one black thread and one white thread over his hand, and when he could tell the difference between the two, he would call.

When I listen to that tape now, I can see in my mind's eye the men moving purposefully out of their houses in their *thobes* and *ghutra*, moving silently across the dirt roads and the sandy vacant lots, moving toward the mosque to worship.

The music from even the farthest church calls us all.

LISA OHLEN HARRIS

The Pied Piper of Damascus

From July/August 2005

You will come to our home.

SHE SPOKE TO me in Arabic, in the imperative, her hand gripping my arm. I felt like a third grader trapped by a gang of playground bullies—no one could see my distress, surrounded by this tent of veiled women all wearing long black robes on a warm day in Damascus. I pulled my arm down and away; she held on and jerked back. They stood in a tight circle around me, touching my arms, my shoulders, reaching under my sleeves to feel my fair skin. When my scarf fell back, exposing my blond hair, I heard one of them say the Arabic word for gold.

I lived with an Arab family in the Old City and had been on my way home from the university, pushing through the usual crowds in the big covered bazaar, Hamadiyye Souk. There was something slick on the ground, a bit of gunk there in the *souk*, and I slipped on it. When I stopped to scrape the sole of my shoe, I saw that what I'd stepped on was a mouse—a dead one. It had probably been run over by a watermelon cart, as it was getting to be summer. I scuffed my foot on the ground with every other step, attempting to clean my shoe without actually touching it. The Old City was full of mice, and rats, too, I'd been told.

Hamadiyye Souk empties onto an open-air breezeway with Roman columns. Ruins of an ancient temple, the Temple of Jupiter, line the walkway from the end of the *souk* to the big mosque at the edge of the Old City. I passed the temple and started to cut around the mosque wall, over on the southern side where the gold merchants have their shops all in a row. Dozens upon dozens of 18- and 22-carat bangle bracelets, necklaces, and rings hung in tiers along window-length display rods. The jewelry formed glimmering curtains in gold so pure it was nearly orange.

Back at our Old City home I was forcing myself to read through a chapter or two in the Book of Exodus each morning, sitting alone in our open courtyard, my feet propped up on the side of our stone fountain. Seeing the windows of gold shimmering there in the market, I thought about those Exodus passages detailing how much gold was to be in the tabernacle: God was greedy for gold. It was a reverse-Midas thing; everything God might touch had to already be pure, heavy, glorious gold. Most folks couldn't even see the glory of it, though, because God ordered curtains of goats' hair be made as an outer tent over the whole thing.

The Bedouin live in goats' hair tents even today. They weave the coarse, dark hair with loose stitches, allowing for ventilation on the many hot days. When it's rainy, the threads swell and tighten, making the tent waterproof. But don't get the idea that the Bedouin are poor, because they're not—at least not all of them. These days, it's common to see a satellite dish nestled in the truck bed outside a goats' hair tent, generator humming in the background. And the Bedouin women wear plenty of gold under their robes, adorned like every Middle Eastern bride. It's a convenient form of riches, really, because you carry it with you. I never thought about gold much until I lived in the Middle East, where women safely walk through alleys and poor neighborhoods wearing hundreds of dollars worth of it. It's such gorgeous stuff. Perfect for the nomad.

I passed one shop window with necklaces crowded so tightly on a display hook that they looked like a rope. And this was also when I saw the group of women up ahead of me. They wore strange clothing, dark robes embroidered across the bodice. I could tell they weren't from Damascus. There were five women but only two men, all of them wearing wedding rings.

In Damascus, not so many guys took multiple wives, even though Islam and the Syrian government allowed it. It would be an economic hardship for most men, because Islam requires fair and equal treatment for each wife. If these robed women were multiple wives as I suspected, then under their sleeves each of them carried exactly the same amount of gold jewelry as the others, gram for gram. The women had been window-shopping when I first spotted them, but as I approached, they stared at my fair features, distracted from the rows of bracelets and necklaces and rings by a better prize.

Lost in my thoughts of gold and goats' hair tents, I bumped into one of the women and pardoned myself in Arabic before moving to go around her. She looked directly at me and stepped back, opening the circle to draw me in. I stopped instead of continuing on my way, and their black robes closed around me.

The woman I'd bumped into wore some kind of bright head wrap—a twist of red peeked out from under the black veil. And now that I was beside her, I heard the bracelets under her sleeves, dangling into one another, making music as she gestured. This was before she grabbed me, but already she was standing so close I could smell garlic on her breath. Her sister, or maybe a fellow wife, was beside her; I saw one of the sister's front teeth was capped in gold. And both of them had *blue eyes*.

Now most of my Arab friends were dark-skinned, dark-haired, dark-eyed. Arab coloring is a study in desert shadows: olive skin and browns and tans. I did see green or blue eyes from time to time, and it always surprised me. My own blue eyes come from a family tree rooted in northern climes of Sweden, Germany, and France. They're a recessive trait, European. But these women—nomads, probably— were part of the ancient Middle Eastern desert where the sun bakes everything brown. Why did they have blue eyes like mine? Though I was trying to think in Arabic, I kept coming up with the word swarthy as they jostled and grabbed at me. I thought of pirates and of slave traders. Now, what I'm about to say sounds like some sentimental poem I would have written back in those college days, but I can't think of another way to get this across. That woman's blue eyes met mine and held them, as in some fairy tale I'd forgotten. Her gaze calmed me, and again I heard the tinkle of gold bracelets under her sleeve. It was all so familiar. I felt as if down deep I had once known this blue-eyed woman, or else someone very like her.

I couldn't understand much of her Arabic. This language spans dozens of countries and cultures over two continents, unified, one like Allah, but still there are dialectal differences making mutual intelligibility tricky, impossible for even the native speaker. The effort of listening made me feel as if I were underwater, holding my breath in order to keep my focus. I felt dizzy from the closeness of black fabric and the heat of their breath around me. After each question, I guessed at the meaning and answered yes or no in Arabic. The woman was pleased. Delighted, really. She embraced me and then kept a hand on my arm, gripping. This was when I understood every word.

You will come to our home.

I could almost see the Bedouin camp where they would keep me hostage, everything so different and isolated and all out in the desert far away from embassies and other foreigners to uncover my plight. Why did she want me, anyway? Did she see something in my eyes, something of her own blue-eyed ancestry, something connecting us back through time and culture?

It may be myth set in the heart of history because the records are questionable, but accounts of the Crusades speak of children's movements in 1212, between the Fourth and Fifth Crusades. In France, thousands of children—young ones not yet teens—left their carts and flocks and whatever else they were doing and ran one after the other, swarming the hills, leaving homes and lands, journeying to Jerusalem. Whether their parents tried to stop them or felt their hands were tied by a divine call, we don't know. But the children went in droves, following after a 12-year-old peasant boy, Stephen, who called them all to come. History doesn't tell us much about Stephen, except that he was a skinny orphan kid with bushy brown hair and bright blue eyes. And that Christ came to him in a vision and told him to gather some friends and head on over to Jerusalem. The children—girls along with the boys—crowded after Stephen, following him south, toward the sea and the Holy Land. Meanwhile, in Germany, a medieval version of science fiction's parallel universe was at play as a second children's crusade formed under the spell of another preteen magic boy, Nicholas. The old Pied Piper story comes out of these bits of history, so whatever trick it was Stephen had up his sleeve, there was something of mystery or myth to him right from the start.

The children marched south toward the sea, expecting that when they arrived at the Mediterranean, the waters would part for them. When the waves continued to roll but no dry land appeared, some kind ship holders gave the children free passage, cramming ships full from bottom to top with these naïve—by now also ragged and hungry—European ambassadors. And of course the ship holders saw opportunity more clearly than the children did. The kids who survived the ride were sold into slavery in Egypt and the Levant, ironically living out their lives subject to those they thought would bow down at their own little feet when they entered Palestine. Their blue eyes still look out from Middle Eastern crowds through the souls of their Arab descendants.

In my own bed in our Old City home that night, I saw what might have been. I was the fourth wife, making the best of my misfortune. I would be the type to submit, not to plan an escape. Does that make me a victim and not a conqueror? Maybe all of my really courageous ancestors all took off over the hills with that kid, Stephen, pioneering to North Africa and beyond before they even hit puberty. They wouldn't be my ancestors at all if they were sold into slavery in the Middle East and married and had children and grandchildren until nothing was left of the European ancestry except an occasional blue-eyed child. My own forefathers resisted; we were left behind when adventure beckoned with blue eyes.

Meanwhile, the blood of my ancestral cousins—the ones who heard Stephen's call and followed—mixed with their dark-skinned captors, perhaps buying freedom for themselves and their descendants. Those blue-eyed sisters were just trying for a family reunion, and I had resisted. I liked to think of myself as an adventurer, coming to Syria as a college student and all. But I wanted my adventure in premeasured doses. I would have been the child left behind when the Pied Piper came to town. And what did those old myths have to do with my experience in the gold market that day, after all? Genetics and history and fairy tale—they all blend together at some point.

Even in my dreams that night, though, I heard the hidden gold and felt something in that woman's eyes drawing me, blue calling to blue.

But I still haven't told about my escape. It's not so glamorous, hardly even an escape, really. It might have been the glint of the gold tooth in the desert sunshine that knocked me out of my momentary trance in the company of those veiled women by the gold market. I ducked and pulled away from the blue-eyed woman. She held my scarf, and I let it slide off in her hand. It was a blue scarf with metallic threads running through it. I'd searched a long time through a stack of scarves in the *souk* to find the exact blue to match my eyes.

I hurried around the mosque, past the old men smoking water pipes at the tea shop just down from the gold *souk*. I looked back before I rounded the corner—to check and be sure one of them wasn't coming after me.

No one was there. They were gone, as if swallowed up by one of the stone walls. I don't think they could have all crowded into one of those gold shops—they wouldn't have fit. But somehow, when I ran away, they all disappeared.

The whole of Damascus, it seemed, was pushing past me. I stood still, the only one not hurrying off to get somewhere. This was when I noticed that my ankle was hurting—I must have turned it when I slipped in the *souk*, or maybe when I pulled away from the woman with the blue eyes. In fact, my whole foot was really tender and starting to swell. I couldn't go back and find those veiled sisters, even if I wanted to. My pace was too slow with the sore ankle.

As I limped home, I thought about the adventure I might be missing. Now the blue-eyed women were going back to their village or camp, riding in the truck bed and feeling the desert wind tug at their head coverings. They would tell tales of the pale girl with the golden hair who refused to come. I imagined them laughing and singing, and one of them tying my blue scarf about her wrist and reaching her arm up high into the wind, where the scarf stretched and flapped like a banner above as the black-robed women sped across the desert, gold threads sparkling in the sun.

MELISSA WILEY

Falling Backward

From April/May 2015

THERE ARE PEOPLE in love everywhere, you can't help but notice. Beautiful people, too, so many it leaves you breathless. Both happen largely by accident, though some irradiate their hair with debris from flailing comets. Why they take so much care with their appearance, I cannot begin to guess. Unless it is to attract a lover, here in central London, where each person is lovelier than the next. Because beautiful people can be as lonely as those who are uglier.

I say this as an American who wears too little mascara perhaps. Beauty has never been a factor in my life at all, I can say with confidence. Then I have hardly had the time for it while love consumes almost all my waking hours. With those remaining from all the love I give, most of it to strangers, I have had to buy groceries, then feed myself afterward.

When daylight savings time began, I went to London, four days before I met my husband in Lisbon. There are no Bibles in the hotels in England, in addition to cream that's clotted for scones tasting sweeter than muffins. Opening all the drawers and confronting only an emptiness, I felt the skin on my face begin to loosen, to unwrap itself from my skull like insect legs from a stamen with all its nectar eaten. The missing Bibles were not the cause, if still a comfort. It was more the feeling of eroticism they engendered. It's the only way I can explain why we bother to unravel, to look each year uglier and uglier as our skin grows looser. To meet any lover, I've heard, is to open all your drawers. To let someone you hardly know empty one after the other.

Americans must go abroad to feel at home and have done so for ages. Had Benjamin Franklin not taken a boat to Paris, we would not fall backward for an hour each morning every autumn. We would stand straighter, yes, but miss the pleasure of the collapse onto the carpet. Sometimes falling backward is as much a luxury as eating cake beneath a blanket. Because fall and you just might fall into someone's arms, even if they're anonymous. Franklin liked to air his wit in public, and so he was not long in Paris when he wrote that residents could economize on candles if they rose an hour earlier once the sun slept longer. He was only joking of course, though candles have no sense of humor. And so the world soon adopted a system similar to that used by the Romans, who deployed different clocks made of water for different seasons so the daylight would seem longer. The Romans, who agreed men and women should take public baths together. Who thought gods and goddesses sometimes slept with humans, so best perfume yourself with oils distilling the essence of herbs or flowers.

I spent very little time in the Tate Modern, though it was one of the reasons I'd cited to my husband for flying first to London. This while he worked inside his office with his fingers numb from typing. I spent far more time inside the gift shop than the actual museum, where I bought a print of a nude woman painted by Picasso—a painting, though, I had seen first in person. The woman lies supine beside a plate of apples while the bust of a man looks down on her, impassive. Her body is blushing the color of a strawberry sheathed in vernix while she is bound by two wide, black straps—perhaps they are leather?—one around her neck, the other below breasts dangling like pears with no skin upon them, the only feature of hers you see clearly besides a skein of yellow hair and the crack of her vagina, a slit without any darker hair layered over. Some might say Picasso rendered her abject and powerless, an object of desire bound by the man's gaze above her and the straps that seem to bind her ribs, keeping her from breathing as freely as she might have. Only, the man is made of marble, remember. He doesn't exist below the neck and has no phallus. No real eyes, either. He is equally naked as the woman, just less vital, with his hard chin resting on a pedestal.

Later, a man at a café gave me a free lunch in exchange for my smile, which he said was too honest to charge me for the meat pie I'd ordered with mashed potatoes. "I don't love you," the smile said, "I know you, which is better," as if I were the marble statue and he the woman naked upon the floor. Then I leaned back so he could study my proportions. Had I tilted any farther backward, I would have hurt my spinal column I'm sure, because I can only fall back so far. However much we may like to stretch backward, then slump alternatively forward like clocks bending with the earth's rotation about a star, the body is designed for the blood to drain from the head earthward. Fall backward at your peril unless you are a woman in a crowded room full of men who want to hump you.

I only wasted the money the waiter saved me buying myself chocolates, then a bouquet of flowers at Harrods an hour or so later. I put $90 on my credit card I would not pay off, not ever. The woman who sold me the flowers asked if I wanted them wrapped, and I said yes, because I thought a plastic, shivering sheath would protect them from who knew what dangers, the more so as a ribbon was also wound round their stems to keep them from straying into another garden. And on Regent Street where the Christmas lights were as yet unlit, the crowds were so dense I quickly realized the flowers—mostly irises, named for the eye color on your driver's license—were trembling and nervous. Rather than shielding, the plastic bag frightened them. But then I understand the fear of suffocation, how you can start breathing shallowly while there's still plenty of oxygen. So I soon untied the ribbon, then held them closer to my chest, when even the drumming of my pulse I saw made them twitch. And I realized the plastic bag needed discarding altogether, though I saw no trash receptacles. So I freed the irises the color of no eyes that were human and unwrapped them from their innocuous prison while pretending briefly to chase the plastic into traffic, until a family of too many bright blond children prevented me from being hit by an ambulance.

So with the plastic protective covering forever forsaken, I hugged the irises mixed with baby's breath of no babies close to my breasts. I cradled them on the Tube as if they were waiting to feed at my nipples, which were milkless. And by the time I reached the station nearest my hotel and walked past a passel of men selling soap made from beeswax, the irises were staring blankly, wondering about the etiology, then the purpose, of all this. The pupils were lightless while fixed on my profile, as if in blame for picking them in the first place. We were suddenly enemies.

My hotel room had only one trash can, beneath my bathroom sink. It was filled with cardboard tubes bloodied with the refuse of an expelled ovary, and to those I added the colored parts of the eyeballs of no one who could ever see.

I realized then I should have bought something more lasting, something that would grow dusty and fade with the sun that also bleaches our furniture, and which I could display for company. I might as well have stayed home for Thanksgiving rather than wasting all my money coming to Europe where the daylight ends so early.

All my possessions I have amassed indiscriminately and with no system of arrangement or labeling. I have collected nothing of things more or less the same. The best thing to have collected, of course, would have been the teeth of babies, if only to build a maw large enough to say everything that needs saying. And because I also know there is no tooth fairy. As it is, the baby teeth are decaying somewhere secretly, chewing no food, keeping no one from lisping.

The truth is I collect sunlight only, which looks all the same—it's only the clouds that change. Only I cannot keep it past dusk, if that late. I have to surrender the whole of my collection at the end of each day, which comes earlier thanks to Ben Franklin's need to regale the Paris literati. Had I collected teeth or even buttons in place of photons streaming from a star just far enough away not to boil all the skin off my face, I might have seen more value in saving certain pleasures for later dates.

There is very little pleasure to be had, however, while traversing oceans aerially, thinking happiness lies on another continent you will have to leave by month's end anyway.

After I had dispatched the withered bouquet, I examined my face in the mirror above the sink. I saw a large pimple below my lower lip, bulging with white pus pure beyond trusting. Only my bones could ever match its sterling quality. Then I remembered baby teeth might compete and give the pimple a run for its money. I never do get pimples except when traveling to other countries. Also, the window of my hotel room was left open by the maid, ushering in a chill that only made the pimple harden while I closed the curtains and watched the moon begin to wane. Because I didn't want to undress in front of my neighbors, though American women are known for taking sexual license when crossing continents. I have never been so deliciously cool in autumn, however. The sky is dark here by four o'clock. I almost wish it were sooner.

Any place you travel, even to your own home after a day of labor, is all by way of answering this one question: Just who are you, you sweet human? You're a very messy person who might be messier yet, is always my answer. Your pimples are cleaner than the rest of you, too, is common. This isn't quite what I want to hear, so I keep asking. Any answer that comes is always insufficient, too meager for so much drawer space when the word of God has left me free of all restrictions. But no answer could be big enough to account for all these thoughts and feelings, always boiling like water to cook something, yet still leaving me hungry. So I keep traveling, to places farther and unseen. Though this is my fourth time in London, no more than three days each stint, and now I've eaten twice in the same Indian restaurant, of which there must be thousands.

I knew it was the same by the narrowness of the corridor through which even one wide person could not easily fit, through which I had to turn sideways to avoid bumping into those tables nearest the doorframe. The waiter was different, I was fairly certain, from the time before, though almost as unsympathetic if not quite hostile to me. I looked prettier when I came in with my husband four years earlier. I must have, because I was younger. The first time the service was curt, we both noticed, while a woman in a headdress sitting across from me had the widest pupils I'd ever witnessed, and she had no irises—not flowers or the colored parts of her eye, either—the easier for her to swallow me with those wells of darkness that still swallowed light nevertheless. But she did not appear again, which would have been too much coincidence not to seem ridiculous. Maybe I was just too foreign. And knowing I had made a mistake by walking inside again, I ordered only an appetizer, which the waiter told me would be insufficient. Of this, I told him, I was already certain.

What do you call the inside of your elbow? The part that usually lies in shadow but when you extend your arm, its whole length looks like a bow strung with an arrow? Whatever its name, mine is beautiful. Its inner veins are patchworked close to the surface so they look to me like a daedal brooch you might inherit if you're rich. Perhaps the waiter in the Indian restaurant didn't notice them, though. Had he seen my elbows' interiors, shocking in their delicacy, like a species of coral, he might have given me water when I said I was thirsty. It is a beauty, though, people don't expect to see. Sometimes it astonishes even me. Even I forget to look for it, which is perhaps a blessing, similar to a Bible missing.

The museums in London are largely free; you only have to pay for special exhibits, those they take more time to curate and whose paintings they print on umbrellas and plates. The William Morris was among them, and I like his drawings as well as furniture from what I've seen on documentaries. Only I didn't know the exhibit was a special one—everything looks so splendid to me—so when I smiled to the security guard standing beside the entrance, he asked for my ticket, please. I told him I didn't know I needed to buy one, then whispered I was sorry. At which he rolled his eyes extravagantly, because I spoke with an American accent, which made me sound even less intelligent. Because I was not beautiful enough to face directly, and so his eyes rolled back inside his head, where he would no longer have to see me and could stare at his own brain.

So I walked upstairs to the main collection and stared at the only extant portrait of the Bronte sisters, with their brother smudged into an ocher vapor behind them. A man beside me explained to a woman standing to his left that their cheeks were flushed from tuberculosis. He acted as if this were a photograph, not allowing the painter to take any visual license. He also sounded erudite, at the very least confident. Charlotte, the one with the most rubicund complexion and to my eye the prettiest, died in childbirth, though, I thought I remembered from Victorian literature class. I dared to offer this to the man still speaking to his companion, but he said the cause was TB, madam, then turned to a portrait of William Thackeray and after that Dickens.

The man was wrong, though I was wronger. Charlotte didn't die of tuberculosis or of childbirth either one. She died of typhus while pregnant, and her unborn child died with her. Please excuse my poor grammar, however. Some things, however, are more wrong than others, though some people say there's no such thing as wrong anything. So long as you are still breathing. So long as you can make a living. Some people think money is everything, but I say dying. Were I immortal, I'd waste far more time adding to my sunlight collection.

And outside the museum, men were levitating. I walked round and round them and couldn't fathom how they had risen several feet and didn't succumb to gravity. And when I later described them to my husband, he said I must have missed the platform that connected supportive tubing through their costume. The platform must be fairly large, though, and I saw no such thing, I told him. There was, he said, laughing. It must have been painted to match the sidewalk, he added, when I felt as if I were the one sinking. I only hoped the floating men were comfortable, though, looking down on everyone, hanging like precipitation that never lands. When I walked past them and the lions of Trafalgar Square on which children were climbing, the walk was slicked with rain.

Walking past a family in Mayfair next morning, I heard a mother say to her young son that maybe next lifetime he would be an animal rather than a human being. A salamander, I hope, I offered in passing. The woman glanced at me strangely, squinting her eyes like Anne Bronte in the portrait at the gallery, olive and rueful to the point she began flushing and I feared she might be dying, but the boy looked hopeful. His skin shone with oil that looked less than human already. His face was dripping with it in the London chill, and he had no acne.

Salamanders never wear clothes, I'm sure you know already. They copulate in the open air or under leaves for privacy. Amphibians, they live half their life subaqueously. They are the only vertebrates to regenerate limbs lost or eaten by a predator—like starfish in that respect, only more free roaming. If you dip their bodies in fruit juice that's fermenting, you'll begin to hallucinate, which is the point, I'm guessing. Some indigenous peoples, in the Andes in particular, quaff brandy infused with the skin of salamanders for aphrodisiac reasons.

Meaning they could hallucinate to the point they'd make an ugly person so beautiful they would want to conjoin with them. Because desire itself is desirable, sometimes more so than its object. These are people who trust their intuitions, people we revere for ancient wisdom and whom colonial populations have all but decimated with guns and sexual diseases. No such men would have to drink juice made from the blood of salamanders to find the inside of my elbows almost too beautiful to witness. It is a wonder more people besides myself don't notice them. Sometimes we look for beauty in the oddest places.

I could have been a good tribeswoman were I born in a remote South American village, I feel quite certain. Instead, I am here alone in London, waiting to spend Thanksgiving with my husband in Lisbon, where the holiday goes unnoticed.

Walking to Paddington to take the train to Heathrow and fly from there to Lisbon, I saw a man talking to a manhole just opened. The hole was talking back and with a cockney brogue, lilting into a laugh. For the last two days I had spoken to no one except waiters and museum guards and was glad to know sewer systems were still convivial.

And while Americans everywhere ate Thanksgiving dinner with their families, falling asleep from mild tryptophan poisoning, my husband and I paced Lisbon's Museu da Marioneta, where I stood rapt watching a video of Hanoi puppetry. The puppets perform ancient stories staged on water when the rice fields flood traditionally, and as the video played on and fishermen jerked their jointless arms covered in silk thimbles, I stood waiting for the puppets to drown, though they kept afloat while rain deluged the museum grounds. There in Lisbon where the ants are smaller than they are in Chicago, and so I didn't mind them marauding through our bathroom. My husband suspected they had crawled inside our sheets and pillow slips, though I denied it when I saw them scaling the mattress, knowing that without his glasses they would blur into invisibility for him. When he saw some crawling on the sheet in the morning, I said they were only crumbs of chocolate I had brought from Westminster Abbey. I also tried not to look at them too closely.

Two out of three evenings in Lisbon we ate in the same tavern. We sat across from a fireplace with no fire, only charcoal, because the nights were not yet cool. All the lights in the room were glass turtles. At every table except ours the turtles were blue, while ours was tinted greener and looked quite natural, though it never moved. Electricity flew across a fraying filament beneath its shell mottled with iron webbing, and while we waited for our meal, I covered it with my palm, eclipsing the light while warming my hand a little. And no matter how tightly I held my fingers together, green light escaped between them, so that the turtle's shell was one carapace over another one, both fairly colorless because my skin is largely pallid. Beneath all, what luminescence, almost too much for me to witness. Like grass that glowed.

Then in Madrid two days before we flew back home, I saw a bearded woman in the Prado. It was the only painting I really noticed, though my husband walked right past her, breezing toward more Titian Venuses. I stood before the face of a man who looked elderly with a forehead deeply furrowed, but from his robes bulged a breast at which he was feeding a baby red as an apple. The man was a woman, though, I read, on the placard just left of the painting. The woman wasn't much older than me.

I have noticed my face falling, though. Farther toward the ground, as if it were reaching for sleep and had begun to dream of solemn things. For have you not noticed that when you are tired, you feel a stronger pull of gravity? No wonder the waiter in the Indian restaurant treated me as if he wanted to make sure I didn't return to his same establishment four years from now, though I now have no plans of returning to the United Kingdom—it costs too much money.

The special exhibits were all too special for me, and there was no bringing back Charlotte Bronte.

After flying home and falling to sleep eight hours later than I had been doing, I saw a man waiting for the elevator in my apartment building whom I hadn't seen in what he said had been longer than he could even remember. He lives two doors down and beside the bin where we throw our rubbish, and I had always assumed he was married, because his daughter wears a purple jacket and whose eyelashes look wet to the point of never drying. He asked what I had been doing, and I told him I had just flown back from Spain, where I had eaten tapas awash in so much olive oil they were practically drowning. When he asked me what city specifically, I told him Barcelona, as if there had been no London, no Lisbon, and no Madrid with its bearded woman, she who might be me if I only grew a goatee. Then I found myself blushing, for the lie that I had told for no good reason—God, how I loved Gaudi, I told him, while the elevator shot several floors higher, like a street performer rising within his robes— yet after I waved goodbye to him, I knew the lie had been spoken for another purpose. None of Gaudi's buildings had any corners. When time falls back an hour, you look for a softer landing.

And when I mentioned Barcelona, his eyes lit up with phosphenes darting antically through them. He said that of all the places in Europe he had visited in his 20s, that was his favorite, the one to which he would return could he only afford it. Only he was bound to stay in Chicago, at least until his daughter graduated high school. His wife was moving out of state. A judge had awarded him custody.

In Spain, though, I added, caring nothing for his daughter and all her travel restrictions, it had rained in torrents. And then rather than the pig's ear I had eaten along with the octopus on Thanksgiving, I would have preferred turkey with dressing. Perhaps he would as well if given the chance to be so selfish. Perhaps he had eaten nothing but spaghetti, because he looked thinner to me. Then there was no reason to keep talking.

After we each closed our doors, I took off my coat and started scratching. Something had started biting me. Three raised red sores were on my chin looking like pimples, but there was no popping them—something other than pus white as the bone in which our blood is made was inflaming them, with fire that only spread as I itched. The Lisbon ants, I knew, were different. Instead of harmless, they were virulent. The placement of our bed had displaced their nests. They were carpenters bent on rebuilding and had punished us for creating distance between their home and place of business. Our bodies had so many bulges on them it made their walk into a pilgrimage. The human body is the best of all continents to travel for insects.

And taking off my shoes, not bothering to unlace them while yanking each off from the heel layered with a dried gum exoskeleton, I palpated the three inflamed sores upon my chin that had not shrunk in some few days. Sensation is its own intelligence, I told myself while resisting the urge to scratch. I will not tell it what to say. And feeling is easier when the sky grows blacker, when my eyes are resting from too many dazzling specters. At 4:30 the sky was black, while any stars were smeared by the city lights beyond glimpsing. Daylight was receding, and still I was falling, waking with the sunlight though still missing something. I knew myself only a little, a little less every day.

RICHARD BELLIKOFF

That Was It

From July/August 2010

Cancel my subscription to the resurrection. —The Doors, "When the Music's Over"

IT CAME AS a revelation to me, upon traveling to Greece for the first time, that I could read the Greek alphabet. I hadn't studied Greek, but my math and science education, with its formulas and equations derived from Greek orthography, turned out to be all the preparation I needed. Even a cursory knowledge of college fraternity and sorority names will take you a long way toward mastering Greek spelling.

Since Greek pronunciation, unlike that of English, is mostly phonetic, I was able to work out, syllable by syllable, the illustrious names on statues and busts throughout Greece: Sophocles, Euripides, Plato, Socrates, Pythagoras, Euclid, and even mythological characters like Athena and Achilles. I could also read names less familiar to me, of modern Greek statesmen and politicians, whose likenesses appeared on the nation's currency, the *drachma*.

But the Greek language wasn't what attracted me to Greece. Nor was it the rapturous descriptions of Greek land and seascapes I had read in books like *Prospero's Cell* by Lawrence Durrell and *The Colossus of Maroussi* by Henry Miller. What actually drew me there was my fantasy of dancing the *Sirtaki* on Greek soil, as Anthony Quinn had done while playing the title role in the movie *Zorba the Greek*. I would be accompanied by Mikis Theodorakis's infectious *bouzouki* music from the film. Following local custom, people dining in Greek tavernas would shout "*Hopa!*" and smash their plates into pieces on the floor in appreciation of my artistry.

My dream suffered a rude collision with reality. Like youth in many developing countries, Greek teenagers had turned their backs on their own rich musical heritage. What they wanted was trashy and ephemeral American popular culture, and who better to purvey that than the King of Pop, Michael Jackson? The release of his megahit *Thriller* album—one of the best-selling recordings of all time—coincided with my arrival in Greece. And so I witnessed young Greeks taking to the dance floor, lip- and hip-syncing to the music videos for "Beat It" and "Billie Jean." They weren't very good at it, but they didn't seem to mind.

The real Mecca of Greek and Middle Eastern dancing turned out to be Southern California, where I live. I was initiated into the local ethnic dance scene when I played guitar with an Armenian band. Although there were occasional concerts and club dates, what we usually played at were weddings. The dancers we often accompanied were Middle Eastern wannabees, enchanted with the exotic romance of the region while oblivious of its poisonous politics. In the 1980s, when I first traveled to Greece, a Greek woman attempting to emulate Zorba on her native soil would have been driven from the dance floor with boos and catcalls, the *taverna* being a strictly male province. And a bellydancer in a city like Baghdad or Tehran, under the baleful watch of Saddam Hussein or Ayatollah Khomeini, respectively, would have suffered a far worse fate. It's no accident that the best bellydancer I know is a Jewish woman from San Diego.

The day Michael Jackson died, I happened to be in Cherry Hill, New Jersey, visiting my parents. My elderly father, who had survived a stroke that left him vulnerable to losing his balance and tipping over, got up in the middle of the night to shut off the air conditioning, tripped and crashed to the floor, breaking the fall with his hand and gashing his palm. He somehow managed to do all this without awakening me or my mother. Bleeding profusely because of the Coumadin that he takes since his stroke to thin his blood and prevent clots from forming, he stanched his wound with some hastily applied band-aids, then slipped on a white latex glove to hold the thick and unwieldy dressing in place.

The next evening at dinner, one of my cousins asked my father, "What's with the glove?"

"It's a tribute to Michael Jackson," I blurted out. "He's a big fan."

A few days later, we were all at a family wedding in Ithaca, New York, a city named after both the modern Greek island and the Homeric home of Odysseus. The band played no Michael Jackson songs. They must have realized that none of us could even contemplate doing the moonwalk without winding up in intensive care. But everyone—even those Greeks I had seen decades earlier trying in vain to dance to Jackson's *Thriller* album—could imitate the young John Travolta just by striking that iconic pose from *Saturday Night Fever*, with our index fingers in the air, accompanied by the familiar Bee Gees music the wedding musicians could probably play in their sleep.

I didn't enter the online lottery for tickets to the Michael Jackson memorial service at Staples Center in downtown Los Angeles, only a half hour's drive from my home, but watched the television broadcast instead. The program was produced by AEG, the world's largest owner of professional sports teams, owner of Staples Center and operator of London's O2 Arena, where Jackson's *This Is It* 50-concert comeback tour, his first in over a decade, was scheduled to take place before it was aborted by his death. AEG was also the promoter of that tour, as well as the producer of the tour's rehearsal movie, also titled *This Is It*. In corporate circles, this is called synergy, where different operations of the same company combine for a better result than each could accomplish separately—the whole being greater than the sum of its parts—all in the service of higher corporate profits. The word is derived from the Greek syn-ergos, meaning working together.

After Jackson died, AEG offered refunds to concert ticket buyers, but they also made a more spurious proposal: anyone waiving their rights to a refund would receive what AEG euphemistically called "souvenir tickets." Since the tickets were already paid for and buyers would have received them anyway if the tour had gone on, this scam suggests that when it comes to financial flim-flam, AEG isn't all that different from AIG, the recipient of the largest corporate bailout in US history after peddling the inscrutable financial instruments known as credit-default swaps that contributed to the worst US economic meltdown since 1929.

The televised Jackson memorial service turned out to be a slick, highly professional production, featuring an all-star cast of performers and none of the wardrobe malfunctions exhibited by Jackson's sister Janet at the 2004 Super Bowl halftime show. I found it surprisingly moving, with some unexpected literary touches such as Queen Latifah's reading of a Maya Angelou poem titled "We Had Him," containing memorable phrases like "...he was ours and we were his... we had him, and we are the world"—although I think John Lennon captured the feeling better in his acid-tripping and Lewis Carroll-inspired lyrics for "I Am the Walrus": "I am he as you are he as you are me and we are all together."

Watching all the celebrity tributes to Michael Jackson, those Greek adolescents I had seen in the 1980s, now matured into paunchy middle-aged adults, must have concluded he was not only a brilliant entertainer but also one of the world's foremost humanitarians, joining the ranks of Albert Schweitzer, Gandhi, Martin Luther King, and Mother Teresa. Equating creative talent with benevolence is *de rigueur* in our celebrity culture—or as Gore Vidal once said in an interview, "Americans think that only a good person can write a good book." Award-winning actors are habitually described as "distinguished" and "acclaimed," suggesting virtues they probably don't possess. I've come to believe that narcissism is practically a requirement for artistic achievement. I gave up long ago trying to convince my father that Richard Wagner was a musical genius despite being a vicious anti-Semite and Hitler's favorite composer. My father insists on pronouncing Wagner's name as if he were American and the name of the city that houses his theater, Bayreuth, as if it were the capital of Lebanon.

Among the many luminaries paying homage to Jackson at the memorial service was Smokey Robinson, who delivered a eulogy ending with the phrase, "And he will live forever and ever." Whoever wrote it was, however unintentionally, plagiarizing Charles Jennens's libretto for the Hallelujah chorus from Handel's *Messiah*, but since Jennens has been dead for over two centuries longer than Jackson, his work is in the public domain and there will be no copyright lawsuits.

Carl Anderson played Judas in what could be considered the modern counterpart of *Messiah*—*Jesus Christ Superstar* by Andrew Lloyd Webber and Tim Rice. I ran into Anderson once in a seedy motel parking lot in upstate New York while I was touring as a guitarist with a deservedly unknown rock band. The group's leader, a trumpet player, fancied himself the heir to Herb Alpert's musical legacy and included in his repertoire the arrangement of the *Zorba the Greek* theme from Alpert's *Going Places* album with the Tijuana Brass.

His wife, the group's lead singer, struggled to hit high notes and misfired on some of the lower ones as well. Standing behind her out of the spotlight and invisible to the audience, I would exchange thumbs-down hand gestures with the drummer and bass player. It was reminiscent of the scene in *Citizen Kane* where Kane's girlfriend butchers an opera aria on stage while the camera pans high up into the rafters, where a couple of stagehands look at each other and hold their noses.

When I met Anderson that night, he was touring as well, trying to launch a solo singing career that never reached the heights he had hoped for. He eventually returned to performing as Judas in revivals of the musical. But then, so did Ted Neeley, the actor who played Jesus. On Broadway, there's always one more resurrection, but in real life, Carl Anderson died in 2004 at the age of 59, his life spanning nine years more than Michael Jackson's.

A few hours after watching the Michael Jackson memorial service, I was driving to the Hollywood Bowl—an arena where Jackson performed just once, as a member of the Jackson 5 in 1971—to see a performance described in the concert program as "Peter and the Wolf with Fireworks," featuring the beloved children's classic accompanied by one of the Bowl's typically crowd-pleasing fireworks displays. My route took me past Forest Lawn cemetery, parodied as Whispering Glades in Evelyn Waugh's novel *The Loved One* and site of the private Jackson family funeral that morning. Fans were still gawking at the gates, perhaps hoping for a glimpse of their hero's casket. Plated with hand-polished 14-karat gold, covered with red, yellow, and white roses, and lined with crushed blue velvet, it must have been more lavishly furnished than most of their homes.

Twenty-four hour security at Forest Lawn's Great Mausoleum, whose other permanent residents include Clark Gable, Jean Harlow, and Carol Lombard, should keep Jackson's crypt from becoming like

Jim Morrison's grave in Paris's Père Lachaise cemetery: a pilgrimage destination, perpetually festooned with flowers, love notes, and assorted drug paraphernalia from teenage girls who weren't even born when the Lizard King died, and garnering far more attention than the final resting places in Père Lachaise's huge necropolis—Paris's largest—of Oscar Wilde, Molière, Balzac, and Proust, all of them having a far greater literary impact than Morrison, even if they couldn't match his sales figures. The quality of Morrison's poetry, some of it published posthumously, is debatable, but his lyrics for The Doors' song "Roadhouse Blues" sound like a prophecy of his impending residence in Père Lachaise: "Well, I woke up this morning, got myself a beer. The future's uncertain and the end is always near." There's nothing like this in all of Michael Jackson's lyrics. The poetry was in the motion, in his dancing.

Despite the advertising tag line for the concert rehearsal movie *This Is It*, "Discover the man you never knew," I experienced no epiphanies while watching it. Performers don't usually reveal themselves while on stage. That would require a look into Jackson's private life, which we already know more about than we probably want to, thanks to years of celebrity gossip columns and TV shows.

In the film, he usually appears in full or three-quarter shots rather than close-ups and wears sunglasses most of the time, with the footage often edited into split screen views showing costume changes. It's all seemingly designed to obscure his visage. But would we really want to see that grotesque mask?

A friend of mine was once married to an assistant director who worked on the long-running (1968-80) TV series *Hawaii Five-O*. He claimed that the show's star, Jack Lord, had so many face lifts, the surgeons could no longer locate any unstretched skin on which to perform the additional operations that Lord, living up to his name, demanded in his quest for eternal youth. Michael Jackson must also have exceeded his lifetime quota of cosmetic surgery, whether or not it was effective in banishing his personal demons. If only he had limited himself to Botox injections rather than daily prescription drug cocktails, he might still be alive.

Throughout most of *This Is It*, Jackson exhibits professionalism, maturity, and generosity in his interactions with his director, backup singers, dancers, and musicians ("It's your time to shine," he tells his guitarist Orianthi Panagaris, encouraging her to take a solo). But then he reverts to the naïve and inarticulate Peter Pan man-child character familiar to viewers from press conferences and interviews, making vacuous comments on the environment during an Earth Song music video of a young girl wandering through an enchanted forest: "I love it. I really respect those kinds of things... We've got four years to get it right, or else it's irreversible damage that's done to the planet." Al Gore wouldn't be envious.

Of course, it's not unheard of for celebrities to spout inanities while being venerated as role models and spokespersons. In his essay "How Tracy Austin Broke My Heart," David Foster Wallace tried to come to terms with why the sports memoirs of Tracy Austin and other professional athletes are so banal, superficial, and predictable. Wallace was thwarted in his novelistic desire to get inside the athletes' heads and find out what makes them great. He concluded that their lack of perspective and self-consciousness might be precisely what allows them to become stars: "It may well be that we spectators who are not divinely gifted as athletes, are the only ones able truly to see, articulate and animate the experience of the gift we are denied."

Had Wallace lived to read Andre Agassi's autobiography *Open*, he would have found it a welcome exception. The book lives up to its name; it could be subtitled "Agassi on the Couch." But then, Agassi has always been an uncommon athlete, analytical rather than instinctive. He won by playing strategically and exploiting his opponents' weaknesses—in contrast to his archrival Pete Sampras, who was able to coast on his natural talent and whose cliché-infested autobiography, *A Champion's Mind: Lessons from a Life in Tennis*, would have left Wallace in despair. There's no telling what Wallace would have thought of Michael Jackson's 1988 autobiography *Moonwalk*.

In *This Is It*, Michael Jackson, with anonymous singers and dancers standing in for his four brothers, Jackie, Jermaine, Marlon, and Tito, performs several Jackson 5 hits. But in the A&E cable TV reality series *The Jacksons: A Family Dynasty*, the surviving Jackson brothers discover that they're The Jackson 4, with Michael upstaging them from the grave, as they first announce and then abandon—amid personality conflicts, disagreements, and recriminations—plans to record a 40th anniversary album and launch an accompanying concert tour. The series ends inconclusively, with viewers left to wonder what's next for the Jackson brothers. Is this *it*?

Things have turned out far better for the Michael Jackson estate. They've made the largest recording deal in history: a multi-million-dollar distribution contract with Sony Music Entertainment for a variety of projects, including previously unreleased music recordings, DVDs, video games, a reality show modeled after "Dancing with the Stars," and Jackson memorabilia. This is another example of corporate synergy, with the memorabilia promoting the DVDs, CDs, games, and reality shows, which in turn beget the sale of more memorabilia, and so on, in an endless upward spiral of revenue.

Similar agreements have been made over the years with the estates of Elvis Presley, Jimi Hendrix, and Frank Sinatra (the Jim Morrison estate is a notable exception, requiring the unanimous consent of the three surviving Doors members for any business deal). The rereleases of old albums by these and other "legacy acts," as the recording industry describes them—borrowing terminology from the computer industry, which calls old and outdated programs "legacy software"—

continue to sell by the millions, casting doubt on the marketing strategy of a prominent Los Angeles rock radio station whose advertising billboard promises "Less Music by Dead Guys."

Beatles albums are also still in great demand, despite the group's having broken up over four decades ago and being a 50 percent legacy act. In fact, the Jackson estate's most lucrative asset is its share of the publishing rights to music by The Beatles and Elvis Presley, among other recording artists.

I haven't listened to those recent rereleases of old Beatles albums—I actually heard quite enough of the Beatles' music the first time around—but I imagine the digitally remastered sound is so clear you can hear in the background Paul McCartney and George Harrison asking George Martin to throw Yoko Ono out of the studio and Michael Jackson negotiating to buy the Beatles' song publishing rights—and then using them as collateral for massive purchases of Xanax, Zoloft, and Propofol.

Jackson's music hasn't fallen out of favor, either. In fact, since his passing, over 30 million of his albums have been sold, about two-thirds of them outside the United States. Those Greek fans I encountered in the '80s must have bought a lot of them. The Jackson estate may end up making more money now than if Michael had survived and gone ahead with his *This Is It* comeback tour. In show business, death can be a smart career move, but we'll never know whether Jackson shared Woody Allen's sentiments: "I don't want to achieve immortality through my art. I want to achieve it by not dying."

In the early 1980s, before my maiden voyage to Greece, I lived with a woman who had been a high school classmate of Farrah Fawcett's in Corpus Christi, Texas. It was Farrah's misfortune to die on the same day as Michael Jackson and have her memorial service overshadowed. The final indignity was omitting her from the 2010 Academy Awards broadcast's annual film montage of celebrities who died during the previous year. Her best known acting credits are the TV series Charlie's Angels and the TV movie *The Burning Bed*, but her real claim to fame is the pinup poster that adorned the walls of male college students' dormitory rooms in the '70s. She popularized a hairdo—a long-layered feathered shag with backward-facing curls— that would look quaint today amid all the multicolored Mohawks, lurid tattoos and nasal, labial, aural, and genital piercings. The King of Pop and the Queen of the Curling Iron are now joined in eternity.

I have a morbid habit of keeping lists of such death coincidences. My computerized catalogue of celebrity necrophilia includes Sergei Prokofiev, composer of *Peter and the Wolf*, who died on the same day as Joseph Stalin. With Prokofiev's funeral delayed for days while the Kremlin paid tribute to its fallen leader, his body had to be kept on ice even longer than Michael Jackson's. There were no fireworks for Prokofiev until the summer of 2009 at the Hollywood Bowl.

Aldous Huxley, the title of whose book *The Doors of Perception* provided the name for Jim Morrison's group, died on the day JFK was assassinated, as did C.S. Lewis, who went through another kind of door—in a wardrobe—into the magical land of Narnia. I was bedridden with mononucleosis during the JFK assassination. With nothing but network television available in those pre-cable days, I saw the film of the event, shot by Abraham Zapruder, more than anyone else on Earth—including Oliver Stone, writer and director of the film *JFK*.

The media loves around-the-clock "saturation coverage" of celebrity deaths, so although politics, wars, crime, and natural disasters will continue to dominate news reports, we can anticipate Michael Jackson stories occasionally surfacing. This phenomenon is not new, as Gail Collins pointed out in one of her *New York Times* columns: "The practice of churning out stories about a deceased celebrity for as long as possible is an old tradition. It used to be known as the 'John

Garfield Still Dead' syndrome, after the extensive postfuneral coverage of a movie star who had a fatal heart attack in 1952 in the bed of a woman other than his wife."

Garfield died in similar circumstances to Nelson Rockefeller, who was Governor of New York throughout my childhood. He seemed in fact to be Governor-for-Life, the way Franklin D. Roosevelt must have appeared as President-for-Life to my parents' generation. I remember a notorious radio newscast blooper that began, "Governor Rockefucker said today..." This carnal epithet turned out to be appropriate when he had a terminal heart attack in 1979 at the age of 70 in his Manhattan townhouse while in the company of a 25-year-old female aide.

There was much media speculation about a possible intimate relationship between the two, but neither the aide nor her family has ever commented on Rockefeller's death. Nor has his widow, Happy—nicknamed for her sunny disposition rather than her reaction to the circumstances of her husband's demise—ever addressed the issue, and the details of the incident remain a mystery to all but that proverbial fly on the wall. I can only imagine the hysteria that would greet this event if it took place amid today's 24/7 cable news, Facebook, YouTube, blogging, texting, and Tweeting multi-media circus—not to mention the ammunition it would supply to late-night comedians. The ancient Greeks would have had to settle for the satirical plays of Aristophanes.

Undeniably, Michael Jackson was an exciting and dynamic entertainer. But for all his talents, he turned out to be just another aging Baby Boomer, discovering too late what the rest of us already knew: you can't get away with taking the same drugs at 50 that you did at twenty-five. According to the Los Angeles County coroner, Jackson succumbed to a lethal combination of sedatives, anesthetics, and anti-depressants. He apparently combined the worst habits of Judy

Garland, Marilyn Monroe, Glenn Gould, Heath Ledger, Anna Nicole Smith, Karen Carpenter, and the German filmmaker Rainer Werner Fassbinder—a drugged-out workaholic who went for weeks at a time without sleep and told his concerned friends, "*Schlaf kann ich, wenn ich tod bin*" (I can sleep when I'm dead), a philosophy he soon had the chance to put into practice, at the age of thirty-seven.

And then of course there was Elvis, known not as the King of Pop, but simply The King. Appropriately, he died while seated on "the throne" and was found on the bathroom floor. The official cause of his fatal heart attack was described as "straining at stools." That's not surprising, since all narcotics, prescription or otherwise—and Elvis's many addictions ran the gamut—have the side effect of immobilizing the bowels, as I discovered once when I took Vicodin for a toothache and wound up needing several weeks' worth of laxatives.

I remember watching Elvis's television debut on the *Ed Sullivan Show*. In those days, he was known as "Elvis the Pelvis," and his hip-shaking was considered too risqué for prime-time, so TV audiences saw him only from the waist up. His choreography would look tame today compared with Michael Jackson's pelvic thrusting and crotch grabbing. It's the difference between a society where, as Philip Roth once described Eastern Europe under Soviet domination, "nothing is permitted and everything matters," and contemporary America, where "everything is permitted and nothing matters."

Elvis sightings continue to be reported over 30 years after his death, which conspiracy theorists maintain was faked in order for him to make a surreptitious exit from a performing career he had tired of. There have been no Jackson sightings yet, although rumors persist he was unhappy with the length of his planned comeback tour—50 concerts at the age of 50, a fortuitous numerical symmetry, but perhaps too great an effort for the middle-aged moonwalker—in which case *This Is It* should have been titled *I'm Outta Here*. It's only a matter of time before Elvis impersonators give way to Michael

Jackson mimics. Maybe the current generation of Greek teenagers will be more proficient at that than their parents were in the '80s.

Despite my flair for the Greek language, I've never become fluent in it. I had little incentive to do so. Even before traveling to Greece, I had read several Nikos Kazantsakis books in English translation, including *Life and Adventures of Alexis Zorba*, the novel that inspired the movie, and found Greece's best known novelist to be overrated, so I didn't feel compelled to reread them in Greek. I preferred the movie version of *Zorba*, thanks to the exuberant charm and charisma of Anthony Quinn and the freely adapted screenplay by the director, Michael Cacoyannis. In fact, one of the best lines in the film, Zorba's credo— "A man needs a little madness, or else he never dares cut the rope and be free"—comes not from the novel but from a nonfiction Kazantsakis book, *The Saviors of God*.

There was, however, a Greek literary figure whose work I had admired very much in translation: Constantine Cavafy. Poetry is always preferable in its original language, but Cavafy's poems are allusive and written in a blend of demotic Greek, the vernacular of the people, and Katharevousa, the officially sanctioned dialect. I didn't want to make reading Cavafy a lifetime project, as James Joyce had desired his readers to do with his work.

Meanwhile, much literature remains for me to read in English, including such classics as *Moby Dick, Uncle Tom's Cabin, The Grapes of Wrath, The Pickwick Papers* and *The Lord of the Rings*, just to name a few. On the other hand, I've worked my way through nearly all of Gabriel García Márquez and Carlos Fuentes, along with much of Italo Calvino's output and several major novels by Gunter Grass, all of these in the original. Foreign language fluency is like a muscle, requiring regular use to avoid atrophy.

With increasing age, I've become far more selective about what I read, and I feel a perverse pleasure whenever I discover I don't like the work of some prolific writer—Kingsley Amis, for example (I prefer his son Martin). So many books, so little time.

I haven't returned to Greece in quite a few years, and a great deal has changed. The Greek *drachma* coins and bills, with their images of statesmen and politicians whose names I once took such delight in reading, have been replaced by the Euro, with its neutral imagery, intended to foster European unity rather than nationalism. The Greek version of the Euro depicts no political or cultural figures, but only mythological ones: Europa being abducted by Zeus disguised as a bull on the two-Euro coin. The bull has turned out to be an apt symbol for the advice dispensed to Greek authorities in 2002 by Goldman Sachs, which, for a hefty fee, counseled the Greeks on how to conceal their indebtedness—and thereby meet the stringent debt requirements for admission into the European Union—using complex financial instruments called cross-currency swaps (I have an MBA and understand how this worked, but all you need to know is the phrase "cooking the books"). When the true extent of the Greek government's red ink came to light in early 2010, the EU and the International Monetary Fund took steps to bail it out, while administering a harsh dose of fiscal discipline, with dire consequences for the Greek populace, including job layoffs, public service cutbacks and tax increases. There's even the possibility the Euro will fall as a result. Perhaps, as Greece tries to resuscitate its economy, it could also resurrect the *drachma*, this time sporting some appropriately symbolic iconography of Michael Jackson rising from the dead to achieve a posthumous comeback. Mythology comes in many guises.

JASCHA KESSLER

...Leave Not a Rack Behind

From April/May 2014

WHEN ONE IS entered into old age, one wakes in the morning and sighs, "I kiss the day!"—as a departed friend then in his early 80s remarked as we strolled around the block. He'd just come from visiting an ancient uncle in hospital, a roué and gambler like Nicky his older brother, who'd left him with a motto: "Boost a booster! Knock a knocker! Fuck a sucker!" That could have served for his epitaph, a legacy recalling a 20th century life evading hit men from Broadway to Miami to Chicago, from Las Vegas to Los Angeles. As an afterthought he asked Bill, did he recall having met one of his track pals whose sobriquet was The Stooper? "Well, he's gone, and I'm going, too." How come, Stooper? It seems that character had made his living from the track, traveling from meet to meet, patrolling grounds adjoining course railings, walking the box seat rows, and hanging about the betting windows. He'd carried a broomstick with a nail embedded at one end that he used to spear winning tickets discarded by disappointed bettors. And a good life it had been for him!

I'm going on 84 now. That deathbed counsel drifts on the sea of memories remaining to me, my friend Bill aged 86 having keeled over one morning several years ago as he stood waiting at the counter of a Brentwood patisserie to buy pastries for tea-time guests. It returns suddenly like a forgotten parlay ticket scribbled with something that now seems to read like an insight into Shakespeare's last play. Glimpses of insight are a common-enough experience in one's latter years; they gleam amidst the flotsam accreted during a lifetime of confusion, action, as the many-too-many fardels of belief that once burdened us drop off like dead limpets and float away. Thoreau cried, "Simplify! Simplify!" Whether or not one attempts to simplify the works and days of a lifetime, simplification comes of itself to scour more or less clean the ruined barrel of one's "identity." Emotions, opinions, beliefs, ingrained dogma, all drift like tattered, tropical fish through the void that fills it with a sort of new clarity. Altered now are perspectives that decade after decade framed one's views. Truly, when one was a child, one thought as a child. Later, after having secured what's called "man's estate," I wrote these lines in a poem called "The Poets" to epitomize its "existential" situation:

> It was an endless parade,
> and they jammed Sixth Avenue:
> Armies, Navies and Airplanes,
> Clerks, Workers and Bosses,
> Actors, Dancers, Deep Thinkers...
> I knew you waited for me,
> but I couldn't cross the street.

There followed an epoch during which one mourns its passing— this latest era brought surprising flashes revealing simplicity's features. They come not like the fractured quarks nestled in the heart of the heart of an atom, but rather run across a field of immateriality. Conceive labile essences like those recently-observed Higgs bosons, tracing the presence of the substrate within the infinitely small construction of a quark's quantum by leaving tracks on a laboratory screen to mark scarcely measurable instants of space's/time or time's/space, thought of as the foundation of matter itself. Indeed, an extravagant comparison: things that are, yet are not. If such things do exist, they tell us our "universe" is... and is not... and both at once. Granted our universe is. Is it all there is?

In the Epilogue to *The Tempest,* Prospero intones Shakespeare's elegiac prophecy. It presents what today's physics would describe:

> ...the baseless fabric of this vision,
> The cloud-capped towers, the gorgeous palaces,
> The solemn temples, the great globe itself—
> Yea, all which it inherit—shall dissolve,
> And like this insubstantial pageant faded,
> Leave not a rack behind.

Spoken to Prospero's daughter Miranda and the play's bevy of chastened characters, were these words intended also for us? Like ourselves, the audience of the Globe Theater daily tended to the world's business. Did they hear it? And do we who lie in darkness hoping to wake, rise, and "kiss the day," ponder what truth may wait in what Prospero says? Can we sense what flickers like some will-o'-the-wisp through the drama, like the tutelary Puck in *A Midsummer Night's Dream* who misled lovers, blinded Oberon's Queen Titania, and set a jackass's braying head on Bottom the Weaver—or Ariel, who moves not only people but the very sky and sea?

Strip from *The Tempest* plot-line and action, tropes familiar from make-believe, fairytale worlds. Consider its characters existentially, so to say, not as if they were performing assigned roles, but persons like ourselves acting in front of the scrim of "this insubstantial pageant" we think of as our world. Shakespeare's "melancholy Jacques" a decade earlier had spoken words presaging this Epilogue in *As You Like It*:

All the world's a stage,
And all the men and women merely players;
They have their exits and their entrances,
And one man in his time plays many parts.

Today it might be asked if the thought of oneself playing at this or
that persona does not provoke a sensation of falling down a well
deeper than Alice's rabbit hole, the bottomless well of our existence.
When Alice finds her footing down that hole, who should dash by her
but a White Rabbit worrying at his watch, regretting his tardiness,
fearing himself late for some appointed meeting. Was it that same
appointment we go to, the hour that must shroud us in the winding
sheet of nothingness? Was Carroll's tale meant just for children?

Prospero, Duke of Milan, ruled benignly until supplanted by his
younger brother, exiled to a desert island. One could suppose it was
not tragic to have outlived his reign years. Think of that usurping
brother as the next generation. There in isolation Prospero studies,
practices, controls power to rule the heavens and earth, and raises
Miranda to restore her to her proper inheritance. Native to the isle
and entrained by magic, his familiar spirit Ariel loyally serves. Caliban,
a brutish creature sprung from the loins of a sorceress who kept him
trapped in a tree's split trunk, is adopted, taught to speak, and
conscripted to menial labor. One cares for him with whatever
affection a supernatural being can hold for an earthly creature; he
labors grudgingly, stuffed to bursting with hatred for his enslavement.

Again, thinking existentially of Prospero, one might imagine him
as one's self, a lone being condemned to live out years surrounded by
the Ocean Sea, as it was known then. He is not discontent. Like
hermits of old, he contemplates that desert isle, purposing to regain
his former rule in a busy world. Like us he knows challenge and
difficulty come from others, and as for his, he plans to settle old scores
with them. As though one's adversaries are what they once were! As
though yesterday's self is today's! (Heraclitus puts it that the man who

leaves his house in the morning and crosses a stream—Time's?—is not the same as the one who returns at night. When we say nobody steps into the same river twice, we have it the wrong way round.) He dispatches Ariel to stir up a tempest to shipwreck his enemies. Their behavior, though they sense they survived miraculously, is what it was: the commonplace strife of mean ambition. Among them is Ferdinand, a youth fresh as Miranda, a proper choice for a match tomorrow notwithstanding the influence of nasty court companions and servants coarse and dissolute. A mirror of society as it ever was.

From the conjured tempest that casts Prospero's antagonists ashore to their final discomfiture, we relish the entertainment of Shakespeare's stage, its "two hours traffic." Self-possessed, Prospero the dispassionate mage observes them as in a glass darkly. Hapless puppets they may be, if not helpless, though Ariel arranges confusion to confound them with despair. Were it not a lot rife with bitter comedy more or less implicit in our lives, we would not sit to watch it played out.

There is little to offer the library of commentary on *The Tempest* except what has lately occurred to me. It is as if I were to peer through the wrong end of a spyglass watching the surrounding world grow distant while I drift towards an end. I think of it Shakespeare's gift: an insight into old age. Oldest old age.

Consider the little scene he presents in which Miranda and Ferdinand her intended are "discovered" playing chess. Chess may be regarded as a metaphor of society: opposing armies of kings, queens, bishops, knights, and pawn soldiers fielded in a war to the end. They are moved in mortal combat by unseen hands according to fixed rules, placed in squares on a board. After the first move, the game is fought through strategies evolved from one player's move, the other's response. Whatever the outcome, it is realized in the interplay of force. In *The Tempest* a young couple sits at chess, unaware their game is life's game. That life's but a game ruled by chance is unthinkable. Still, that's what we're told by the Epilogue. Montaigne believed chance was determined by a goddess named Fortuna. In the mid-20th century, we were offered the philosophical opinion that our existence was a manifestation of the Absurd. Whether the Absurd be goddess or god, it is as unapproachable and implacable as ever Fortuna was for our most remote ancestors.

After having moved his pieces here and there about that desert isle, Prospero discharges Ariel and shows himself as he has at last become, a free man. Today Ariel might be thought of as his creative power, which is as much as to say his imagination, the faculty inspired by Socrates's Eros. Prospero puts down his pupil Caliban, an unregenerate creature of flesh personifying the animal within that nevertheless knows itself well: "You taught me language, and my profit on't, is I know how to curse. The red plague rid you. For learning me your language!" Prospero no longer needs them in this closing hour of his age. He discards his magical rod, no longer needing a wonder-working staff like the one Moses wielded against Egyptian wizards who had such an instrument themselves. He sees the world as it was and always will be: a dream.

As one is relieved of lifelong illusions, whether malefic or blessed, whether imposed or pursued, there remain still some tasks. If the mind be clear in oldest age, Thoreau's *Simplify!* is answered. I recall our first friends on our arrival in California on Labor Day of 1961. They were Joan Wight, an intelligent and worldly Englishwoman, and Frederick Wight her husband. We'd been referred to them by a mutual friend back East. An artist, novelist, and director of UCLA's gallery, Fred chaired the Art Department. Our relationship, sealed immediately, was to be close during a half-century; it remained so after Fred died of prostate cancer in 1986. Joan was that rarest of persons, a "classy" woman, to put it in vernacular. When she declined and grew disabled, my wife would take new books to her. Twenty years vanished like morning mist, and a day came when she said to my wife, "Don't bring a book this week. I need to concentrate on dying." Clear as diamond after the play of words and action—the staged business and busyness of drama—is set aside, what's left is *The Tempest's* Epilogue. Think of it as saying what Joan's concentration that last week of dying may have said to her.

Prospero's dispassionate, even godlike phrases are moreover the quintessence of Comedy. Not the low clowning of a Trinculo and Stefano but that undefinable thing a baffled Socrates proposed. He thought of it as a mixed form, a blending of Comedy with Tragedy. As Chesterfield put it in a letter [1750], it is a *je ne sais quoi,* to both our experience and mind inexplicable.

The Tempest's Epilogue has been heard by audiences since 1611. Yet not until this epoch in my life when I must acknowledge mortality has that Epilogue seemed the vision that ought to be recognized before the hour of death. Montaigne writing in 1576 his famous essay "An Apology for Raymond Sebond" recurs there and elsewhere in the *Essais* to our notions of death, observing that the thing itself, the thing in itself, no matter myriad conceptions ancient and modern, cannot be known. Whatever is supposed to be the state of things afterward is vainly supposed. How we cope with or seek to command our lives is the subject of his *Essais.* In the manner of Socrates, his favorite, he reviews efforts whether by ordinary folk or philosophers to contemplate what we are. Socrates wrote no books. At his end he talked with friends about the ethos of living the good life— until a draught of hemlock took him off to what in Italian is called the *aldila,* or perhaps into nothingness nowhere.

Two things regarding Socrates are to this hour obscure. We do not know what he thought about Diotima, the Sibyl he'd once left Athens to consult. As Plato records it in *The Symposium,* he returned from her with news of Eros, the god or mysterious power that inspires the making of poems. Eros is what the young Dylan Thomas named "the force that through the green fuse drives the flower." Socrates also gained from her a notion regarding the aim and purpose of life, expressed by the simile of steps ascending to love, a ladder to Love. What his thoughts were as he quaffed that mortal cup are unknown. Scholiasts have more or less concluded Montaigne, all things considered, was a skeptic, even near Pyrrhonic. Contemplating humanity in his *Essais,* one may imagine his eyebrows raised in amusement at the folly of our presumptions regarding all and everything mankind believed, prescribed as laws by virtue of being held sacred. John Florio's translation in three volumes having appeared in 1603, it is likely Shakespeare read Montaigne. In any case, the thought recognizable everywhere in Montaigne's *Essais* is distilled into six lines of *The Tempest's* Epilogue.

It may be worth noting that poetry per se was sung and spoken long before philosophy, and that philosophers have been at pains to supersede poets. I remind students that most of what is taught as the principal subjects in college in whatever field that is not mathematics, biology, or physics and engineering—that is, the social sciences, history, literature, philosophy, the Humanities, in short—is about events. Whereas a poem says out what was, is passing, or to come, as Yeats puts it elegiacally in "Sailing to Byzantium." Poetry, understood as what the Greeks termed "making," "creating," emanates from that force; call it the energy of Eros primordially released in speech, recorded or written in poems.

Regarding the three greatest poets of Western civilization—Virgil, Dante, and Shakespeare—George Santayana (d. 1952) ranked Dante above the others, considering Shakespeare lesser because he is godless. Notwithstanding, for Shakespeare as with Montaigne, it is not a matter of gods, or the god of monotheism. Nor of knowing what death may or may not be according to whatever articles of faith. When well over a half-century ago I happened to say to our Calvinist chaplain Colin Miller at Hamilton College that I knew no God, he declared, sonorous and stentorial as though he preached to me from the Sunday morning pulpit—I recall him standing left arm atop the refrigerator at a faculty party—"But God knows you!" Out of respect for my kind friend, I let that pass, assuming it was the glass of scotch whiskey in his right hand fueling his Scottish hubris. *Oh,* I thought to myself, *is that so?*

At any rate, today's cosmologist studies a monitor's screen and calculates the birth and death or being and non-being as it occurs in infinitely small particles, constituents of the substratum of matter, even as they are caused to appear instantly into being and pass from it. They are traced as the radiation saturating the universe since the Big Bang inflated, expanding from a mere 20kg mass containing the energy that makes up our universe. Santayana had his god just as had Presbyterian Colin Miller, but no matter what name they use and worship, concerning His being, nothing can be known. It is the same with death. Montaigne says that. Shakespeare says the same.

It may be painful to ponder the Comedy revealed by Prospero's last words. It may be difficult to accept, distressing to deny them, yet there they stand. A possible modern response to them comes to mind, darkly bright yet brightly dark in these my latter days: what the poet Yeats composed for his own epitaph. After a life's suffering through social, political, personal, sexual, and intellectual confusion, he set it down:

> Cast a cold eye
> On life, on death.
> Horseman, pass by.

J.J. WYLIE

On Eavesdropping, or Can You Hear Who You Are?

From April/May 1997

DO YOU KNOW what other people really think of you? I do. Actually, I just know what two particular people think of me, not the thin slice of the populace that is even aware I exist (nor the even thinner slice that cares). And, speech not being a transcription of thought, all I really know is what has been said about me. Still, it's interesting.

It began as a classic set-up. I was at work when two of my fellow employees began a conversation just outside the open door of the room in which I sat. Well, it was less a room than a cubby-hole just off a larger conference-room, and I was where I was because I was reading the instruction manual of some software I had been ordered to install on the obsolete PC my boss had seen fit to squirrel away in this outsized closet.

The manual had apparently been written by a graduate of the Phenobarbital School, where students learn to turn words into tranquilizers (their most famous alumni being James Michener). I kept yawning every line or so, actually having to shake my head to stay conscious. At one point, I even drooled right onto the page. If anyone had seen me sitting there, hunched over that hefty book and bobbing my head, they would have thought I was headbanging a silent mantra over the lyrics of Led Zeppelin. (And if they had seen me drool, I would've had to piss into a cup to keep my job.)

Now, I had heard my two coworkers come into the conference room, but I was too preoccupied to take much notice; I was busy enough just maintaining consciousness. I want to stress this point lest I am later accused of sneaking around like some Hearing Tom.

It wasn't until one of them said, "So tell me what you think about JJ," that I awoke enough to tune in.

The novelist Don Delillo, in his first book *Americana*, writes of what he calls "the universal third person," whom he says "we all want to be." What he's writing about is the imaginary perfection we all wish for, as expressed in cultural terms: the physical prowess of Michael Jordan, the hyperkinetic wit of Robin Williams, the winsome beauty of Sandra Bullock, etcetera. "Advertising has discovered this," Delillo continues, and advertisers use it to suggest "that the dream of entering the third person singular might possibly be fulfilled."

Thus advertisements lead us to believe we can become something separate from our workaday selves, something defined as good by how it is perceived by other people. We achieve perfection, it seems, by becoming a symbol for it.

Honestly, I'm not overly worried about what other people think of me (or so I've learned to be through therapy), especially since I have spent years analyzing the effect I have on people and have long ago concluded my case is hopeless: I have all the personal charisma of your average Vice President (though Al Gore does do a better macarena).

But the situation at hand was this: I was being slowly tortured by a styleless tech-manual and the only way out of the cubicle in which I was trapped was to show myself to two people who were already discussing me. And I have at least a passing curiosity about how my "third person singular" matches with my first.

Besides, what would you have done? Well, that's just what I did. I sat there.

In order to protect the innocent, I won't reveal the names or descriptions of the two people I overheard, except to say they were a man and a woman. And I quickly figured out that, though they were speaking about me, I was not the real impetus of their dialogue. What they were really interested in was each other, which made the request quoted above doubly complex, for it was the man who made it.

Workplace romance is tawdry enough, and nothing I could reveal here (like names) would broaden the horizons of such a subject any more than your average talk show, except to say this: what I have often noticed about illicit liaisons is that public discussions of them carry an undercurrent of rivalry. It's as if the gossipers begrudgingly identify with their respective counterparts in the coupling-at-hand and thus feel somehow defeated for being left out.

In other words, as we dish the dirt, we feel somewhat akin to the writer Gore Vidal when he said, "Whenever I hear about the success of a friend, a little part of me dies." So, as we (consciously or not) feel that "So-and-so's getting some and I'm not, so I'm a loser," there's an element of revenge in gossip.

Thus, not only was I interested in eavesdropping on someone's candid assessment of me in order to get a better idea of my public persona, insignificant as it is (and not only was I wondering whether my male coworker was going to run me down in order to build himself up via what my friends call the "Pulley Method of Self-Actualization"), I also wanted some dirt.

But what I heard, amidst all the knowing giggles and innuendos that characterize professional flirting, shocked me. What I heard about myself was so wildly exaggerated, so maliciously intended, and so factually untrue, all my qualms about eavesdropping were quickly overcome by my growing indignance.

It's tough learning how you really look in public. The public never gets it right. Celebrities are constantly bemoaning this, and the Argentinian writer Jorge Luis Borges calls fame "a form of incomprehension, perhaps the worst." Imagine how bad it can be for those of us who can't afford publicists.

An inaccurate public persona can even cause a person to retreat from the world. Thus, because he feels persecuted, Mark Fuhrman moves to Idaho. Thus the unnamed hero of Ralph Ellison's masterpiece begins his story by telling us, "I am an invisible man," whose public persona has been all but erased "because people refuse to see me."

Well, apparently I had been seen, although through very dirty lenses. In fact, public perception is nowhere near close to being accurate enough to be used as a lens. Nor is it a mirror into which one can look at oneself. It's more like an inkblot revealing more about whoever is interpreting it than who is being interpreted. What we're looking for is what we want, not what's actually there, and few of our desires are pure. Thus the very impulse that had made me listen for dirt on my eavesdropees had caused some dirt to get dished on me.

I'm a little different than the people I work with, and many of them react to this difference with derogatory speculation about who I am. I'm as guilty of doing this as anyone, but it's alarming to realize I'm also a target of it. Finding out who people think you are is a little like finding out you're adopted: it calls your own conception of yourself into question. The aforementioned Delillo, in his novel *White Noise*, has his narrator characterize himself thus: "I am the false character that follows the name around."

So, without going into a blow-by-blow rebuttal of the inaccuracies that were leveled at me, I want to conclude by addressing only the most answerable slanders:

First, I am not related to my boss. I attained my position in the company through merit and effort, not nepotism. Believe it or not, I work for a living.

Second, I don't live with my mother; nor are my living expenses paid through a parental trust fund. (Again, I work for a living.) At birth, the spoon in my mouth was plastic, not silver.

Third, I am not "so serious that it would kill me to smile." In fact, I've always thought of myself as rather witty, and I laugh a lot. Especially at myself.

Finally, my sexual preference and experience are my business. Suffice it to say, ANYONE'S conclusions about those aspects of my personality should be considered wrong by default. So, barring those of you who are close enough friends of mine, if you think I'm heterosexual, you should reconsider. And if you think I'm homosexual, you should do the same.

All of this talk of public persona, gossip, and misperceptions brings to mind a line from Michael Ondaatje's novel *The English Patient*. It is particularly appropriate, given my citations concerning Delillo's defining of publicly-perceived perfection: "Death means you are in the third person."

I prefer the first. I'd rather be me than not.

DAVID GRAHAM

Man with Gun: Photographing Violence

From July/August 2004

1

IT SOMETIMES SEEMS, in these days of cable news and instant access on the internet to almost every dark thing, that whatever proprieties and taboos once held for the mass media have long since been deeply eroded if not obliterated. But as I write these words, two stories dominate the news, both from the war in Iraq, and both having to do not only with photographing violence but also with the propriety of what may and should be shown to the public. As everyone now knows, a group of American soldiers photographed themselves abusing and sexually torturing Iraqi prisoners in Baghdad; and, explicitly in retaliation for such abuse, a terrorist group released a gruesome video of an American civilian hostage being decapitated.

And, of course, everyone from the President on down recognizes these news stories simply wouldn't be stories in the same way if they had not been unforgettably recorded visually.

When these stories broke, I thought almost immediately of incidents in Vietnam, a generation ago, when I first became aware of the role of the mass media in the body politic. Very likely we will be debating the parallels between Iraq and Vietnam for another generation or more. What follows is my meditation on these issues, taking as touchstone one of the most horribly indelible images from that conflict.

2

General Nguyen Ngoc Loan, South Vietnamese police chief, was driving around the streets of Saigon one day in February 1968. It was the time of the Tet Offensive, and the capital city had been infiltrated by guerrillas who had captured and blown up a radio station. They had also killed a number of policemen and some civilians. Since General Loan was known as a particularly ruthless cop, he was a good person for photographers to follow, and they did. His mission was bound to be photogenic.

An Associated Press photographer as well as an NBC cameraman thus chanced to film and photograph one of the most memorable images of the war—perhaps only the photo of the screaming, napalmed girl running naked toward America is more famous. In any event, I imagine everyone knows this scene: a Vietcong prisoner was marched up to General Loan, hands bound behind his back, wary look on his face. He was wearing black shorts (at least in the still photo and on my black-and-white TV set) and an untucked plaid sports shirt. A skinny, ordinary looking man, he might have been eighteen. General Loan pulled out a snub-nosed revolver, placed it without hesitation against the prisoner's temple, and pulled the trigger.

The man flinched and crumpled to the street as General Loan casually holstered his gun and walked off. Presumably one of his subordinates hauled the body away. No doubt the TV cameraman and still photographer felt at that moment a perverse surge of joy, even as it was mixed with horror at this wordless brutality. They couldn't have helped knowing they had found a great image, which is to say, an unforgettable one. Very likely General Loan did not mind the event being filmed. Perhaps he even wanted it recorded as an example of his efficient justice and command. The event soon became world famous, in any case, not because it was more brutal or shocking than others, but simply because it had been well photographed.

Along with millions of others, I saw the TV footage on the news the next night. The televised scene, I realize now, was hardly more informative than the single still shot now found in many books on Vietnam, though more grisly. For here was a drama without exposition. We simply saw a man, frightened-looking and helpless, shot down without warning or explanation by a dour gunman dressed in fatigues. The prisoner had possibly been caught in the act of some other no less atrocious act, but as I recall, the TV announcer gave no such explanation. (Maybe there was some mention of context, but even if so, it could hardly compete with the power of the naked image.)

There are other distortions as well. The film I saw, as I only came to understand later, must have been edited to eliminate the spurting blood, the exploding fragments of bone and flesh that surely were visible in the original footage. (In a similar way, the Zapruder film of President Kennedy being killed was normally shown in edited form.) The man simply grimaced and sat down, dead without the intervening stage of dying, gone without mess, like a Hollywood hero. Is it this unreality that makes the image particularly terrible?

Difficult questions are raised here. If the purpose of showing the film in the first place was to shock us—and who could deny it?—then why not go all the way? If the TV producer's intent had been to avoid sheer sensationalism, I would surely remember at least an attempt to put the scene in context: statements by the General, interviews with bystanders, list of the prisoner's alleged crimes, something. No, what we were given was mostly pure sensation, brutality unmoored. So why the decorum of editing away the blood? We had seen blood before, in many film clips, in some *Life* photographs, not to mention the copiously spilled stage-blood of film directors like Sam Peckinpah. We knew well enough (or would, given thought) that when a gun is fired point-blank into someone's skull, there is going to be a mess. Yet I wager we all would have known instinctively, just as the TV producer did, just where to draw the line in 1968. To the extent that he rationalized his decision at all, it must have been in terms like these: "We'll show the violence and cruelty," he might have said, "but we won't wallow in it. We must spare the feelings of our viewers, consistent with our obligation to report what happened." Or so I imagine a high-minded producer may have argued; more likely, he simply knew the scene would shock and arouse and therefore was good footage. In any case, the decision to edit would have seemed entirely proper and normal—just as, a generation later, news outlets around the world mostly chose not to show viewers the actual decapitation in Iraq, just the prelude to it.

Yet I think there is a fundamental sense in which you can't have it both ways: the producer may have been cynical or high-minded, but not both, because one cannot simultaneously act to spare the audience's feelings and also to arouse them. And in fact, it seems most television, especially documentary and news programming, has as a main function arousal, not merely the conveying of information. If this were not true, news shows would be immune to competition for high ratings. We would have more 30-minute segments on economic policy, and fewer clips of airline crashes, terrorist violence, all the predictably photogenic aftermath of freak accidents. Public television would not need taxpayer support.

Was I aroused? Of course I was, and not just because I was an impressionable and naïve 15-year-old in 1968. I enjoy the scene at more than one uncomfortable level, even today. For one thing, the scene is clearly pornographic, in that we see another person being humiliated publicly, his suffering exposed to the world, his humanity denied, his last moment transformed to gruesome theater. I am shamefully drawn to this scene because it is forbidden, because I am not the man being humiliated but can imagine being him. Photography has many and various powers, but chief among them is what Roland Barthes called each image's "certificate of presence," which explains the fascination we feel before photos of all kinds, but especially those portraying the forbidden, the strange, the hideous and uncanny. This fundamental pull toward unfamiliar reality links such apparently dissimilar uses of photography as news photos, tourist postcards, pornography, and microscopic imagery.

The potential perversity of photographic imagery is nowhere more aptly illustrated than in the collection of Pulitzer Prize photos titled *Moments*, an anthology of news photographs dating from World War II through Vietnam. With surprisingly few exceptions, the award-winning images are appalling, frequently recording fatalities. General Loan's murder is included, as are a dismaying number of other violent occasions, including assassinations, battles, traffic accidents, racial brutalities, riots, and plane crashes. The few nonviolent images—a baby's birth, a candidate with a hole in his shoe—stand out as welcome exceptions. The editors are aware of this bias, though they remark rather ingenuously that although there is violence aplenty in their book, it simply reflects "the violence in the lives around us," and that nevertheless we also see "bravery, compassion, dedication, joy, and so much more of the day-to-day human qualities that surround us." The fatuity of their uplifting language here very nearly masks the completeness with which they beg the question: why are prize-winning photographs so uniformly miserable? Why not record moments of unadulterated joy, dedication, and compassion, rather than always seeking these qualities within disaster?

A particularly ghastly sequence from 1976 shows a Boston woman and her child trying to flee their burning apartment. The fire escape they stand on suddenly collapses, sending both of them plunging down toward the lucky photographer in the street. He is able to capture several shots of the two in mid-flight. The woman died on impact, the caption rather needlessly informs us, but it turns out that this information is merely the prelude to a further grim twist: the fact that the child survived its fall by landing on top of the mother. A miracle. Clearly the purpose of this caption is to allow us to savor the full shock of the moment, both from the woman's and the child's perspectives.

Not to mention the perspective of the photographer: the text throughout *Moments* records more about the photographers' feelings than it does about the events themselves. Their luck, skill, and excitement at finding themselves in the right place at the right time are continually emphasized. More than one photographer expresses a certain unease at being so close to violence and yet remaining unscathed, but the deeper implications of this unease are barely touched on. And it is striking to note that several of the photographers make the same sort of remark about the murders they have recorded. As Eddie Adams put it, describing the taking of his photograph of General Loan's summary execution, "When he fired, I fired."

This identification of camera with gun remains disturbing, however commonplace it has become in books on photography. So an even less admirable reaction to the Vietnam photo derives from my identifying not with the dead man but, through the camera's lens, with General Loan. I cannot help my questions: how much did the gun weigh? What were his thoughts as he pulled the trigger? Righteousness? Secret glee? Self-satisfaction? Weariness? Or, worst thought, nothing at all? My own worst thought, I suppose, is simply the thrill of the absolute: imagining that satisfaction, its casual deployment in ending life. Bang-bang, you're dead. News photography not only allows a viewer to engage in this sort of shameful daydream; I suspect that in its very nature it encourages such thinking.

I suspect but cannot prove this point. The larger issue is context, however, and it seems inescapable that there are significant dangers involved when photographs and films of violence are objectified, removed from their original situations. A full accounting would demand more information than any book like *Moments* is prepared to offer. For example, what happened to General Loan? The last I heard, he was living in exile in the United States, had started a restaurant business and a new life, and was unrepentant. It seems useless to judge him now unless we know the full circumstances surrounding his act, unless we recognize how many other brutalities went unrecorded, and unless we fully admit our own guilty attraction to viewing his action. Yet I imagine something even less pleasant than judgment has descended on the General. For as the still photo of his murder has of course outlasted the film footage in popular memory, it has become a shorthand symbol for a whole complex of feelings about Vietnam with which he can hardly be expected to agree.

For instance, in one of Woody Allen's movies (*Stardust Memories*, I think), we find Allen's character has hung a huge blow-up of this photo in his apartment, along with other frightful scenes. His point is both humorous and not, an example of his character's (and probably his country's) showy neuroses. As I understand it, Allen must be both expressing and criticizing liberal unease over the War, the guilt of those who did not go, especially those whose social status protected them. I don't expect anyone but an American who has lived through the Vietnam era would completely understand the complicated levels of irony in Allen's black-comic use of those photographs. The untethered cruelty of the original scene has further escaped its own context to become, in Allen's hands, a crudely effective symbol for an entire social and psychological malaise. Thus we may say that by now this photograph, taken for commercial and documentary purposes, has passed through its role as propaganda to become, finally, art. The photographer, after all, won a prestigious award.

This tendency of shocking photographs to lose their potency and eventually beautify all manner of ugliness has troubled many commentators. Photographer Robert Adams, in his book *Beauty in Photography*, comes to the rueful conclusion that, with notable exceptions, "the static visual arts are not well suited to the direct exploration of evil. Various media can report on evil, but a single painting or sculpture or photograph rarely resolves our feelings about it into that balance of emotions toward which art has traditionally been understood to progress." He continues, asserting "the arts that do the best job with evil as their avowed subject are the narrative arts such as drama and fiction; good and evil are important to us finally as matters of choice, and to show the reality of choice requires that time pass, time for decisions to be made and paid for."

If we have a legitimate complaint about the way television news is presented, it lies here: by focusing so doggedly on shocking moments, even film manages to approach the static quality of a work of art. Of course, there is good art and bad art. The problem with both still photo and televised scene lies not in the images themselves, but in the way they are shown. The film footage of General Loan, so long as it is shown without appreciable commentary, will remain more symbolic than documentary—an effective figurative indication that war is indeed hellish, but not much of a specific commentary on the Vietnam War itself. In other words, as time passes, the very real differences between the two forms of this scene (film and still photo) will inevitably diminish.

Thus General Loan, whose version of this event will never, even if known, attain the currency of the photographic image, is in a sense trapped. Just as the film footage I saw removed him from context, the still photo has in turn replaced the film's action with utter stasis. He will eventually be stripped of all his virtues and faults except one—he will be the man with the gun. And the blood that was edited away, which he may also have cropped from his recollections, will gradually vanish even as possibility, leaving only this eerie tableau: an extended arm, sun glinting on polished steel, a man's head recoiling from the bullet that we don't and won't see, only feel.

ANTHONY BROWN

You Can't Have Him

From May 1997

HE DIDN'T KNOW what it was about the footsteps that woke him up, but Jimmy Lee Vaughn snapped to awareness to their sound amongst the normal, subdued night noises. Living in dormitory conditions, with the entrance, stairs, shared showers, sinks and toilets at one end of the huge room, prisoners moving around at night was not so unusual. There were 60–75 men living on his floor, each with a bunk, locker, and writing desk in a space separated and surrounded by a four-and-a-half foot painted plywood partition, with either a swinging or a sliding panel for a door. The cubicles were all that passed for privacy in the "E" Unit, one of two housing blocks out of 11 with open dorms instead of cells at what was then, in the late '70s, called the Federal Correctional Institution at Lompoc, CA. "E" Unit housed all the prisoners participating in a long-term substance abuse program.

Glancing at the illuminated face of the clock, he saw it wasn't Count time, but the footsteps were moving closer, pausing every few seconds, and they were somehow "wrong." Movement in the half-light caused him to look up just as the head and shoulders of a man appeared over the cubicle wall, stopped so their owner could peer in at him, and then move on. It wasn't a guard. The head had a face belonging to Mansfred "Kurt" Kurtizt, and seeing it now could only mean he'd thought of a solution to his problem.

In prison, problems were most often rooted in the perceived disrespect of one prisoner by another, an unpaid drug or gambling debt, the extortion of commissary, property, or cash, or an unwanted homosexual advance, even rape. But Jimmy Lee knew about Kurt's problem, and it was unique.

Kurt was a South African national serving a six-year NARA sentence for smuggling drugs into the United States. His problem was that South African authorities believed him to be a member of a communist anti-Apartheid organization using drug smuggling profits to help finance violent attacks against the government. During his trial he had been informed, in no uncertain terms, that upon his deportation back to South Africa at the end of his sentence, he would be executed. Although Kurt fully expected to be thoroughly interrogated (meaning tortured) before he was killed, the burly, red-faced, Afrikaaner police official had colorfully described the hanging of his "kaffir-lovin' ass" from the hatch of the plane the moment it touched home soil.

Nobody, at least nobody Jimmy knew, was certain if Kurt was actually a Communist or an anti-Apartheid activist. Being seen as a race-traitor was no more popular in American prisons than in white-controlled South African streets, so it wasn't a topic that he would have discussed openly. But no one doubted his fear of deportation. Kurt had peacefully and systematically lost every day of his "good time" credits in order to put off his release and deportation. Most youthful offenders sentenced under the Narcotics and Rehabilitation Act could have normally expected to serve two years inside the joint and four on parole, the felony conviction having been expunged from his record. But Kurt was serving every single day of his six-year sentence; he had no more good time to earn or lose, and he was getting short.

Jimmy Lee threw off his covers and stood up. Looking over the partition and a couple cubicles down, he saw Kurt turn to look back at him, but without a pause he continued to move down the cubes, peering over and into each one. Jimmy Lee wasn't sure what he should do, if anything. It wasn't a question of right or wrong but of consequences. Interfere and he could get hurt or killed. Don't interfere and... his quandary was resolved when Kurt stopped in front of Robert Moore's cubicle and began sliding the plywood panel open. Bobby was Jimmy Lee's homeboy, a fellow Alaskan and contract state prisoner, exiled to the federal system because Alaska had no facilities for long-term prisoners.

Without concern for noise, Jimmy Lee slid his door open, stepped out onto the walkway, and moved toward Kurt just as Kurt pulled a long, fat-bladed shank from his belt. Kurt stopped and turned to face Jimmy Lee, setting his feet and moving the foot-long killing tool down along his thigh in preparation, but he said nothing, just watched as Jimmy Lee approached.

"That's my friend. You can't have him," was all Jimmy Lee said.

Kurt stared at him for long seconds, then nodded his head once and, without a word, turned away to continue his search. Jimmy Lee pulled the door back across the entry to Bobby's cube and returned to his own space, but he continued to watch Kurt over the partition to be sure he didn't return.

Less than a minute later and four cubes farther down, Kurt again slid open a door and this time moved inside. Jimmy Lee sat down at the edge of his bunk. His heart pounded and stomach twisted under the adrenaline onslaught, his ears functioning with a terrible clarity that made denying his imagination impossible. He listened to the sounds of Kurt dropping onto the back of his sleeping victim, the grunt of startled response, the blade thudding again and again through the wool blanket and struggling flesh, the fearful, half-smothered scream-turned-wail of understanding, the sound of Kurt's voice, clear, calm, almost conversational in tone and volume:

"Just roll with it, man. Just roll with it."

DALE BRIDGES

Off the Grid

From October/November 2011

IN 1980 MY father obtained a full-time preaching position at a small church on the Colorado prairie, and our family moved into a pink farmhouse just outside the city limits of a town called Fort Morgan. I was excited about our new residence, primarily because I expected to be living inside some sort of walled garrison, wearing a coon-skin hat and fighting off Injuns with my trusty musket. My pioneer fantasy was momentarily crushed, however, when I learned the city had earned its "Fort" prefix during the 1800s, and since that time the local white men had shed their coon-skin headgear in favor of grease-stained baseball caps, which they wore as they trudged through the streets every morning on their way to work at the local sugar-beet factory.

Ours wasn't a real farm, just a house at the end of a long, dirt driveway, but there was enough land for a chicken coop next to the garage and a small garden, to be tended by my mother. Still, my father insisted this was our opportunity to live "off the grid," a phrase he often used after watching too many episodes of *Little House on the*

Prairie. "Just imagine," he said, "giant carrots plucked right out of the earth! Fresh eggs for breakfast!" We would weave our own socks with a loom and then beat them against a rock on laundry day. When baths were needed, water would be fetched in buckets from the well and soap would be made from lye and lard. Who needed expensive modern appliances? Material trappings were for those hedonistic Hollywood types who graced the covers of celebrity gossip magazines. No more glossy centerfolds for us. In fact, no more television or radio, either. From now on, songbirds would be our pop stars and sunsets our nightly news. We would study the beetles with the same passion and amazement that our peers studied The Beatles. At some point, we might even trade in our Ford Granada for a couple of prancing white horses and a wooden carriage. Could I wear a coon-skin hat? You bet I could. And maybe even a sweater made from coyote pelts to go with it. Anything was possible because we would be completely self-sufficient. Just like the settlers of ye olden days.

The idea was to wean ourselves off the teat of mainstream society and eventually go underground. No bank accounts, no social security numbers, no way for Big Brother to track us down and tattoo barcodes on our foreheads. We were going to separate ourselves from the frills of secular culture by adopting a simpler, purer way of life. True, the world was falling apart all around us—satanic rock bands constantly screamed obscenities on the radio, Godless communists threatened to obliterate freedom-loving countries with nuclear weapons, liberal intellectuals taught their students that human beings evolved from chimps—but if we could just maintain complete control over our tiny section of the prairie, perhaps our souls would escape the chaos uncorrupted.

In spite of my father's histrionics (or perhaps because of them), there was a certain rustic romanticism in this proposed lifestyle that I found appealing at first. I'd inherited more than my fair share of my father's delusional nature and fancied myself quite the heroic frontiersman, despite the fact that I was a small, sickly child who rarely enjoyed physical activities—what is commonly known in playground circles as "kind of a wuss." My pioneer daydreams were indirectly connected to a collection of children's books called the *Little Patriot Series,* which featured fictionalized accounts of notable figures such as Davey Crockett, Jim Bowie, and Sam Houston. I wasn't quite old enough to read them myself, but I enjoyed the pictures and often forced my overworked mother to read them aloud before bedtime. While not altogether historically accurate, the novels were filled with tales of barrel-chested men who wrestled grizzly bears by day and slept under a canopy of stars by night. According to legend, some of these trailblazers could shoot the wings off a housefly at 20 paces and kill a mountain lion with a single, mighty blow to the kidney. The writing wasn't exactly Pulitzer Prize material, but the authors knew how to turn a simile. Tough as nails, fast as a jackrabbit, strong as an ox. It was enough to excite the imagination of any red-blooded, semi-literate boy. Beholden to no man and afraid of no beast, these hardy patriots exemplified the spirit of American freedom and self-determination, and I wanted to be just like them. Or so I thought.

It turns out, living off the grid is a lot more arduous and boring than one might imagine. Chores were assigned, and I soon found myself being forced out of bed before sunrise to water the tomato plants or collect warm, poop-covered eggs from the feathered nether regions of manic hens. On Saturdays, when other children were watching cartoons in their footie pajamas, my brother and I were outside gathering icicles and buckets of snow, which would later be melted down by our mother for drinking water. The work never ended. As soon as you finished weeding the garden, it was time to shingle the roof or dig some postholes or make strawberry preserves in preparation for the upcoming winter. These tasks were neither fun nor patriotic, and I wanted no part of them.

Things seemed to take a turn for the better when my father decided to add a pregnant sow and a hut full of rabbits to our little ark. But my initial optimism dissipated when I learned what real pioneers did with piglets and bunnies. Apparently, Daniel Boone did not take cuteness into account when surviving in the wilderness. The rabbits were skinned and the pigs gutted, the meat either sold to neighbors or dried, salted, and made into jerky. This always happened, conveniently enough, while the children were at soccer practice or visiting relatives for the weekend. When we returned, the rabbit hut would be empty and the kitchen would be filled with the delicious, gamy aroma of stew.

Somehow it was decided that participating in the execution of four-legged mammals would be traumatic for the youngins, but watching poultry get slaughtered would have no adverse psychological effects whatsoever. Therefore, every summer the entire family got together and butchered a dozen chickens in the backyard. My job was to chase down the fat, headless bodies after my father decapitated them with an ax. Normally our chickens were slothful creatures who could barely be bothered to waddle a few feet for their morning feeding, but apparently all they needed was a good, swift whack in the neck to motivate them. Afterward, they flopped around for several minutes, beating their wings as they scampered blindly across the driveway like drunken Olympic sprinters, leaving behind a trail of blood and feces. The phrase "Running around like a chicken with its head cut off" took on a whole new meaning. I followed the headless cadavers until they ran out of energy and fell, seemingly exhausted, to the ground. Then I grabbed their weird lizard feet and dragged them over to my mother, who plucked the feathers and disemboweled their naked remains. Sometimes my brother would put one of the severed heads on his index finger and chase my sisters around the house with it. Chicken-head puppets, we called them.

But, alas, not every day could be as exciting as Chicken-Head Puppet Day, and I quickly grew tired of living off the fat of the land. Apparently, the land had become anorexic. Hard work and sacrifice were not what I'd signed up for. Staring down buffalos and fighting off Comanches were the adventures I was after. The fact that I would have soiled myself at the sight of either was beside the point. If I couldn't have fun being a pioneer, why bother? Freedom and self-determination are nice in theory, but when it comes down to who's going to castrate the farm animals, I think we can all agree there's something to be said for shallow materialism.

I decided my parents were holding me back. It was fine with me if they wanted to live like a couple of Dust Bowl hermits, but it wasn't fair to force that lifestyle on their innocent, postmodern offspring. Why not join the 20th century and live a little? After all, I was fortunate enough to be growing up in the Golden Age of Spoiled Children. It was the 1980s, and juvenile greed was at an all time high. Everywhere I turned, my peers were holding their breath and throwing temper tantrums in an effort to acquire the latest incontinent doll or comic book action figure. Baby Boomer parents seemed powerless against such techniques. Advertisers picked up on this, and soon there were million-dollar marketing campaigns directed at pint-sized customers who did not actually have any money of their own. Rock 'Em Sock 'Em Robots, Twinkies, Cap'n Crunch, Hot Wheels. How could a five-year-old afford such treasures? The goal was to loosen the parental purse strings by encouraging children to behave like jackals feeding off a lion's kill. If we harassed the lion long enough, eventually it would grow tired of our yelping and abandon the Hungry Hungry Hippos carcass. Then we could fight amongst ourselves over what remained of the cheap, plastic cadaver.

My parents raised me to be an obedient child, but I was open to other options. The problem was, I didn't have a role model. My siblings were all respectful and well-behaved by nature, traits that were of no use to me whatsoever in my new position as Generation X Brat. No, it was obvious I would have to look outside my family for inspiration.

My mentor finally presented himself one day in the unlikeliest of places: the breakfast aisle at Safeway. This was where I saw a kindergartner named Tommy slap his mother in the face because she had the audacity to put oatmeal in their grocery cart instead of Count Chocula. When this happened, I was shopping for cereal with my own mother, who politely turned away from the scene and pretended to be engrossed in the list of ingredients on a box of Grape Nuts. However, unencumbered by good manners, I gawked at the little monster and took careful mental notes.

The child was sitting in the fold-out seat for toddlers at the top of the grocery cart, a perch for which he was obviously too big. His fat thighs barely fit through the wire slots designed to hold them, and his mother had to keep one hand on the cart at all times to prevent it from tipping over. The other hand was busy fending off the constant barrage of kicks and punches the boy directed at the woman despite her quiet protests. "Stop that, Tommy." "Put that down, Tommy." "Please don't punch Mommy in the throat again, Tommy." I was amazed. Up to this point, I'd been under the impression the adults were in charge of the planet, but this underage tyrant proved who was really in power. Tommy ruled his household with an iron sippy cup. When he wasn't physically abusing his mother, he was shrieking and throwing stolen Skittles at passing customers. "I'm so sorry," said the mother after a piece of red candy bounced off the permed head of an elderly woman. "He's normally not like this." The old lady looked at the boy sitting in the grocery cart, his pudgy hands and face covered in rainbow carnage, and nodded kindly. It was all too obvious little Tommy was like this all the time, and his mother simply made excuses for his horrible behavior. Somehow the innocent angel who emerged from her loins just a few short years ago had transformed into a Third

World dictator with a sugar addiction. And his mother had been assigned the unenviable position of public-relations director for the regime.

After the old woman moved on, Tommy's mother smiled apologetically in our direction and then bent down to retrieve a box of oatmeal off the bottom shelf. When she stood up, Tommy reared back and clocked her right in the kisser. This was no playful tap, either. It sounded like someone had smacked a chicken cutlet with a spatula. "Chocula!" the kid screamed. "I want Chocula, stupid!"

My mouth dropped open. Surely this full-grown woman would not stand for such treatment. She would rip the tiny prince off his wire throne and beat him with a bag of oranges. She would pull down his pants and paddle his bare hindquarters with a meat tenderizer until he apologized. And then she would light him on fire.

But that's not what happened. Without a word, Tommy's mother meekly returned the Quaker-inspired breakfast food to the shelf and selected the creepy vampire candy instead. The despair and resignation in her eyes as she did this resembled that of a concentration camp victim or a woman who had been trapped for months in a serial killer's basement. Clearly, this woman had been broken. Tommy seemed to understand this, and to complete the humiliation, he smiled and kicked his mother directly in the vagina.

A whole new world opened up for me in that moment. I realized I had been a fool. An ignorant, chicken-chasing fool! All this time I had been living in the past instead of embracing the future. Hard work and self-reliance were no longer part of the American Dream. These days it was all about gluttony and emotional manipulation. When you wanted something, all you had to do was point at it and scream until it became yours. If that didn't work, one shouldn't be afraid to throw a punch every now and then to remind the parental units who was in charge. This was oedipal warfare at its finest.

From that point on, I decided my days of being a pioneer were over. Sleeping late, watching television, eating junk food—this was the true birthright of my generation, and I was ready to collect. As far as I was concerned, Davey Crockett could keep his stupid coon-skin hat; I wanted an Atari.

If it were actually possible to kill someone with kindness, my mother would be the deadliest military weapon on the planet. She could wipe out the whole of Eastern Europe with a polite smile. A few heartfelt *thank you's* would sink Australia. Compared to my mother, Gandhi was just a skinny a-hole wrapped in a bed sheet. Mother Teresa was a poser. I have rarely heard her utter an uncharitable word about anyone. Once, after reading an article about a serial killer who had murdered half a dozen prostitutes in the Chicago area and then had sex with their lifeless remains, my mother put down the newspaper and said, "Well, he sure does have a nice smile."

I knew my mother loved me because she said so constantly. In fact, as I grew older, her affectionate demonstrations were becoming something of an embarrassment. Sure, it was acceptable to administer a casual peck on the cheek before bedtime to help bolster my courage against the various closet monsters, but it was not okay to lick one's finger and then attempt to remove some imaginary smudge from my face while friends snickered nearby. The woman had no boundaries.

In the past, I'd considered my mother's love a source of shame to be endured, but now I saw her devotion for what it really was. A bargaining chip. Her children's happiness was my mother's primary concern in life, and I planned to exploit those maternal instincts for all they were worth.

The fact that she was under a lot of stress worked in my favor. Living off the grid was taking its toll on my mother, who by this time was looking after four young children and operating a small petting zoo, all with limited resources. While my father had been adamant about our frontier lifestyle in the beginning, like me he grew tired of the tedious work that went along with it. More and more, he began to focus his energy on bringing salvation to the masses, an activity he enjoyed because it allowed him to escape the confines of our house. If he wasn't at church delivering sermons on the Apocalypse, he was driving up and down the numerous dirt roads surrounding Fort Morgan, reminding the local citizens they were going to hell. Many advised him to do the same. Eventually, these heavenly road trips took him further away, to neighboring cities and counties, where he brought the good news to far off lands, such as Sterling, Holyoke, and Laramie. He returned late at night, tired, grumpy, uninterested in household maintenance or monetary problems.

Meanwhile, my mother was trying to hold our small, gridless estate together. A farmer's daughter from rural Minnesota, she was no stranger to hard work, but this was more than she could handle by herself. The garden provided a few salads in the summer and chicken eggs made for nice breakfast omelets, but it was not nearly enough to feed a family of six. On top of that, there were a variety of unplanned expenses that kept popping up. My father's income was sufficient to keep us afloat, but it was not enough to cover emergencies. And there were always emergencies. Car engines stopped running and kid noses started. Mechanic and hospital bills piled up. The bank kindly bounced a few rubber checks for us, but despite all that elasticity, the money never stretched quite far enough.

I wasn't much help. After the encounter at the grocery store, I became increasingly lazy and difficult to deal with. Whenever my mother asked me to perform even the simplest of chores, I would groan and roll my eyes as though she had requested one of my kidneys. Every task became a burden and the person who asked me to do it an oppressor. My attitude rubbed off on my well-behaved siblings, and soon I was the leader of a small, whiny insurrection. Together we protested our indentured servitude with furrowed brows and pouting lips, a guerilla army of Che Guevara Jrs who refused to take out the trash.

For the most part, my mother endured this behavior with infuriating grace, patiently smiling whenever I misbehaved, reminding me that I was a good boy at heart, even though I had become rotten, like a jar of mayonnaise left in the sun to spoil. I observed her reactions and decided my initial conclusion had been correct: my mother's love was an ocean. Its depths were infinite. If I happened to miss a wave of affection every now and then, it was no big deal. I just had to wait around for a few minutes, and another would come crashing at my feet. The way I saw it, my mother owed me a great debt. If I had never been born, she would simply be a crazy woman who darned socks and occasionally deboned chickens. My endless demands for time and attention gave her existence meaning. The least she could do in return was to buy me things and cater to my every whim. After all, I was her son. And she was my meal ticket.

Several months passed before I returned to the grocery store alone with my mother. At the time, we were on a mission to purchase cake ingredients for my sister's upcoming birthday, and my mother was in a rush because she also needed to visit the bank and the post office before they closed. I decided it was time to have my mother's love appraised and find out exactly what it was worth. If things went well, I would be setting myself up for life. All I had to do was lay a little groundwork, and my future would be filled with the bounty produced by my parents' desperate attempts to buy my affection. The toy box would overflow with the fruits of my whimpering. Candy would appear every time I stuck out my bottom lip. On my 16th birthday, there would be a new sports car in the garage, and two years later I would drive it to an Ivy League campus, where, after a few guilt-inducing sighs, my parents would write a check for the tuition. Sure, they might have to take out a mortgage or two, but wasn't my happiness worth a little soul-crushing debt? I thought so.

Therefore, with a lifetime supply of M&M's and a Harvard education in mind, I followed my mother through the grocery store, waiting for the opportunity to ambush her. The occasion presented itself when she stopped to ask a woman in a red smock where she could find the birthday candles. The employee was in her mid-30s, plump and matronly, with thick glasses and the type of short, no-nonsense haircut commonly worn by women whose grooming habits have been streamlined by a houseful of children. I figured having an additional parent around would only help my case, as it would cause my mother to feel as though she was being judged by a jury of her peers.

The woman was stacking reading material in a tall, wire display case. At the top of the display, there was a comic book called *Richie Rich,* an illustrated story of a wealthy blond boy who lived with a butler and, for some inexplicable reason, always wore a red bowtie with blue athletic shorts. Like *Archie* and *Casper,* I considered *Richie Rich* a juvenile comic beneath my literary standards, but that wasn't the point. It was the principle that mattered here. I needed to dig my foxhole and dig it deep.

I pointed to the comic book and said, with the most entitled voice I could muster, "I want that!"

My mother glanced down at me and patted my head. "Not now," she said. "I'm in a hurry."

This infuriated me. How dare she dismiss my desires with such flippancy. Who did this woman think she was? I grabbed a handful of her shirt and yanked. "But I *waaaant* it!" I said. "I want it now! Right *now!*"

The look that came over my mother's face was not the defeated, submissive expression I'd hoped for. In fact, I had only seen this particular horrified grimace on one other occasion, during a Fourth of July barbeque, when she accidentally stepped in fresh dog shit while walking across a neighbor's lawn. "That is just disgusting," she'd said as she scraped the foul-smelling excrement off the bottom of her shoe with a pencil.

There were no pencils in sight this time, but the look my mother gave me insinuated that I, too, needed a good scraping. She bent down close to my ear and said quietly, "I said no. That is the end of this discussion. If you don't like it, you can wait in the car."

She stood up and apologized to the woman in the smock. "I'm sorry. He's going through a phase."

The woman waved her hand dismissively, as though shooing a fly. "I have five of them at home," she said. "Believe me, I know how it is. They're *always* going through a phase."

The two women laughed, and my face burned. What was going on? They were supposed to fuss over me and attempt to gain my favor. What had happened to maternal instincts?

Sensing this was a pivotal moment in our relationship, I decided to call my mother's bluff. Wait in the car, my butt. She was just showing off in front of her new friend, but I'd show her. I'd show the both of them.

With a long howl that could be heard all the way in the produce aisle, I turned and kicked the display case with my foot. I'd meant to topple the thing in dramatic fashion, but given that my foot was about the size of a Milano cookie, all I did was jiggle it a bit. *"I want it! I want it! I want it!"*

My mother rolled her eyes and excused herself.

"No problem," said the woman in the smock. "You take care of business, honey."

My mother is five-feet tall and weighs 95 pounds soaking wet, but she's not exactly what you'd call a fragile woman. When she flung me over her shoulder like a bag of cat food, I was so surprised, I forgot to scream. We were through the automatic glass doors before I got out a good wail, and by then it was too late. She opened the car door, sat on the passenger's seat, and placed me facedown across her lap.

"But you love me!" I bawled.

"Yes, that is true," my mother said. And then she proceeded to spank me in the Safeway parking lot in front of the entire world.

It was only three swats, distributed lightly and without anger, and the tears that followed were formed from embarrassment, not pain.

"I don't know what has gotten into you lately," my mother said. "But I am very disappointed in your behavior. This is not the well-mannered little boy I know. I hope you clean up your act soon, but if you don't, I can do this as long as it takes." Then she kissed me gently on the forehead and closed the car door.

After she was gone, I rubbed my skull vigorously to remove all traces of her kiss. The nerve of that woman, administering affection after nearly beating me to death. She would pay for what she'd done. I wasn't ready to admit I'd been in the wrong, and so I ignored the scene I had made in the store and focused on my punishment. I sprawled out on the backseat and placed my right hand on my forehead, palm-side up, pretending I was dying from heat exhaustion, even though it was a mild day and my mother had cracked the window before she left. When I shriveled up like a raisin, she'd be sorry. Then she would understand why a mother was supposed to give her child anything he asked for.

I remained dead until my mother returned with a bag of groceries. She placed the bag on the passenger's seat and told me to buckle up. I did, but only after sulking first. My mother sighed and removed a *Richie Rich* comic book from the grocery bag. "You can read it after you've finished doing all your chores," she said. "And not a moment sooner."

I crossed my arms over my chest and stuck out my bottom lip. "That's not even the right one," I said. My mother rolled her eyes and drove us home.

GREGORY DUNN

Confessions of a Hapless Reader

From July/August 2009

KOTMAN DRAINS HIS glass of beer, sets it on the worn table, and asks, "Have you read *Cod,* by Mark Kurlansky?"

I shake my head. "No, but I remember seeing it on the front table at the bookstore."

"I know from the title it doesn't sound promising," he replies, "but it's really good."

Englesman points his index finger at him. "I didn't read that one, but his *Basque History of the World* is brilliant."

The two of them talk a bit about fish and Basques and Basque fishing. Then Kotman turns to me. "It's a great book. You really should read it." He refills my glass. "You can borrow my copy. In fact, I'll bring it over to your house."

I smile and thank him, but inside I'm cursing. Despite the fact he's a great friend who sometimes buys me beer, I think, *Who are you to tell me what I should and shouldn't read?*

I already know what I have to read. I have a list.

I didn't always have a list. I had stacks. They would start innocently enough—say, with me sifting through a pile of old *National Geographic* magazines at a used book sale. In one issue, I found a photo essay on Hemingway's northern Michigan. Paging through it made me want to reread "Big Two-Hearted River." Once I got home, I pulled a collection of Hemingway's short stories from my bookshelves. Next to Hemingway, I'd placed books by Jim Harrison, another Michigan writer. I remembered what a great book *Legends of the Fall* is, so I grabbed that, too. But then I thought I ought to read something new by Harrison, so I headed to the library and checked out his novel *Warlock*. Scanning the dust jacket, I discovered that part of the story occurs in Key West, where Hemingway also lived. It made me wonder what other writers are connected to the place.

After a quick search, I learned Annie Dillard spent time there. This prompted me to grab my copy of *Pilgrim at Tinker Creek,* a book I love, as well as her later book, *For the Time Being,* a book I found difficult but decided to give another try. Through it, I learned about Pierre Teilhard de Chardin, who I'd never heard of before. Dillard is so enthusiastic about him, I decided to hunt down his *Divine Milieu.* I eventually discovered a copy at a local secondhand bookstore and was pleased, until I remembered I had started with fishing and ended up in mystical theology. I found this somewhat disorienting.

These books—plus six more from the used book sale, three more from the library, and one more from the bookstore—all went on the stacks on my nightstand. But not only on my nightstand. Also on the desk in my study and next to the easy chair in the living room.

Then the anxiety set in. I worried about losing focus. I fretted that I hadn't finished reading a single one of these books. And I grew tired of knocking over all those stacks cluttering my home.

So I started a list. I entered all the books in all my stacks into a word-processing document and returned them to my shelves. In the habit of a highly effective person, I even prioritized the titles. When I finished, the list was nearly a full page, in two columns, in eight-point type.

I promptly ignored this list and began stacking as before. The anxiety returned. I lengthened the list and returned the books to my shelves. And then I made more stacks.

Clearly, I needed another approach.

I purged my list, which was easier than expected. The justification for half the books had evaporated with time. (Why, again, did I want to read Peter Drucker's *Effective Executive*?) Another quarter of them, upon reflection, no longer interested me. (Did I really want to read an 800-page history of the city of London?) The final cut was harder, but eventually I trimmed the list to 32 books. I got out my typewriter and typed the titles onto a three-by-five index card, ten of them in red ink to indicate they were bona fide members of the canon.

When I finished, I put my typewriter away and set the index card in the center of my cleared-off desk. The list was perfect. Thirty-two books, ten of them genuinely great books, the others entertaining or edifying works of fiction, theology, ethics, history, and biography. An utterly manageable list contained in a convenient three-by-five format that could double as a bookmark.

Three years later, I'd read exactly three of these books. I also had two new piles of books on my nightstand, two more on my desk, and one by the easy chair. In addition, I had a second list, also on a three-by-five index card but handwritten, of 22 books, mostly fiction. This list I made a year after the first, when I realized those edifying books weren't nearly as interesting as I expected.

I'll concede that my reading anxiety may be idiosyncratic. People, probably most of them, simply read—pull a book off a shelf and then read it without reservations, just because they want to. I envy such people.

So why make lists at all? Partly for the pleasure of crossing things off the list. To confess, I am a habitual—some might argue, compulsive—list-maker. Things-to-do lists, daily, monthly, and seasonally. Lists of errands to run, movies to rent, trips to take. Grocery lists, project lists, address lists—if it's listable, I've listed it. I've even made lists of things I've already done, just for the joy of crossing them out. "See what a good person I am," I want to say. "Look at my crossed-off list."

Which brings me to a second kind of list I keep: books I have read. I started keeping this list after a friend mentioned that, since grad school, he kept a log of each book he read and the date he finished it. It struck me as an interesting experiment, so I tried it. From it, I see that over the past three years I have read 41 books, 26 of them fiction, seven memoirs, and the rest nonfiction.

I felt pretty good about my reading pace until I read three books: *Education of a Wandering Man* by Louis L'Amour (number 32 on my "have read" list), *The Polysyllabic Spree* by Nick Hornby (number 39), and *On Writing* by Stephen King (number 40). These guys kept lists of books they read, too. Hornby, according to his list, reads nearly 60 books a year. King reports he reads from 70 to eighty. And L'Amour claimed in his youth to have averaged over 100 a year.

It's hard not to find that depressing.

According to the harsh reality of my list, I read about a book a month, a little more if I really push myself. A dozen books a year, give or take. It will take me over four years just to get through my index cards, and that's only if I read nothing else. And comparing my "have read" log with my "to read" list shows that's not going to happen.

What chills my heart are statements like Thoreau's: "Read the best books first, or you may not have a chance to read them all." Or this one from Harold Bloom's *Western Canon*: "Who reads must choose, since there is literally not enough time to read everything, even if one does nothing but read." Bloom, of course, made a nice living telling people which books are worth their precious time and, so, presents his own list of what one ought to read. It reaches well over 1,000 books. If

I started today, at my current pace, I'd need to live to be 120 to read them all.

It's hard not to find that *really* depressing.

But it gets worse. The problem with sticking to the canon is summed up neatly by Joseph Epstein. "If one tried to read most of the world's good books," he writes, "there would be scarcely any time to read many of the world's interesting books, for, as any veteran reader will tell you, good and interesting books are sometimes but not always the same."

For me, book catalogues are a maddening source of this kind of book. I used to receive one such catalogue called *The Common Reader*. Initially, I was excited when it arrived in my mailbox. I dutifully thumbed its pages, usually in the bathroom, and dogeared particularly interesting ones. I promised myself that after I made a little headway on the books on my list and in my piles, I'd order some. I never did. Every couple of months another catalogue would arrive, with new interesting books, and I'd thumb and dogear again. I did this for years. Although I never ordered any books, I did accumulate an impressive stack of yellowing, dogeared catalogues on the top of the toilet tank. I finally contacted the company and asked them to stop tormenting me.

Add to this situation other lists of interesting books I've come across—lists of "Best Adventure Books" and "Best Nature Writing," the Modern Library's list of the best 100 fiction and nonfiction books of the 20th century, lists of the Pulitzer, Nobel, and Booker Prize winners—it's clear that if I added the interesting books to the great books, I would need several lifetimes to read them all.

It's too depressing to even consider.

Merely spending time in the bookstore is now a challenge. This is difficult, since my wife and I go there every Sunday after church. At first, it's not so bad. The light is good, and the air smells like books. The new-release table stands right by the door, and, though one or two always look tempting, I am prepared for them and am able to resist their advances.

Then I walk deeper into the store for the complimentary coffee, browsing as I go, and things start to go south. To the left is the history section, and I am reminded of my resolve to include more of it in my reading diet, maybe a book on the McKinley administration or on the development of bathyspheres. Behind the information desk is the section on religion and theology, and I think maybe it's time to read Calvin's *Institutes* or make a study of Zoroastrianism.

On the way back to the front of the store, paper cup of coffee in hand, I weave my way through the fiction area. I see all those books I think I want to read, or ought to read, or should have already read. By the time I return to my wife, I have a mental list of another three dozen books and a new anxiety attack.

My wife finds this hilarious. "It's not a test," she says. "Just read what you want to."

I do not find her attitude helpful.

Near the front of the bookstore, the management reserves a table for books being discussed by local reading groups. Most are pretty good. Some are even on my list. I often browse the table, sip my coffee, and think it would be nice to join one.

Until I remember how reading groups stress me out. As I said before, I know what I have to read. I have a list. A couple of them. The last thing I need is another book I haven't read, sitting on my nightstand, highlighting my shortcomings as a reader.

This is especially true if that book is borrowed and carries an imperative to be read, preferably soon. A friend once loaned me a copy of Michael Pollan's *Botany of Desire*. I spent a whole year not reading it. From time to time, my friend would ask if I had finished it.

"Not yet," I'd reply, "but soon."

He eventually stopped asking. Now and again I'd unearth the book from a pile and make a resolution to read it as soon as I finished what

I was reading at the time. I once even leafed through it, glancing at the table of contents and author's foreword. Usually, though, I just weighed it in my hand, considering its mute accusation, and, in shame, hid it away.

A couple of years later, I came across a copy of *Botany of Desire* at a used book sale, bought it, and returned the borrowed copy.

"I was wondering where this was," my friend said. "I thought I loaned it to my brother-in-law." Then he added, "Did you read it at least?"

"Yes," I lied. "It's a fine book."

I still haven't read it.

I once read that the disciples of the political philosopher Leo Strauss read and teach only some two dozen books. I've not yet found a list of these books, but I can guess at them, and the purity and simplicity of such a rule appeals to me. These surely would fit on an index card. Indeed, they could all fit on one shelf, greatly freeing up room in my house for other things. But such a rule isn't really feasible. I'm not sure it's even desirable. Life is too riotous to accommodate such attempts at simplicity and purity.

My wife is right. Reading is not about passing a test, implementing a system, or, even, working through a list. It is not a task, something that can be itemized, crossed off, and finished. Reading is a practice. Being well-read means reading well.

Nevertheless, I still like my lists. Maybe it's the promise of focus a list asserts. Maybe it's a result of too much schooling and a residual reverence for syllabi. Probably it stems from the sense of being in a broad, unknown country and the need for a map and an expedition log, a sense of where I'm going and a record of where I've been. So I'm going to keep my lists. I'm going to keep making them. And I'm going to keep ignoring them.

ALAN KAUFMAN

Things Carl Little Crow and I Did Together to Stay Sober in San Francisco

From August/September 1998

Carl and Me

I WAS 37 and a half years old, raised in the Bronx, penniless, prideful, a paranoid-schizophrenic, overeducated transplanted New Yorker with 22 years of severe alcholism under my belt, newly arrived in San Francisco off a Greyhound Bus with $67 in my pocket.

Carl Little Crow was half African-American, half Native American; a former back alley drunk from Chicago with 18 years of sobriety to his name. He was half my size and had a face like an alert animal. He wore an embroidered West African shaman's cap, a cowskin vest, baggy corduroys, scuffed black shoes, and carried a befeathered Native American tom-tom drum he beat as he walked down Haight Street.

The Things We Did

1

Healing ceremonies atop Buena Vista Park in Haight Ashbury. Carl claimed a satanic sacrificial cult was operating in the area, abducting and murdering people, and that as spiritual human beings we must "cleanse" the area with our souls. For this ceremony, Carl's mentor, Rolland, drove in from Arizona in a rusted brown stationwagon. Also in attendance was Mike, sober ten years, known thereabouts as the Captain of Haight Street.

With only two months booze-free, I was the novice and appointed to carry the healing plant, a ratty-looking lobby plant with withered leaves Carl had salvaged from the trash outside a Tenderloin Hotel. Carl took the plant home and gave it food, sunshine, Native American chants, petting strokes, water, and whispers of love until it was able to lift its head again, which it now did proudly. It still looked like a shitty plant from a flop hotel, but it was vibrantly alive. As I carried it, huffing, Carl led the way, chanting in a trance, beating the drum, walking in a slow processional march up the slope of the park to the top of the hill. Deadheads and crack dealers watched us with interest. According to Carl, the Devil worshippers were spying on us but chances were excellent we wouldn't see them. It was strange, I thought, about the ceremony. I'd showed up in SF paranoid and delusional, clinging to my sobriety by bloody fingernails, gibbering about being pursued across the continent by Devil worshippers, and suddenly Carl, who's been 18 years without booze, declares that yes, they do exist, are a definite danger, and now for once and all we will rid the world of them. I felt both terrified and reassured.

Bringing up the rear was Mike, the Captain of Haight Street, tall, bone-lean, with a mean-looking handlebar moustache and a combative black beret set at a jaunty angle on his old gray skull. He had cold blue eyes, and a big key ring jingled from his belt. He was scanning the turf with sweeping looks, warning off anyone with the wrong idea. There were lots of such people around, and they knew Mike and knew that while he might not beat you one on one the first time around, Mike would make it his religion to get even, even if it took 20 years, and would not cease until you were effaced from the earth. His other hobbies were amateur photography, of which he was a very fine practitioner, and archiving local historical information and artifacts. Like, he could show you, hidden near a drainage ditch covered over with dead leaves, a row of little white tombstones embedded like teeth into the cement, belonging to a party of goldminer 49ers who were killed in a drunken brawl 'round these parts nigh a hunnert and 50 summott years ago' as Mike would say. The accent was an affection. He was really a marvelously bright and well-educated man whom alcohol had laid low, like the rest of us.

Rolland walked behind Mike at a remove of ten paces, and I was surprised at how average-looking he seemed. Like any road dog you might come across in the Arizona desert. That hermit smile and blue eyes bleached kind by extreme loneliness. He wore just a plain old black tee-shirt, stone-scrubbed blue jeans, and embossed leather cowboy boots. Was more a dude than a hierarchically royal medicine man of the Blackfoot tribe. But, I figured, what the hell did I know about it, anyway?

My job was to carry, and I did. My arms grew heavy. I wanted to drop the damned plant. But I held on as we inched our way up, led by Carl's mournful voice and the *boom boom boom* of the tom-tom, and soon we were at the top where we proceeded briskly to a ravine and slid down the slope to a wide shelf, which Carl declared to be our healing ground.

It was a godforsaken place of dead trees and amputated branches. We sat in a circle, and Carl Little Crow said something in Native American tongue, and Rolland nodded and smiled. Then they all looked at me. "What's your spirit animal?" Carl asked.

Surprised, I shrugged. "I dunno. "

Carl's eyes burned into mine. "What? Name it!"

I couldn't think of any. We don't have animals in the Bronx. What should I say? Cockroach? Rat? This is how I knew I was really in

California now. Someone named Carl Little Crow asking me to name my Spirit animal.

"I dunno," I said again.

Once more he burned into me with his eyes and said, "Name it! Name it now!"

Suddenly the word "hawk" popped into my brain, so I blurted out "Hawk!" and Carl hissed, "Look up!" and I looked up, and O, my God, O my ever-loving fucking God, right there, over us, circling, two of them, enormous, right here in Haight Ashbury. What were hawks doing there anyhow? And right at that moment, no less?! Now I felt the presence of what he called the Great Spirit, others call God, or whatever they call it. I felt it. Absolutely absolutely. And it freaked the living daylights out of me. In a good way.

2

Walking down Haight Street together, Carl beating his drum, me holding onto his shirt, afraid to let go, afraid if I did, I'd go drink. He'd lead me up to trees and stand there talking to them, waving his hands with this ecstatic look on his animal-like face, nodding his head vigorously with a look of delight, as though answering questions.

"What're they saying, Carl?" I'd ask.

"They're saying: 'Don't drink!'" he'd reply.

3

Taking astral projection trips around the world. Actually, he took them while I sat there and watched. Usually, we did this in the Café International on Haight and Filmore, down in the Lower Haight. Sat at one of the scratched up wooden tables embedded with hand painted tiles, surrounded by electric new paintings by young, unknown geniuses, worldbeat music playing, and Carl would close his eyes and begin to sway from side to side, and it would seem as though the colors in the room were running together with acid-like intensity, and Carl seemed to... how to describe this? Know how a gif looks on your computer if the server crashes? A kind of graphic ghost? Carl turned into that. If you'd clicked on him, nothing would have happened. He was elsewhere, transported by spiritual metasearch engine into the hard drive of the Amazon jungle, or appearing on the interactive screen of the Himalayan mountains. He was rapping with the Dalai Lama. He was reading poetry to the King of Sweden.

Once, he opened his eyes and I saw two white ghost buffaloes galloping in his irises.

When he did this, it scared the shit out of me, but I preferred to stay by him than take my chances alone with my own mind, which was detoxing with D.T.'s and hallucinations that wanted to kill me. Each cell of my brain, my body, Carl had explained, had been perforated after years of drinking by a little hole, each of which I'd previously filled with alcohol but which was now empty, yearning, yawning, craving, desperate to be filled, an almost sexual need, but I must fill it with something else now. I must fill it with my soul. I must fill it with the Great Spirit of the Universe. And for this I must not drink but allow my mind and body to recover. I must learn to know my spirit. We were like two separate entities calling each to the other across a great gulf now. But soon, we would be reunited. So I sat and watched Carl Little Crow cavort with Dakota sandpainters and Ludwig Von Beethoven. Ludwig, Carl informed me, was an abused child, like me.

4

Eating Bar-B-Q chicken wings. Carl had a shameless love of Bar-B-Q chicken wings. It surprised and disappointed me. I thought someone so spiritual would want to eat, say, a bowl of brown rice and a cup of green tea. Instead he'd take me over to Chicken Charlies on Divisadero, across the street from the Kennel Klub, and order up big buckets of greasy orange Bar-B-Q chicken wings and get all messed with juices and greases and wing bits and bone smattering his grinning mouth, ecstatically cooing "YESSSS! OH, YESSSSSSS!" when I took a nibble off one and smiled happily despite myself. It just didn't fit the picture, him tearing at those chicken wings and slurping up a 32-ounce Cherry Coke. I noticed he had a bit of a belly, too. But worse still, he had this ugly weal of a scar worming down the center of his chest where'd he'd had open heart surgery, during which he'd died twice and been revived.

During the time he was dead, he had floated above the table smiling down at everyone and then left for a few seconds to take an astral projection trip to New York City, where he danced, he said, with a seniorita in the Spanish Harlem section of New York. That, too, shocked me. I mean, that's what one can think of to do at the moment of one's death? Dance with a woman? "Not just any woman," said Carl Little Crow. "A Puerto Rican woman." He looked at me and jumped up and down in his seat, laughing like a happy kid with the grease all over him, and I said very gravely unamused, "Well, that shit's real bad for your heart, Carl, and seems like you already had one heart attack and..." I got all choked up here, and Carl grew still, and I fought back tears but lost and sobbed out, "And what if you die, man! What am I gonna do? How am I gonna stay sober!?"

And Carl's eyes grew moist, and he said, "By helping another... Remember! It's always by helping another that we are healed ourselves."

And I am crying even now, seven and a half years later, to remember those words.

5

Consuming a whole half-gallon of peach melba ice cream. Another of Carl's peculiar weaknesses. First he'd have me at night seated on the floor of my tiny room near the Hayes Street projects in the "Mo" as we called the Filmore district, with the gat guns of battling crack gangs going *pop pop pop* outside our windows, and squealing tires and screaming voices, and a bundle of burning sage smoking in a bowl as we sat and breathed in and out, in and out, watching our breath, calming our bodies—it is all in the breath—and then we chanted a mantra, "God grant us the serenity to accept the things we cannot change, the courage to change the things we can, and the wisdom to know the difference," and then he'd have me up on my feet, dancing a slow spirit dance around the room, waving my hands, moving the energy fields around, as he put it. And when we were done, we then adjourned to the communal kitchen I shared with a bunch of potheads and grunge maniacs, and took out a half gallon of peach melba ice cream and two spoons and Bob's Your Uncle!

The sugar wacked Carl out for sure. His eyes would get all red, and he'd feel giddy and sway and stagger as he walked, and for a moment I could see 18 years ago to the back alley drunk he must have been, a little lethal menace. And it amazed me he could have gone so long without a drink, and I'd feel hope. Then he'd leave, and I'd sometimes find a ten spot on the bed, maybe his last since he was always short of money and mostly unconcerned about it. I'd stretch out on the bed with my boots on, head pillowed on my hands, listening to the gunfire and the shouts and watching the fog roll over the last vestige of the San Francisco moon. I was flat broke, my Welfare General Asistance due to expire, and all that I had been—a father, a soldier, a lover, a boss, a highly touted this and a well-regarded that—all lay behind me now. The park bench where I had laid down to die in Thompkin Square on Avenue A in Alphabet City, Manhattan, New York City, and from which I rose to live—damned if I understand even to this day how or why?—when every blood vessel in my flesh demanded booze and booze and more booze, and when this disease I have, this disease of alcholism believed it would continue to drink even after I had died. Instead I found help in the rooms of recovery and against the advice of the recovered drunks I met, boarded a bus with $67 in my pocket and a California sun rising in my addled, sleep-deprived detoxing brain. And this is what it means to be happy: to want nothing and sit listening to the calm beating of your own heart as big wheels carry you off into a Mystery lined with fast food concession stands.

6

Getting a man to detox. We happened upon him sitting on the steps of a Haight Ashbury Victorian recovery home that had once been the former residence of Janis Joplin, just a few doors down from where the novelist Kathy Acker once lived (we'd see Kathy in her leather jacket handpainted with skulls and roses and she, being a real dear woman under that tough exterior, always had a kind word). He dressed for business in a tie. He wore spectacles, his hair was thinning, and his hands were trembling violently. An over-flowing suitcase lay open on the sidewalk, and he was staring at its contents and moaning ""hhhhhuuuuuhhhh, God, uuuuuhhhhhhhhh, Oh, God," and Carl said, "What is it my brother?" and he said "You God?" and Carl Little Crow breathed out meditatively and said, "No. I am a drunk like you," and the man looked at him angrily, then at me and snapped, "I'm no drunk!" and burst into tears.

"I AM A DRUNK! OH, I AM A TERRIBLE DRUNK!" he keened.

"What happened?" I asked softly.

"My friend lent me his apartment for three days, so I got permission to leave the recovery house on a pass and went there and dropped all his acid and drank all his brandy and smashed up the house, and I ran back here, and they saw that I'd gone out, and they threw me into the street! Now I have no place to go! My friend's back by now. He's probably looking to kill me. What'll I do? What'll I do?"

"Go to detox," said Carl.

The man looked at him, astonished. "Detox? I can't go to detox!! I'm middle-class!"

How well I understood that pretense. But booze strips some of us down to our essentials. "It's your only option," said Carl. And the man nodded his head and sobbed, and I went up the street to the phone booth to call the MAP van to take him in. For hours we sat with the man, waiting. And I told him the story of my last run. There I was, I said, living in Park Slope, Brooklyn. Had a $60,000 a year job. Married to an English actress and had a year-old daughter, a little blond and blue-eyed angel named Isadora who would say, "Da'ddy, Da'ddy" over and over to herself as though I were ambrosia to her little soul. Had a garden out back where I'd sit at night in a lawn chair under a tree of heaven, counting stars. Had sworn off the liquor for good, figuring that nothing, nothing must ever spoil my chance for a beautiful life with this little girl, nothing on this earth! Belonged to a gym, too. Got into peak physical condition. Was up for a raise at work, bringing in a lot of new accounts and money. Inside I felt miserable, but I thought, "What the hell, I've always been miserable, it's just the way it is for me."

One day on my way home from work, passing through the twilit streets of my little neighborhood, I passed a local tavern, a real nice place for a respectable clientele, and I thought, "Why not? Why the hell not? Don't I deserve it? Look at how beautiful my life is. It'll be the proverbial cherry on the pudding." So I entered the bar to cherry my pudding.

A bartender dressed in a red Eisenhower jacket was toweling a tumbler dry by candlelight. "Good evening, sir," he said as I settled onto a plush red leather bar stool and rested my elbows on the polished mahogany counter.

"Evenin'." I smiled with a terse nod.

"And what will you be having this evening?"

I lifted a finger into the air. "Chevas Regal," I said, and as he turned, I lifted a second finger. "Make it a double."

When he brought it, I held it up to the candlelight and swished it around in the brandy snifter, its golden elegance proclaiming the vigor and achievement of my adulthood. I slammed it down with a gasp and said, "Gimme another," and that came, and no candlelit reflection now, just down the hatch, and another and another, the bulkhead filling fast. I don't remember anything after the sixth.

I experienced a black roaring pain in my head, and my eyes winced open to the vague chilly paleness of a Manhattan dawn sky. I was still dressed in my London Fog raincoat, still clutching my attaché. And I was lying in bushes in a projects on 23rd Street in Chelsea, covered with vomit, urine, and blood. I staggered to my feet to stumble off to work. And now I tore through my little daughter's life with cyclonic ferocity; took to sleeping at the office on an inflatable boyscout mattress and spent the nights in Billy's Topless on sixth avenue and 24th Street, one of whose dancing girls was found decapitated and dismembered, her body parts boiled for soup and served up to the homeless in Thompkin Square Park. It was front page in all the papers. They found the killer, too, a local nutcase version of Charles Manson. I remember the girl, a sweet Swedish dancer. I had stuffed a few bills myself into her G-string. It was that kind of place and those sorts of people. I'd only go home to stuff some of my cashed paycheck into a measuring cup in the cupboard and then leave again to ride the subway back into Manhattan to Billy's. Once, late at night, I came home to leave some money. My wife didn't even bother to rise from bed. I put the money into the measuring cup and was heading for the door when I heard behind me the patter of little feet and turning saw Isadora, all of a year and a half by now, rush up and clasp my leg with her tiny arms and press her cheek to my shin and cling there, as if to say, "Please, Daddy, don't go." Never in my life had I ever loved anyone or anything as much as I loved her. I lifted her up, pressed her to me, kissed her cheeks with tears in my eyes, cradled her in my arms and returned her to her place beside her mother, who lay there in the dark staring wordlessly at the ceiling. Then I turned and left. I went back to Billy's.

When I need to drink, nothing, no one, can stand in my way, I told the drunk on the stairs as we waited for the MAP van. It's not a thing that normies fathom. Nor should they have to. I am living proof that life is not fair. Because if life were fair, I'd be dead, slaughtered by the way I drank. Yet here I was, sober, and here was my friend and mentor Carl Little Crow with 18 years. If we can do it, I told our middle class friend, then so can you. And I knew he believed me, as only one drunk can believe another who has been down the same road and lived to tell the tale.

7

Finding a higher power. From across the street a man with glowing eyes leered at me. Further on a pair of tattooed and toothless motorcycle freaks eyeballed me, plotting my murder, as I hurried down Haight Street. Like the man with glowing eyes, they had been following me for days and were all part of the same conspiracy. So, too, was a tall black man with a shaved head and wire rim spectacles who received a signal from them and registered my presence as I passed his Mercedes Benz. I knew he thought I was an FDA agent sent to spy on his cocaine-smuggling operation. His eyes promised me a slow, painful death. By the time I reached the corner of Church and Market, I was faint with fear. I looked around for shelter, spotted a shop called Aztec Taqueria, and made for it. But as I crossed the threshold of the steamy little shop, I realized this was the headquarters of an Aztec sacrificial cult who knew I knew what they were. I had tricked myself into the lion's lair. Now I was really doomed. I couldn't leave, though. Paralyzed with terror, I stood at the counter.

"What'll you have?" asked the counter help, a Mexican with tired eyes. My eyes shifted nervously to the open door of an office near the kitchen. Someone in there was staring at me. There was a video screen monitoring traffic. So that's how they did it! I watched to see if someone would emerge to close the store's front door, entrapping me. But the counterman's voice was adament: "What's it gonna be man?"

"Burrito," I stuttered.

"Refried or whole beans?"

I didn't know what to answer to this obvious test. The wrong response would unleash hidden minions in white uniforms, rushing out from every corner to throw me onto the counter and hold me down for the high priest with the butcher knife.

"For here or to go?" the counterman asked as he wrapped the burrito. He was looking at me strangely. Another test.

"Here," I said. It was obviously the right answer. Only, I had a plan. With shaking hands, I received the burrito and paid him. A cauldron of white hot panic boiled in my solar plexus as I made my way on wobbly legs to a table and sat down. I stared at the burrito without appetite, sure that 100 eyes watched to see what I'd do. I must have looked white as a sheet. I just sat there. Had run out of steam. Felt ready to give up, stand, shout, "OK THEN, MURDER ME! MURDER ME!" It is what people who have completely snapped do in public with violent abruptness. Stand up on a bus, begin to shout about their crossover into the fifth dimension of insanity. Their way of saying they hereby renounce their residency on Planet Normie. My plan was to sit thus until they tired of my surveillance, looked away.

I waited, enveloped in sickening fear. When I felt it right, I jumped up, burrito in hand, and ran out the door. I hurried down the street, sure they were on my heels, and halfway down the block, my legs wobbled, lost all feeling, and I sprawled over the sidewalk. I lay there, 37 and a half years old, paralyzed with terror, unable to walk, rise, or speak, certain of imminent execution, not wanting to die, and so alone, so very alone. "Carl, " I whispered, "where are you, Carl Little Crow? Help me. Help me."

And I saw Carl Little Crow's face before my eyes. He said, "Pray for help to whatever you call your Great Spirit. Ask for protection." And so I did. I called upon the name of God in Hebrew, Elohim, remembered from my Bar Mitzvah, without a clue about what it named or meant. I called out that name in sorrow, anguish, and defeat. And my legs regained sensation. And I stood up. And I began to walk normally. I did not feel the need to hurry. I still felt threatened by death but walked in the Valley of its shadow without fear. This was on Church Street in San Francisco, where later I bought a Jewish prayer shawl for a buck off a junkie selling stolen goods on the sidewalk.

My Life Now

8

Carl Little Crow, where are you? Often I think of those times we spent together. It's been over seven years and can you believe it, I have gone that long without a drink, and I have become a well-known poet. It happened because you said to me one day as we walked down Haight Street, "What do you want to do with this great gift that you have been given?"

"You mean sobriety?" I said.

"Yes. How will you use this miracle for the benefit of others?"

I didn't know. I said, "Maybe I should get a good job and set myself up, you know, more comfortably."

And you stopped and looked hard at me. "What were you doing when you went on your last run?"

"Earning 60 grand" I said.

"And was this true to your real nature?"

"Nah," I said. "It wasn't. I knew it. I hated it. And I hated myself."

"And haven't you learned here, 'To thine Own Self Be True?!' is this not the motto of our recovery? To Thine Own Self Be True!"

"Yah," I replied.

"So what is it you would do with the gift that is true to your being? Because sobriety is the Great Spirit's gift to you, but what you do with it is your gift to the Great Spirit."

And I said: "Wellll, I've always had this fantasy to be a poet, ya know?"

And you jumped in the air, literally, finger pointing at my eyes and howled, "HO! Then that is what you must do! And never waver until the last breath of your life! And remember, the hawk is your spirit in your work! Call upon him when you most need help!"

And I have done as you advised. Since then, I have performed my work before audiences around the world. I live in a beautiful apartment with a woman, a kindergarten teacher, named Diane. My life is so beautiful now that sometimes I sit in a chair in my study just listening to the sound of my heart. There's a garden outside my window, where birds sing. Doves and hummingbirds and sparrows and bluejays and robins. And there's a garden inside of me. It is a Buddha garden of Zen flowers. There is a pond in which a great blue carp rests at ease in the shadows unmoving for days.

I miss you, Carl Little Crow. I want to show you this place I have found within, because it is you who first led me to it and helped me to plant the first seed. I see you laughing with glee, slapping your sides, rolling on the ground. I see you wacking at a coffee can with an oar, trying to get it open because we couldn't find a can opener. I remember you as though you were in this room with me now, strolling like a warrior down Haight Street, the proudest man I have ever known. I remember how your head bobbed like a mongoose and your eyes fixed on me with unflinching compassion when I told you my mother had been in the Holocaust and had beaten me as a child. You said, "She was wounded and passed her wound to you. But that wound is the flower from which all will grow, if only you don't drink, and instead turn your thoughts to love and service for others."

I am crying now as I write this, Carl Little Crow, unashamed of my feelings, another gift you gave to me. How your face, like a bust carved out of rock by a Mayan, would suddenly bear bright ribbons of tears caused by another's expression of pain. How you felt. How you saw. How you loved. Do you remember the trees you introduced me to in Golden Gate Park? There was the short black tree with white and yellow blossoms that you asked me to hug and I did, in front of a group of Japanese tourists. There was the immense redwood you slapped on the trunk with a shout, "HO! MY BROTHER!" and danced around while I stood by, bewildered by your energy and ignorant of your purpose. There was the eucalyptus whose leaves you snapped open under my nose to inhale and later brewed me tea from and told me of its healing properties. I remember how, at your approach, the little black birds who crowded the sidewalk outside the McDonalds on Haight Street would swarm around your feet and dive out of the trees and sometimes land on your shoulder. Everyone around was too oblivious, consuming their hamburgers, maybe consumed by them, to notice this extraordinary thing. "Yessssss, little brother," you sighed to the birds. "Ohhhhhhh, how are you my friends? How is the food gathering?" And you'd listen. I swear they chirped back.

MONIKA LANGE

The World and I

From July/August 2007

ON THIS LONELY Saturday, the sun shines just as bright as it did on Tuesday, September 11. In front of our San Francisco Bay Area house, my teenage daughter Anahita (Ana) and my husband Bei install a new American flag. As the flag blows in the breeze from the lagoon, the wind seems to play Chopin's *Mazurka*.

"Mom!" Ana's voice brings me back from my reverie. "Where are you?"

Where indeed? In Poland, in Warsaw, where in my dad's study I began to discover the world.

Poland, a small country in Europe, sandwiched between her potent neighbors, forever occupied, cut and divided, as if it were a piece of cake. Chopin's music in the willows—the constantly weeping, eternal sadness of freedom lost. Among all this at the end of the 1950s, my father's study provides a safe haven, where I can sit under the desk, or find a book on one of the floor-to-ceiling black shelves holding many languages, countries, and religions in their wooden embrace. I can sit on a black lion adorning the Danzig sofa, or on Dad's lap, which I obviously prefer, and read or listen to him telling me about distant lands, different cultures, and religions. From the wall, a South American mask with black horns looks upon us with bloody eyes. From the table, a serene Buddha sitting in the lotus position guards us, and a dancing Shiva engaged in his eternal cosmic prance offers his protection. And so my little country grows, embracing the world.

My mother supplements father's tales about foreign lands and people with the story close to home. She reminisces about her best friend, Roma, a Jewish girl who "went to an oven" in Treblinka. Mom tells me how initially she visited Roma in the ghetto and later sent her food and books, whenever an opportunity presented itself. She also tells how my grandfather, the physician, surgeon, and ObGyn of German descent who stayed in the Nazi occupied town, refused to sign the "volks list" stating his German citizenship, treated and operated the Home Army freedom fighters, all the while under scrutiny of the Nazi occupant. While the non-Jewish citizens were forbidden to enter the ghetto under the penalty of death, he not only repeatedly asked the new county captain, Dr. Glehn, for passes to visit his friend Dr. Mordkowich in the Tomaszow ghetto, but he also helped treat the ghetto Jews during the frequent outbreaks of typhus. He repeatedly pleaded with Glehn to ameliorate the ghetto's living conditions. He helped some Jews to escape initial deportations by employing them on his estate, like Dr. Schindler. They had risked their lives and survived.

At nine, I broaden my little world when we visit Italy. I fall in love with the history of the Roman Empire, immediately deciding to become an archeologist. Every day I run to the Colosseum, where I almost can hear cheers of spectators, roars of lions and tigers, and sounds of gladiators' deadly battles. I pick up a black piece of a mosaic and hide it in my pocket. I keep this ancient relic for many years to remind me of human history.

A year later chemistry casts its spell, so even while writing historical novels for my friends, I decide to major in chemistry. Many years later, I will. However, different events occur in the meantime. My beloved father dies when I am only 12, my mother and I are suddenly alone. My half-brother Christopher, who lives in England, invites me there for summer vacation. My summer trips to England become a custom, and every summer I travel to London, Manchester, Wales, and Cornwall. I love it. I meet so many different people—Indian, Jewish, Asian, Black, American, and South African—people from the distant countries I know of, others I still have to learn about. My friend Patsy from South Africa tells me, "During the apartheid I filled in questionnaires, 'race: human, color: pink.'"

Meanwhile, my own country prepares to give me a hard lesson in history and life. In March of 1968, I am in the 9th grade. Unexpectedly, a Star of David appears on my best friend Ela's desk. Until then, I never think of Ela as being Jewish. What does it matter, anyway? Now I learn that for many people it makes a great difference! Friends from my girl scout troop and the local boy scout troop are leaving Poland. How is it possible? It seems just yesterday we all took a pledge at the Warsaw Citadel, the symbol of Poland's struggle for independence. A hundred years ago, during the Tsarist Russian occupation, *kibitkas,* or horse wagons, were leaving the Citadel's gallows filled with Polish political prisoners. Horses' hoofs clicked on cobblestone streets in the rhythm of the Polish national anthem: "Poland shall not die, as long as we live..." The journey and the lives of the freedom fighters from the Citadel ended in Siberian lagers. Now, a century later, my friends' journeys result in exile. I still see the surreal image of the empty train station, the hugs and the tears, and the train for Vienna, reluctantly pulling away. My lips emit no sound as I sing in my mind, "Poland shall not die, as long as we live..."

Another shock comes at the end of the school year, when our principal, who is also my beloved history teacher, gets kicked out of our high school. Ela and I visit him some time later, only to learn that he, too, will leave Poland. Meanwhile, we feel discriminated against by most teachers—I for sticking to my friends and my values, Ela also for not having left when all other Jews did.

"Do you want to change schools?" my mom asks after one particularly unpleasant day.

I refuse. So does Ela. We don't want to give in to the anti-Semitic bigots.

In the summer of 1974, I arrive in the US. It's been the year of Joan Baez and Bob Dylan's "Where have all the flowers gone?" and the never-ending Vietnam war. Now it's the verge of President Nixon's impeachment. When I come to Washington DC, the White House is closed for visitors. People gather in front of the gates.

"Do you know why it's closed today?" I ask a female tourist.

"President Nixon resigned last night, and we are waiting for President Ford's arrival," explains a young woman, her face shaded by a straw hat.

I decide not to wait, and I visit the city instead. Again I come invited by my brother, who this time lives in Rochester, New York. The Greyhound Bus Company provides me with a tour of Canada and the States. I love it, but even on the Navajo Reservation, I miss history that in Europe surrounded me everywhere.

Back in Europe, while visiting Paris, I meet Jamshid, an Iranian whom I will marry the following year. I reach further back into the history of humanity, all the way to ancient Persia.

With my new husband, I travel to Iran in August 1977. The country stands at the brink of an Islamic revolution, but we don't realize it yet.

The next eight years are sometimes difficult, sometimes happy, sometimes just uneventful, but always fascinating. I meet with Islam, this time not in a book but in real life. I discover a compassionate religion of giving and sharing with the less fortunate, of helping fellow human beings, the qualities almost forgotten in the Western World I come from. Iranians are hospitable, caring, and fun-loving people. They embrace me like one of their own.

A few years later, I'll also meet with Islamic extremists who call for girls to marry at nine and who send little boys into war as minesweepers. The fanatics will carry out the Jihad, or the holy war, against the Arab invader, Iraq. A horrifying picture emerges. Little children become instant martyrs who are to open Heaven's gates with a plastic key each carries around his neck. A man on a white stallion, dressed in white robes and white turban, walks his horse toward the minefield. "It's the *Imam*, the Spirit of Saint Ali," the children are told, and they run to become martyrs forever. Their small bodies torn in half, decapitated. Little limbs scatter across the minefield. Mothers will never see their young sons again. Tired, the horse rider returns to camp. Tomorrow, he will play his role again. Such religious fanaticism teaches me a bitter lesson.

In 1980s Poland, great things are happening, but they are too far removed from me as I have given Iran my heart. Yet, eventually, the fanatics will drive me away from the country of Saadi and Hafez, the country that will change its "roses and nightingales" into guns and martyrs.

America turns out to be my destiny after all. A weary traveler, I reach the East coast, running away to save my daughter from bombs falling on Tehran and from life in Communist Poland. A gypsy, a vagabond, I travel from New York to Texas, and on to California, planting my roots temporarily in each home and in each state, until a few years later I get grounded by an enemy, the biggest of all: Multiple Sclerosis. The illness comes upon me unexpectedly, in the midst of the Mexican Rainforests, and enslaves me, chains me, cuts my wings. Revenge of Montezuma? Ahriman? Some god I have offended?

Fate has been so unforgiving. As if I have not been punished enough, today I face another, brand new Jihad, this time against my new country. New York is burning. America bleeds. Terror shows its ugly head. My heart aches for all the lives lost, for all the people who will perish in senseless wars. Have human nations forgotten they are one, that their humble creation lies with a common ancestor who originated somewhere deep in the heart of Africa?

Sometimes I feel the world and I are alone in this endless fight for common sense, understanding, and love of mankind. Yet, I have moments of glory. On a Saturday in September, I, a Polish woman, watch my Muslim-born daughter Ana, a typical American teenager in denim shorts and a tiny white tank top. Her long blond hair blows in the breeze. My Chinese husband Bei, her stepfather, usually stern and disapproving of Ana's skimpy outfits, silently shakes his black mane and works with her in unity to install a new American flag on the lagoon in front of our house. The sun reflects on the water and bounces off the surface, creating tiny disks of light. As Ana and Bei hoist the flag in the air, I recall my small country in Europe and my father's study, where among thousands of books I learned that all people are equal. I believe I have understood this lesson well. The flag flutters in the breeze, and I hear Chopin's *Mazurka* playing in the weeping willows on the other side of the water. Slender poplars, so much like the ones that flanked the driveway of my grandparents' house in Tomaszow, join in the Chopin concert. The world and I have come full circle, and we still have hope.

Contributors' Notes

Norman Ball has published poems and essays in *Asia Times, Counterpunch, The Berkeley Poetry Review, Rattle, Liberty, Foreign Policy Journal, Global Research* and elsewhere. He has a new poetry collection, *Serpentrope*, from White Violet Press and his book on TV Culture, *Between River & Rock: How I Resolved Television in Six Easy Payments* is available from Giant Steps Press with a viewable excerpt at the Museum of American Poetics. Prior essay collections, *How Can We Make Your Power More Comfortable?* (2010) and *The Frantic Force* (2011), both widely available on the web, are published by Del Sol Press and Petroglyph Books, respectively.

Richard Bellikoff is a transplanted New Yorker living in Southern California. He regularly performs his nonfiction stories—including a much shorter version of *That Was It*—at various spoken word venues in Los Angeles. A starving musician before he became a starving writer, he began his writing career on TV sitcoms. Life imitated art, as his own existence became a sitcom. After years of writing documentary scripts for public TV and executive speeches and communications, marketing, and training materials for ruthless and predatory multinational corporations, he discovered he was far too educated to make a living in today's globally outsourced economy. He has a BS in chemical engineering and an MBA in finance. Both are available for lease or purchase.

Dale Bridges is a fiction writer, essayist, and freelance journalist. His writing has been featured in more than 30 publications, including *The Rumpus, The Masters Review,* and *Barrelhouse Magazine*. His book of short stories, *Justice, Inc.*, was published in 2014. He lives in Austin with his wife and two cats, working on his first novel.

Anthony Brown went to prison at 21 and did not again live outside of concrete, steel, and barbed wire until he was fifty-six. While serving a Life Sentence for the state of Alaska, he was imprisoned in facilities operated by state, federal, and private entities in Alaska, California, Arizona, and Colorado. Writing about life in America's prisons, while not usually expressly forbidden in writing, is openly and harshly discouraged. "You Can't Have Him" describes a real incident, and only individual names and the identifying details of "Kurt's" nationality and crimes have been changed for the protection of all involved. Anthony and his wife, Michelle, were married in 1991 at the Spring Creek Correctional Center in Seward, Alaska. He was granted parole in 2011, and they now live in Anchorage, where they are happy to finally be together.

Ana Doina is a Romanian-born writer now living in the United States. She left Romania during the Ceausescu regime due to political pressures and social restrictions. Her poems and essays have been published in numerous American and international magazines and anthologies. She was nominated for a Pushcart Prize in 2002 and 2004. Ana co-edited and typeset four anthologies for Bergen Poets, one of New Jersey's oldest community-based poetry organizations. She is the coordinator for Leonia Poetry Forum, a community based poetry study group, and a workshop instructor in the JOY poetry workshop for the Oakland, New Jersey, middle school district. Her poem "The Extinct Homeland: A Conversation with Czeslaw Milosz" appears in the textbook *Approaching Literature in the 21ˢᵗ Century*, and her poem "The proper English word" won honorable mention in the Anna Davidson Rosenberg Awards for Poems.

Gregory Dunn is a farmer. With his wife, Michelle, he runs Blackbird Farms, a small-scale, organically managed produce operation located northwest of Grand Rapids, Michigan. His essays have appeared in *Swink* and the *Pebble Lake Review*, among others.

Fernando Morro Emerson is the nom de' plume of Marvin Douglas Emerson. The name Fernando is in homage to an older cousin who was an early casualty of a little known disease called AIDs. The author originally wrote under his own name until he was blacklisted in his industry for the believability of a controversial first-person character. The author divides his time between an industrial loft in Brooklyn and a penthouse in San Juan, Puerto Rico. The author races vintage motorcycles at racetracks in the Northeast and belongs to the United States Classic Racing Association and the American Historic Racing Motorcycle Association. The author is the owner of a 38 ft. classic blue-water sailboat and sails in the Caribbean. The author wrote his bio in third-person.

Lyn Fuchs is a university professor in Mexico, the editor of *Sacred Ground Travel Magazine*, and the author of the critically-acclaimed books *Sacred Ground & Holy Water: One Man's Adventures In The Wild* and *Fresh Wind & Strange Fire: One Man's Adventures In Primal Mexico*.

Stuart Gelzer grew up in West Africa and India and wanted to be an archaeologist. Instead he's been a screenwriter, a film editor (*Fallout*), and a high school drama teacher, and these days he teaches film in New Mexico and mostly writes novels. He's also a singer specializing in folk music from the Republic of Georgia, and he's got some stories. "The Watermelon Hunters" forms one chapter of *Six Reasons to Travel,* a book-length memoir about some of those adventures. "Immigrants," an excerpt from that memoir, is forthcoming in the winter 2016 issue of *Harvard Review*; other excerpts, "Song Collectors" and "Guns and Dogs," have appeared in *Hippocampus Magazine*. "Dolls," an excerpt from his novel *Earthworm,* set in a fictional former Soviet republic (not Georgia), appeared in the Spring 2015 issue of *Carolina Quarterly*.

David Graham has published six collections of poetry, including *Stutter Monk* and *Second Wind.* He also co-edited (with Kate Sontag) the essay anthology *After Confession: Poetry as Autobiography*. Essays, reviews, and individual poems have appeared widely, both in print and online. In May of 2016 he retired after 29 years teaching English at Ripon College in Wisconsin.

Lisa Ohlen Harris is the author of *The Fifth Season: A Daughter-in-Law's Memoir of Caregiving* and the Middle East memoir *Through The Veil*, which includes "The Pied Piper of Damascus." She teaches memoir and essay writing online for Creative Nonfiction Foundation and mentors nonfiction writers via her editing and critique services.

Ikhide Ikheloa came to the United States from Nigeria armed with a blue suitcase and the hopes and blessing of his ancestors. He is still here, taking short breaks from his demons and credit card bills to indulge in romantic hagiographies of his lost youth. He writes for a living, crafting inane memo after inane memo for a thriving bureaucracy in a thriving American village. He says, "I also write to process my personal issues, and so I write virtually non-stop on the Internet and I think that I'll never write that book, because, who cares, the book as we know it is so analog, and it is dying a long slow death. Long live the Internet. The Internet is probably the greatest revolution that has ever afflicted mankind. The World Wide Web will reshape the world in a way that is unimaginable by even the world's greatest thinkers. The best is yet to come. The worst is yet to come. I love it."

Stanley Jenkins has been published widely in electronic magazines, print journals, and anthologies, including *The Best Creative Non-Fiction, Vol. 2*. He holds the record for the greatest number of appearances in *Eclectica* and is the author of *A City on a Hill: An Indirect Memoir*.

Alan Kaufman is a critically-acclaimed novelist, memoirist, and poet and an author-in-residence in NYC Public Library's Frederick Lewis Allen Room. In addition to the "*Outlaw*" anthologies, *The Outlaw Bible of American Poetry*, *The Outlaw Bible of American Literature* (co-edited with Barney Rosset), *The Outlaw Bible of American Essays*, and *The New Generation*, his books include the novel *Matches* and the memoirs *Jew Boy* and *Drunken Angel*. His most recent book of poetry is *Straight Jacket Elegies*. Kaufman is the former Dean of the Free University of San Francisco and has been a lecturer at the Academy of Art University in San Francisco. His essays on culture and politics have appeared in *The Los Angeles Times, The Huffington Post, San Francisco Chronicle, Salon, Partisan Review,* and others.

Jascha Kessler has published nine books of his own poetry and fiction as well as six volumes of translations of poetry and fiction from Hungarian, Persian, and Bulgarian, several of which have won major prizes. In 1989, his translation of Sándor Rákos's *Catullan Games* won the Translation Award from the National Translation Center. A two-time *Eclectica* Spotlight Author, Jascha has the added distinction of having had his work featured in the magazine in four different categories: fiction, nonfiction, miscellany, and poetry.

Julia Braun Kessler was a journalist and novelist who was published widely over several decades in *Seventeen, Family Circle, Travel & Leisure, Geo, Modern Maturity,* and others. Her novels under the pseudonym Julia Barrett are sequels to Jane Austen's works: *Presumption, The Third Sister, Charlotte,* and *Mary Crawford.* A frequent contributor to *Eclectica Magazine,* Julia passed away in 2012.

Dorothee Lang is a freelancer, multilingual writer, and traveler. She lives in Germany and recently dealt with too many things that start with "c." For more about her, visit her website, *blueprint21.*

Monika Lange has a master's in Chemistry and is the daughter of Oskar Lange, a world famous economist. She composed poems and stories from early childhood, even before she learned how to write, and shared them with her father. At the age of nine, she wrote her first novel. After many turbulent years in her life, Ms. Lange returned to her old passion. A statuette on her father's desk inspired her novel *The Dancing Shiva.* Another novel, *Opium,* is set in Iran where she lived for several years. She based her novella *Lala* on a true story from the past. She also writes essays and short stories and is working on a family history project spurred by the 19th century grave-monument, and on a series of children stories. She lives in California.

Thomas Larson teaches in the MFA Program at Ashland University, Ashland, Ohio. A journalist, critic, and memoirist, he is the author of three books: *The Sanctuary of Illness: A Memoir of Heart Disease, The Saddest Music Ever Written: The Story of Samuel Barber's "Adagio for Strings,"* and *The Memoir and the Memoirist: Reading and Writing Personal Narrative.* He is a longtime staff writer for the *San Diego Reader* and Book Reviews editor for *River Teeth.*

Barbara Lefcowitz, a noted Maryland-based poet, artist and essayist, authored nine collections of poetry and won writing fellowships and awards from the National Endowment for the Arts, Rockefeller Foundation, and Maryland Arts Council. During the 1970s, she was a visionary co-founder of the Writer's Center in Bethesda, Maryland. She was born in Brooklyn New York in 1935, earned her BA in English Literature from Smith College and a PhD from University of Maryland. She died in Rockville Maryland on October 8, 2015 and her work is in the permanent collection of the Smith College Poetry Center.

Bobbi Lurie is the author of four poetry collections, most recently *the morphine poems*. She is currently working on a book about/with Marcel Duchamp. Her writing can be found in *Eclectica, Berfrois, 3 A.M., Vol. 1, Brooklyn, APR, New American Writing* and *Fence.*

Kathleen McCall is a freelance writer living in Northern California. She writes poetry and essays, and spends her spare time studying West African drumming.

Clinton Daniel McKay is pursuing a PhD in Information Science at Indiana University in Bloomington, Indiana, where he also works for the university in web application development. His recent work consists mostly of generative digital art inspired by painting, drawing, and printmaking.

Andie Miller is a writer and editor who lives in South Africa. She is the author of *Slow Motion*, a collection of stories about walking.

Kevin O'Cuinn comes from Dublin, Ireland, and lives and loves in Frankfurt, Germany. He is fiction editor at *Word Riot.*

John Palcewski has enjoyed an eclectic career as a publishing house copywriter, wire service photojournalist, corporate magazine editor, music/drama critic, short story writer, and fine arts photographer. His work appears in the literary and academic press as well as in a substantial number of online publications. He has a BA in Journalism from Moravian College, and studied photography and videotape production at New York University. Palcewski's profile of jazz great Miles Davis appears in *Miles on Miles*, an anthology recently published by Lawrence Hill Books, an imprint of Chicago Review Press.

Rolf Potts is the author of two books, *Vagabonding* and *Marco Polo Didn't Go There*. He has reported from more than 60 countries around the world, and his work has appeared in venues such as *The New Yorker*, *Slate.com*, *Outside*, *The Believer*, National Public Radio, *The Best American Travel Writing*, and *The Best Creative Nonfiction*. When not traveling, he is based in rural Saline County, Kansas.

V.K. Reiter has translated French novels, including Maryse Condé's *Tree of Life* and five of Daniel Odier's "Delacorta" series, and has had nine novels of her own published in the US. She has ghostwritten three films and served as a freelance editor on several bestselling books. While living in France, she wrote and translated narration for documentary films, wrote English subtitles for French films, was a reader, editor, and translator for Les Editions Robert Laffont and spent five interesting years as editor and consultant to Maurice Girodias, publisher of The Olympia Press both in Paris and New York. She worked as a consultant, scriptwriter, and editor for Michel Thomas, owner of the Michel Thomas Language Centers and publisher of the Michel Thomas Language System. Her creative nonfiction pieces have also appeared in *Smoke Signals Magazine*. Her essay "Transport" won the X.J. Kennedy Award and was published in *Rosebud Magazine*. She lives in New York.

Piers Michael Smith teaches literature at the Gulf University for Science and Technology, Kuwait. He has published essays, poems, and short stories and maintains a travel blog for those who have too much time on their hands and infinite patience.

Robert Walsh is a longtime columnist for Hersam Acorn Newspapers and a regular contributor to *The Huffington Post*. Most important, he is the luckiest English teacher in history and an amateur cocker spaniel wrangler.

Melissa Wiley is the author of *Antlers in Space and Other Common Phenomena,* an essay collection forthcoming from Split Lip Press. Her creative nonfiction has appeared in places like *DIAGRAM, Juked, Drunken Boat, PANK, Superstition Review*, and other literary magazines. Her travels in Lapland are also anthologized in *Whereabouts: Stepping out of Place.*

J.J. Wylie graduated from the University of Nevada Las Vegas and then spent several years in middle management before getting permission from his wife to quit his job, do some freelance writing, self-publish a vampire novel, and open an independent coffee shop with an old fraternity brother. As of this writing, Grouchy John's Coffee Shop is still thriving, and so is J.J.'s marriage. The sequels to his vampire novel remain unpublished, for which most people are thankful.

Recommended Online Nonfiction Publications

1966: A Journal of Creative
  Nonfiction
aeon
Arts & Letters Daily
Brevity
Commentary
Creative Nonfiction
Critical Inquiry
Fourth Genre
Hippocampus Magazine
Jacobin
Lapham's Quarterly
Longform
n + 1

Nowhere Magazine
Orion
Punctuate
River Teeth
Southwest Review
The American Scholar
The Baffler
The Believer
The New Inquiry
The Point
The Rumpus
The Sun
Under the Gum Tree
Zocalo Public Square